FIRESIDE

YOU CAN TRAIN YOUR CAT

Jo and Paul Loeb

A FIRESIDE BOOK
PUBLISHED BY SIMON AND SCHUSTER
NEW YORK

PHOTOGRAPHS OF JERZI CAT BY TERRY CLOUGH

FIRST FIRESIDE EDITION, 1979
PUBLISHED BY SIMON AND SCHUSTER
A DIVISION OF GULF & WESTERN CORPORATION
SIMON & SCHUSTER BUILDING
ROCKEFELLER CENTER
1230 AVENUE OF THE AMERICAS
NEW YORK, NEW YORK 10020

MANUFACTURED IN THE UNITED STATES OF AMERICA

1   2   3   4   5   6   7   8   9   10
1   2   3   4   5   6   7   8   9   10 Pbk.

LIBRARY OF CONGRESS CATALOGING IN PUBLICATION DATA

LOEB, JO, DATE.
        YOU CAN TRAIN YOUR CAT.

        (A FIRESIDE BOOK)
        INCLUDES INDEX.
            1. CATS—TRAINING.   I. LOEB, PAUL, DATE,
JOINT AUTHOR.   II. TITLE.
SF446.6.L63   1979   636.8   79-13463

ISBN 0-671-22578-2
ISBN 0-671-25147-3 PBK.

TO STEPHANIE

With special thanks to Joel Bergstein, on whose desk this book was written

Contents

7

CONTENTS

Foreword

Jo and Paul Loeb have taken their love and deep understanding of animal behavior and applied it to the feline. Through careful observation and research they have found that the mysterious and aloof cat, once understood, responds favorably to love, good care and proper training. It is not necessary to have a pet that rules the home and is independent to the point of having to have any bad habits tolerated.

Training of cats is both possible and enjoyable, and the added happiness they bring us makes the effort worthwhile. This well written book has long been needed, both by the confirmed cat lover and by those who are just experiencing their first pet cat.

Martin DeAngelis, D.V.M.
Yonkers, N.Y.

PART ONE

TRAINING YOU
TO TRAIN
YOUR CAT

1

OUR PHILOSOPHY ON CATS

The door of a pretty little suburban house opens up and out walks a sleek red tiger cat. She strolls down the walkway, along the street, and into a crowded shopping mall. Occasionally she pauses to look into a store window. People stop and turn around to stare at her. Paying them no heed, she keeps walking until she reaches a supermarket. She hesitates a moment at the door until the electric eye opens it, and then walks in. Once inside, she heads straight for the cat food, stands up on her hind legs, and knocks her favorite brand off the shelf with her paws.

A supercat you say? But she's not. She's just a plain little six-month-old house cat who, through proper training, has been taught to do tricks for commercials.

This is the kind of training almost anyone can do with his cat if he is willing to put in time and effort. Cats have long been considered untrainable, aloof, and disdainful of affection and people. It's about time this fallacy was disproved once and for all.

We both had cats as children, and grew up with the same attitude toward them as most people: Cats are nice cuddly creatures you keep around the house to make sure the mice and roaches stay away, and who take care of themselves as long as you feed them and give them a few basics. However, when we

15

became involved in animal behavior and started working with cats for television and movies, we soon developed a new understanding, deep respect, and love for cats.

We were fascinated by cats and wanted to find out as much as we could about them. Therefore we set out to gather all the information possible on the subject. We soon learned that very little was known about them. Apart from books filled with cute pictures and ones that simply perpetuated the standard myths, not much had been written.

So we started to investigate cats ourselves. Not by experimenting in clinical studies, but by observing and working with them in what has now become their natural habitat—the midst of human society and, more especially, the home. We talked to cat owners, professional breeders, and veterinarians. In addition, we studied the social life, behavior, and habit patterns of the big feral cats in order to better understand the social heritage that makes their little cousins, our house cats, tick. We also researched the strange superstitions that have for so long surrounded cats, to see why these developed and how they have affected the way people feel about cats. But it was from our experience with the ordinary, everyday problems people have with their pets that we learned the most.

We have worked with cats in many households and trained them for hundreds of movies and commercials. The personalities of these cats ranged from outgoing and friendly to subdued, reserved, and even timid. Owners' attitudes toward their pets seemed to be the factor which affected them most profoundly. Therefore the interrelationship between cat and human became our main area of study. And most of our work in researching owner/cat dynamics was in the home, where the habit patterns are formed.

In our work we have discovered that many of the commonly held beliefs about the cat's nature are completely unfounded. A cat can be as affectionate a companion as a dog, can do tricks and respond to you, and can still maintain that special independent quality that people admire in cats.

Today the advantages of cat ownership are becoming more and more apparent. People are discovering how easy it is to care for a cat, and what a satisfying experience it is. However, there is so much misunderstanding about cats that many misinformed people are reluctant to own one.

In fact cats are now on their way to being the pet of the future. Cats are becoming a symbol of freedom to many who are locked into small houses or apartments. When you watch a cat walking around your home it's hard not to be reminded of his wild cousins, the exotic cats. In addition, it doesn't take much time to care for a cat, so you can have a cat without feeling tied down. In fact, since a cat doesn't need to be walked, you can safely leave him for a weekend with an ample supply of fresh food and water. Cats prefer to stay home as long as someone comes in to feed them and clean their litter boxes.

In some fifteen years of working with animals, we have helped train hundreds of cats for individual clients. We have also trained the animal actors for movies, TV commercials, and ads. All the tricks in this book are ones which we have trained cats to master. The simple training techniques used are ones you will soon learn.

We feel certain that even the most ardent cat lover and supporter of independence would like to have his or her pet respond to commands once in a while. Haven't you noticed how proudly a cat owner with a responsive pet recounts the accomplishments of his cat? Even the tiniest things are noted with enthusiasm. Surely all cat owners, deep down, crave some kind of responsiveness from a cat.

Why do you think exotics are better trained than domestic cats? Simply because the people who own and train them know exactly how to do it. They also know all about their cats' physical and mental makeup. This book is going to teach you to

17

know and train your domestic cat in much the same way these pros do. But after reading this book please don't go out and buy a tiger and try to train it, because when it grows up you might be food!

The first thing to do when you think about training your cat is to be honest with yourself about how well trained you really want him. There is absolutely no point in training your cat to do more than you really care about. Once you are basically satisfied with him, your motivation will taper off and your training will be largely a waste, since it will be only a halfhearted effort on your part. If you don't care, you won't even put in the time to do a really good job, and just like anything else worthwhile, proper training takes a fair investment of time and patience plus a strong desire to do it well.

Cats, like people, come with varying IQs and potentials, but all cats have the ability to learn. Underestimating your cat's potential by classifying him as "too stupid" or "too independent" is a mistake. People who look at their cats in this light are missing out on much of the fun of cat ownership. Cats are, of course, living things subject to idiosyncrasies—just like us—and these must be taken into consideration in training. But, no matter what, the basics of training are the same for all cats.

Many people put off training, reasoning that they'll wait until the cat is older and thus better able to understand what is going on. This is their first mistake. Cats learn early and fast. Young cats' minds are really open to suggestion, so start training as soon as possible. It is easier to teach the almost blank mind of a tiny kitten than the cluttered mind of an adult cat. All the trainers of big cats know this; they get a cub at a very early age and bring him up to their way of life.

The best time to start training a cat is when he is very young. In fact, training him before taking him away from his mother is best of all—this way you can get at him during his imprint period, which is approximately three to five weeks of age in cats. However, since this is not feasible for most people, and since kittens should be kept with their mother until they are at least eight weeks of age, you should try to get a kitten as young as is safely possible and start working right away.

If, however, you already have a cat past the kitten stage, don't despair. We have trained hundreds of these for commercials and private clients. They have responded beautifully. It's harder work, requires more effort, and takes more time, but it can definitely be done. With older cats you may first have to break old habits before training can begin. But basically, training an older cat is the same as working a small kitten, only done with more intensity.

Training an unaltered cat is a different story, however. In fact, trying to train a full cat of either sex is almost impossible. The intensity of their innate natural callings can't be channeled into training. If you really intend to train your cat, or just want a better pet, have it altered.

In teaching people to train their cats, we use the same basic methods for third graders as we do for Ph.Ds. It's just that the third graders learn faster. The more intellectual the person, the more he expects this whole process to be complicated. It really isn't.

Just keep in mind that you get out of a cat what you put into him. If you work, you will get a response; if not, nothing. And working with your cat doesn't mean doing something once. Like anything else, training your cat takes effort. Most well-behaved and trained cats have had time and concern spent upon them. When you were learning in school it didn't happen overnight— so give your cat the same consideration you were given.

Our training doesn't follow a precise sequence other than to teach a cat the basics before expecting him to learn complicated tricks. But no matter what you teach him, you should first train your cat in exercises that can be performed indoors. Even teaching him to walk on a lead should be done indoors before he goes outside.

Make sure he has each command down pat as a separate and distinct exercise before you begin linking them together. If for several times running you follow one command with another, there's a good chance he'll start associating the two commands and become confused. Thus, if you teach him to sit and to jump close together, he may jump when you say "sit" and sit when you say "jump."

Constant repetition is very important. One of the big secrets is doing an exercise over and over: gradually the cat accepts it as something you want him to do and does it. Habits are established readily in cats, and once established are extremely durable. And so, if you establish a training pattern properly, he will stick with it. Your cat will probably enjoy performing tricks once he's gotten them down pat. Just be sure to follow any work well done with something rewarding for him.

If your cat sees some advantage for himself in performing, he will. If he can see none, it is nearly impossible to get him to work. Cats tend to work to achieve some kind of physical pleasure or comfort. Praise doesn't give this. Use the fact that cats love their physical comfort or pleasure when working with them.

We often use food as a reward in training, and we recommend you do the same, though you should bear in mind that a fat cat never does anything he doesn't have to do. But never starve a cat to get him to perform.

Keep a second type of food for use in training. This should consist of special treats that are never fed to your cat at his regular mealtimes. These treats should be really super, a complete change from his normal diet. And they should be kept as an exclusive reward for obeying or doing something you like. Never give treats to your cat other than as rewards for obeying. If you give them to him for no reason, why should he perform?

The commands should be taught by one person. Of course, eventually every person in the house can give the cat the same commands, but it's best to wait until the cat has learned them from one person first.

Keep in mind that cats don't respond to people who are busy doing other things while trying to train them. You can't teach your cat to sit while chatting with a friend about the latest gossip. Training takes your full attention. You need the time to learn about your cat just as he needs a while to learn what you want from him. Therefore, before giving your cat a command, be prepared to make sure he goes all the way through with it no matter what distractions crop up. A cat quickly learns that a doorbell or telephone signals the end of a lesson, and he'll hang around waiting for one or the other. If he does get away, go and get him and then put him through his paces. Let him know that, no matter what, he has to finish each exercise once the command is given.

Most owners are interested in having their cats perform for their friends. The cardinal rule here is to pretend that there are no other people present. Your cat should be performing for *you* and *your* satisfaction, not your guests. In short, concentrate on your cat, not on your audience. Some people are embarrassed when their cats don't perform and just laugh it off, leaving their pets to their own devices. Such cats will never perform properly. A cat must go through with the command once it is given, so you must not be capricious about the times you decide to command your pet.

If the cat knows what he's supposed to do and still doesn't follow instructions, the original mistake was yours, not his. Once you slip up, your cat is guaranteed to foul up on his own. In general, if you let your cat get away with not carrying through with a command, you will have difficulties the next time. If you are not consistent with your cat, he won't know when you are serious.

Too much conversation can confuse your cat. Keep it all as simple as possible. Just the single word of the command is enough. We can't overstress the need for simplicity in explaining to your cat what you require of him. And remember to make it as simple as you can for yourself by leaving as little room as possible for the cat to make a mistake.

Some people push their cats too fast. With a cat you must always be prepared to retreat at least one step for every two forward. You just can't push a cat beyond where he feels comfortable. He won't stand for it and will refuse to obey.

If your cat hurts himself while learning something, he'll probably not do it again. Be careful what happens to your cat while he is being trained. A bad action associated with a command can destroy the possibility of his ever learning that command. You should also be careful about reprimanding your cat while you're training him. Don't confuse him with punishment during training. In fact, never even tell your cat "no" during training. If you do, he is likely to associate his reprimand with whatever you are trying to teach him, and will thus refuse to obey. "No" should be established and reserved for bad deeds, *not* mistakes made during training.

We remind people never to lose their temper with a cat. When you lose your temper, whether physically or verbally, your gestures aren't always methodical and simple. Jumping around in anger will only scare your cat. He will become extremely confused and therefore very reluctant to respond, since he won't know what your reactions might be. (In fact, he's more likely to run and hide than do anything else.) Shouters are the kind of people whose cats never really get disciplined, simply because the owners haven't any discipline themselves. When working with cats use your natural tone of voice.

Not all cats can learn all the commands or tricks we will detail, but most cats can do them. Felines are capable of a lot more learning than their owners usually give them credit for.

But they have to be trained properly. In addition, they must have a close relationship with their owners. Therefore, when you're not working with your cat, be his friend. Hug him, stroke him, love him. Cats respond to love just as humans do, flourishing in loving surroundings.

It's up to you, the owner, to mold your cat's nature, and to adjust it to fit what you want. If you do what most people do, and give him little attention because you think this is what he wants, then your cat will probably be aloof and distant. But if you give him plenty of attention, training, and love you will usually find your cat will become a responsive, trainable, and socially interactive member of your family.

It's cat owners' ignorance about the animals they are involved with that causes most problems. We believe that the owner should be taught to understand the cat and his own role in the cat's life, and vice versa. Common sense is the key word in our approach to working with cats.

Owning a cat is an emotional outlet for most people. People love cats because with them they can share an affection not to be found anywhere else. But many other reasons and factors enter into cat ownership. Many people work at jobs they don't really like and thus feel trapped by society. Owning a cat, with its reputation for maintaining an independent outlook under all conditions, allows people to share vicariously in that independence. Even people who love their jobs and lives may feel this way about their cats. The independent reputation, and the aura of the wilderness that surrounds a cat wherever he is, are magical to many people.

The three major reasons people get cats are for a child substitute, frustration outlet, or fantasy; many owners relate to cats as possessions rather than animals. Whatever view people have of their cats, however, they tend either to overindulge them or ignore them. People who do the latter frequently complain that their cats ignore them completely. But what do they

23

expect? After all, the cats learned their behavior from their owners. A cat will take on the personality traits he feels his owner
wants—and if he doesn't, the owner will often read them into
his pet anyway, simply because he wants—perhaps even subconsciously—to see them there.

Many people feel that cats don't care about them, since cats
don't seem to have the need to feel loved and praised. In fact,
sometimes cats seem to have no real loyalties except perhaps to
their environment or territory. Before condemning your cat,
however, keep in mind his innate tendency to become extremely
attached to a certain home base. It's not really that cats don't
get attached to people—they do. Rather, it's that instinctive primordial reflexes cause them to look for security in their surroundings.

To get your cat to relate more intimately with you, it is important for you to pay attention to him. Put time into being
with him, playing with him. Make him relate to you—gently
but firmly force the issue. He'll begin to relate to you rather than
just to his environment. Man has to cultivate the friendship,
loyalty, and trust of cats. They are remarkably adaptable in their
socializing tendencies but, if not encouraged, they will adopt a
loner's life.

Always keep in mind that, despite all myths to the contrary,
if you give a cat love and affection, he will be an affectionate
responsive pet. This is especially effective if you begin to cultivate the relationship while the cat is a very young kitten. Unfortunately, all too many people tend *not* to hold and pet kittens
and cats because of their reputation for independence. In fact
they tend to over-respect this reputation and ignore their kittens
and cats. This treatment only makes a cat take on an aloof and
distant attitude, thus seeming to confirm the owner's belief in a
cat's independent nature.

We can't promise a bright friendly cat to everyone. Cats'
temperaments differ from individual to individual in extent and

quality of attachment, and differences in personality are often strongly bred in an animal. In addition, many people don't want what they consider to be a fawning cat, but want a more independent pet. In this case just ignore him—but don't expect him to respond to you when one day you suddenly decide you want his attention for some reason or other. If you want your cat to be friendly, you will have to encourage the association.

It is not necessary to overswaddle a kitten. A little stressful stimulation early in life can be beneficial for any infant, be it human or feline. It has been found that the earlier and oftener a kitten is handled—especially during the first thirty days— the more socialized and intelligent a pet it tends to be.

Therefore, when you bring the kitten or cat home, pick him up and hold him. Not too much, but enough to get him used to being held. Cats prefer it if they are simply stroked and petted, and do not like being restrained. Try to break that tendency early but in a nice way. Train your cat to allow himself to be held. Encouraging him to play with you will further establish a close social bond.

Kittens handled by several different people are much friendlier toward strangers than those handled by only one person or not handled at all. Thus if you want your cat to be socially well-adjusted around people he should meet many of them. If an owner keeps to himself and has few visitors, his cat will not be very sociable. This is one of the ways in which a cat grows to be like his owners. By the same token, if a cat has never been around children he will be shy of them.

Never pick up a cat by the scruff of the neck; you could hurt him. (Mother cats pick up the kittens this way only while they are very small.) And don't let children grab the cat around the stomach or pick him up by the forelegs. Treat your cat gently and with kindness.

A cat should be held gently but firmly. The approved method is to slip one hand under the cat's chest, holding his front legs together with your fingers, while at the same time cupping your other hand and part of your arm under the cat's hindquarters and resting under his tummy. A frightened or insecure kitten may squirm and claw. Get young children to sit down before holding the cat, because they will generally drop it the minute it starts to struggle or claws at them. Stick around to watch. Explain to the child the problems with holding and petting. Don't let very young children, who don't understand, grab at a cat or kitten; the cat and the child both can get hurt.

Small children like to pull and squeeze. Cats don't like this kind of treatment, so be careful about getting cats for the kids. If you expect your cat to serve as a toy, a cuddly stuffed toy cat would be a better idea. Unfortunately, some parents think pet animals exist just to amuse the kids. And when a claw goes into a child's eye they wonder why and abuse the cat. In one family, the parents had bought cats as playmate companions for their children. They couldn't understand it when they found that the cats took to one child and not the other, but the answer was quite simple. It seemed that one child was gentle and loving toward the cats, while the other would pull them around and demand their attention. A firm lecture on the proper care and treatment of animals was the solution here.

Bringing a baby into a house with an established pet can be as awkward as bringing a kitten into a home with children. A cat can often become completely disillusioned when a baby appears on the scene. Imagine a cat who is used to getting an enormous amount of attention from his owners, even to being sole ruler of his territory. How do you think he is going to react to the new arrival? One cat disappeared for three days after a new baby came into the house. Explaining to the owners why this sort of thing happens is not particularly easy. The thing to do is to try to get the cat used to children gradually. And don't neglect your attentions to your cat when a new baby arrives.

People think that training simply means training for tricks

and the like. But training a cat also involves teaching him what he is not to do—such as not to eat plants, not to scratch people and/or furniture, not to urinate in the house, and even not to hide.

You must realize that you are the one who sets your cat's habit patterns. If you approve of his habits—great. But if you later decide that what he's doing is not to your standards, the damage is already done—you'll have to break the habit that you set up for him before you can reform him! Problems arise from the fact that people let their cats get away with things, saying, "just once can't hurt." You can't take this attitude with cats. If you let them do something just once, or if you do something just once, or something happens just once, they remember; so try to train your cat to your way of life as early as possible.

Many cat owners fear the idea of discipline, thinking that if they discipline a cat the cat will hate them forever. This is not so; but some people still will not discipline a cat, no matter what the infraction. The cat may jump all over the cooking counter and stove, and regardless how much they don't like it, the owners won't stop it. When talking about discipline we are of course talking about extremely mild forms. Discipline does not have to mean pain. In fact, if overly forceful, physical or verbal discipline may have no effect other than to scare and alienate your pet. Cats in general react adversely to physical and mental abuse. Plain, simple discipline is sometimes needed, but it must be administered logically, with restraint. It must have a specific purpose and meaning that your cat can understand.

Only if something is not pleasurable for a cat will he stop, so you have to make things unpleasant for him. If a cat enjoys something and gets pleasure from it, why should he stop just because you don't like it? Show him why by making it uncomfortable, and thus undesirable. He won't continue with something that has become disadvantageous to him, because it could hurt, is annoying, or is difficult to do. There is little point in

27

trying to reason with your cat as though he were a child. He won't understand.

Patience is ultimately the most helpful factor in training and correcting a cat. Plan to spend time on the problem or project. In working with your cat, repetition, consistency, patience, and a certain amount of authority are very important. And one of the big secrets is never letting your cat get away with things.

2

THE PHYSICAL FELINE: Development, Anatomy, Senses, and Body Language

The house cat as we know it today is generally believed to be descended from the Kaffir (Caffre) or Cape cat* from Africa, a type of small wildcat whose tamed descendants were used by the Egyptians to help protect their graneries. This breed and similar varieties still exist in various parts of the world—in fact they range from Africa through the eastern Mediterranean, and as far as India.

In order to succeed in their association with man, cats have had to make certain adjustments. Living in our environment has necessitated changes in their outlook and behavior. However, you should never overlook the fact that they are still cats. As such, they have certain innate characteristics inherited from millions of years of adapting to the wild before man took them in. Knowing about these will make you more aware of what makes your cat respond and what he responds to the most readily.

Because of the dangerous conditions and because cats in the wild frequently lead solitary lives, it is important for the infant cat to mature rapidly and not have to rely on others for survival.

---

* This is an extremely small wildcat about the size of a large domestic cat. It is yellow in color, with markings like the domestic tabby, but banded with dark stripes on the tail and sometimes also on the legs.

This early independence is facilitated by many innate actions, or instincts, which ensure that the little cat will be able to take care of himself at an early age.

If you were to watch a kitten from the time he was born you'd be amazed at how rapidly he develops. Kittens generally open their eyes between five and twelve days (usually seven); sit up by the twelfth; can walk by twenty-two days; run by the twenty-sixth day; respond to sound by twenty-six days; are able to lap and drink by the twenty-ninth day; and can climb by the thirty-first day. So by the time a cat is four and a half weeks old, all the essential body reactions necessary for minimal survival without his mother are developed. A cat reaches his full physical size by about nine months, with his bone structure completely developed. It takes him until he is about a year and a half old to fill out completely and reach his ultimate size, but he is working at very efficient capacity much earlier. In comparison with humans, as you can see, the maturation of cats is phenomenal. It is almost impossible to estimate a cat's age in "people years" because of this much-accelerated maturation. But, if you want to try, the first year of life should be counted as at least triple and the second year double the amount of each later year. Therefore, rather than the usual seven "people years" per year, we would have fifteen for the first year, ten for the second, and five for every year thereafter.

In order to facilitate survival in the wild, cats have also been endowed with great defense and hunting mechanisms. A cat has long, sharp, curved retractable claws. These are so well adapted for grasping that he could, if absolutely necessary, cling to a cement wall. These claws are normally hidden inside sheaths atop each toe, but they come out fast when needed. Most cats have five toes on the front feet and four on the back. Some cats, however, have six on the front and five on the back. (This has been interpreted as mythological symbolism, meaning that cats with more toes have been reincarnated. No one really knows the reason, however, and it is most likely just an evolutionary quirk.) The extra toes on the front are dewclaws, which are those little claws part way up inside the foot.

A cat's long canine teeth and sharp-edged molars are specially adapted for ripping and tearing. Cats, like humans, only grow two sets of teeth: the first, or milk teeth, and then the adult. The milk teeth usually fall out when the kitten is four to six months old, and are replaced by his adult teeth. This second set of teeth should be complete by six or seven months, and they must last the cat for the rest of his life. (If your cat's second set comes in and his milk teeth remain, so there are two sets, take him to the vet so the baby ones can be removed.)

A cat's anatomy has quite a few decidedly unique features, which help make him such a fantastic physical specimen. For one thing, a cat's skin fits him very loosely. This is an excellent defense mechanism that prevents adversaries from getting a grip on the underlying muscle or flesh, thus allowing the bitten, clawed, or even impaled cat to maneuver within his skin for a better position. In line with this, the cat's skin is only lightly provided with blood vessels and pain receptors. Therefore, when a cat's skin is cut open, he will bleed only slightly, unless of course the underlying tissue is damaged.

The skin also contains a very few sparsely distributed sweat glands. Most of these glands are found in certain places such as around the base of the tail and under the pads of the feet (which, incidentally, help to protect the feet by providing a good padding and thick skin). Since there are not too many over the body, a cat's skin cleans itself not through sweating, like a horse or a human, but through a sloughing off of old skin and hair, which is constantly shedding. This way the cat gives off very little odor, so his enemies and prey can't smell him, thus enhancing his hunting and defense capabilities. This can cause problems for cats if they get overheated. Don't ever leave your cat where he can't get relief from the heat. This includes cars on hot days and poorly ventilated traveling cases. These can become like ovens and the cat could easily go into shock, pass out, or even die.

The main function of the cat's coat is to hold a layer of air close to the skin to help insulate his body against changes in temperature. It consists of a fine-haired undercoat covered by longer, coarser hair. No cat should ever be clipped unless absolutely essential for medical or other emergency reasons. It can sabotage his natural insulation.

A cat's whiskers and eyebrows (vibrassae) aren't part of his coat but rather one of the instruments of his sense of touch. The bulbs at the base of these coarse, wiry hairs are very rich in nerve and blood supply, thus making them supersensitive.

There are, as you probably know, five traditionally recognized basic senses: sight, sound, taste, smell, and touch, which has five sub-senses including sensitivity to pressure, temperature, and pain. There are also some minor senses, such as balance. And in addition some people have ascribed to cats a sixth sense —a sort of ESP, which all animals including humans seem to have to some extent, but which cats seem to possess to a remarkable degree. This special ability is believed by many to be mainly dependent on the keenness of their ordinary senses.

All the cat's senses are well developed, but certain senses are more developed than others, and these are the ones you should make use of when working with him.

A cat's eyes are absolutely super. The sharpness of your cat's eyesight seems to be based mostly on his ability to see movement. Even the slightest movement at a great distance catches his attention immediately.

The eyes of a cat are of prime importance to his survival, and are one of his really interesting features. They are very large in proportion to his body size and are in frontal placement, which is the best for seeing and hunting. All cats have supersensitive pupils, which in strong light seem to disappear and in poor light expand to cover nearly the entire surface of the eye, thus letting in extra light. The pupils also have a special, if strange, mechanism to allow your cat to accurately gauge distance, especially of moving objects, by constricting and expanding extremely rapidly. It's like a bionic eye with a zoom lens attachment. A translucent eyelid comes up from the lower part of the eye to cover it whenever protection is needed. Behind the eye itself there is a reflective layer called the *tapetum*, from which light is reflected to allow the cat to see in dim night light. The tapetum is what makes the eyes shine in the dark. Since both light-sensitive rods and a few cones sensitive to a limited number of colors—namely blue, green, and possibly red—are to be found on the retina behind the eye, your cat, contrary to popular opinion, is *not* color blind.

What the cat doesn't see he hears with his special cup-shaped ears, which enable him to pick up even distant or faint sounds. There are more than thirty muscles in each ear, as compared with man's six muscles. This allows the ears to rotate in any direction, either separately or together, so they can pick up sounds from two or more directions at the same time. The insides of the ears are trumpet- or funnel-shaped to channel the sound so they can pinpoint it with absolute accuracy.

Even when he's napping, a cat's ears are constantly moving around, always on the alert for new and unusual sounds. These are the ones that really catch his attention. (Familiar noises fade into the background unless they have specific meanings for him—e.g., his food dish being rattled—and elicit responses from him.) It is when your cat is in strange surroundings that you will see his ears really moving, picking up clues to his surroundings. He's on edge and can't relax until he has acclimated himself. Cats dislike loud (not necessarily high-pitched) noises; they often run and hide and refuse to come out until they are sure it's safe. Therefore you should try to adapt your cat gradually to unusual noises to secure his confidence. This is especially true if you plan to teach your pet to walk on a lead or do other tricks that necessitate his being outside or around people.

Raised voices and sudden, sharp noises put a cat's supersensitive hearing on edge and are annoying. If you have a large noisy family, eventually your cat will get used to the general noise level, despite his initial reaction. Anything unusual, however, will put him on guard, and this can cause trouble for you. For instance, if a cat is really terrified by thunder when young, he may always run and hide when he hears it. Many people inadvertently encourage such behavior by petting their cats when they show fear. One client had this exact problem with his cat. In fact, it got so bad that he couldn't leave the cat alone. Our solution was to record a thunderstorm and play it back to the cat, almost imperceptibly at first, while he was eating and very relaxed. We then very gradually raised the volume, a little every couple of days, until it was finally raised to full volume with the cat ignoring it, or at least showing very little reaction. But it was a slow process stretching over several months.

Besides the noise itself being frightening to a cat, a certain sound can become through association symbolic of an unpleasant experience. In one case, a client's cat ran and hid whenever he heard a siren outside. It seems that as a kitten he had been in a fire and had had to be rescued. He consequently associated the sound with those hours of fear. Our job was to show him that the noise was nothing to be afraid of—not an easy task, but manageable.

In addition to providing him with superb hearing your cat's ears also account for his incredible sense of balance. This sense is controlled by the semicircular canals of the inner ear. In cats these are obviously well developed. The cat's fantastic balance, together with his special ability to adjust the focus of his eyes to accurately measure distances, allows your cat to jump in the air and make a neat landing on a spot half his size or on a narrow ledge or even a fence. His remarkable balance also allows a cat to land on his feet even if dropped on his back. If you drop him as low as six inches off the ground, he'll right himself. There are always exceptions to the rule, however, so it is not wise to experiment. If you do, please put a pillow under the cat to prevent any mishaps.

The cat's sense of smell isn't one of his best, and its uses seem to be aesthetic rather than informative. In a newborn kitten smell is the most important sense but, once its eyes open, sight takes over. Cats open their mouths to help them smell better. Cats often sit around smelling with their mouths open; but if your cat seems to be breathing through his mouth all the time, get him to a vet—something could be wrong.

One sense that doesn't seem to have developed to a great degree is taste. Food does not stay in your cat's mouth very long, so there is not enough time for the taste buds to savor it. Your cat's taste seems to depend on his sense of smell. This is an important aspect of the human sense of taste also, though not nearly as important as in cats. Hold your nose tightly while you eat: you'll see that at least some if not all pleasure will be gone. The food may even be completely tasteless. Smell is what adds the real pleasure to taste. Cat food companies are fully aware of this fact. They study what preferences cats have in the odor of their food and incorporate these into their brands.

Cats have one of the most highly developed senses of touch of all the mammals. In fact, many say they are the most sensual of all animals. Each hair seems to be sensitized. A cat's coat even generates electricity when you stroke the hair on his back. One engineer claims that the electricity potential on a cat's back is enough to light a 75-watt light bulb. Cats love to have their bodies stroked, but only in the right direction, which is from head to tail; they don't like to be stroked "against the grain."

As we mentioned, a cat's whiskers and eyebrows are an extremely important part of his sense of touch. They act basically as feelers to help protect the face and eyes from injury. It is not true, as is commonly believed, that whiskers are for measuring whether spaces are wide enough for the cat's body to pass through. Just like people's eyelashes, some whiskers are long and some short. Therefore the whiskers of many cats are wider or narrower than their bodies. After all, as the owner of any fat cat knows, the whiskers don't lengthen and shorten when a cat gains or loses weight. But they do help the cat feel what he can't see, especially for night hunting. They also seem to be able to act as antennae and pick up vibrations in the air, allowing the cat to sense coming changes in the weather. In fact, scientists have found that a cat's fantastic whiskers and supersensitive hearing tend to pick up ground and wind vibrations preceding hurricanes and earthquakes. Scientists are now testing the possibilities of using certain animals, including domestic, to predict earthquakes and other natural disasters.

The ability to pick up low-level stimuli has given cats a reputation for having a sixth sense—of possessing ESP and/or being highly intuitive. We don't discount ESP as a phenomenon, but a lot of ESP ability is based on highly developed senses—as, for instance, the way blind people can "sense" a wall in front of them and thus avoid it. They do this by feeling and listening. In this case the vibrations of the wind and air are cut off by the wall, as are sound waves. Instead of using their eyes, the blind use all their other senses, senses most people would never normally use and may consequently think of as "extra-sensory." Of course, some people are more attuned than others, but they have to work at developing these other senses. A cat doesn't; he's born with them honed to perfection.

All objects and people give off energy. This is usually unnoticed by most people, but there are some who can feel the forces that emanate from things. Their senses are attuned to certain energies. Your cat's senses are so highly developed that he picks up all the energy (and smells) around him—whether good or bad. This is why, for example, they always seem to be attracted to people who are afraid of cats. These people are giving off the strongest vibes and odors.

Oddly, cats don't seem to have much homing ability, and usually can find their way home only within short distances. It has been reported that cats, like pigeons, use a sense of "time and sun" correspondence to find their way. However, in the wild most cats live on a permanent hunting range and rarely wander far. Therefore, they don't need much of a homing instinct. They take their cues from such natural landmarks as rocks, land formations, trees. In the apartment complexes and suburban communities of today it doesn't work quite as easily for our house cats. Everything looks the same or is very similar. Each street, house, apartment floor and door, run together in a cat's mind and confuse him. In our building when cats get out of their apartments, oftentimes they can't find their way home even if it's just a couple of floors away. Many times we've had to return cats who live only one flight up or down from us. Each floor looks the same to them! This is one of the many reasons you should keep your cat inside if possible.

Cats do have an accurate internal clock, however, and their sense of timing is great. They seem to know when you are coming home, what time they're going to get fed, and when to expect many other occurrences that happen on a routine basis. People are always amazed that their cats know when and what they are going to do. Really it's quite simple—they use their senses to look and listen to your every move. Your behavior is a direct clue to your plans. If you get dressed, you're going out. If you put out food, you're going to eat. If you do something just once, they remember!

Animals are acute observers and learn the human routine easily. They have nothing to do all day long but think about us and watch us and our actions. You are, believe it or not, the center of your cat's life. You feed him and care for his needs. It's therefore in his best interest to know as much about you as possible. He knows when you're going out, what kind of mood you're in, everything. He's got you clocked. In fact, a cat's knowledge of you and your actions is really quite phenomenal.

It doesn't take a cat long to see which of your actions affect him. Soon he'll be watching specifically for these. Cats quickly get to know that certain things we do give them the go-ahead to do something, or at least to expect something. Perhaps if you spent time watching your cat, you'd learn a lot about him, too.

Don't ever think that you can't communicate with your cat: you definitely can. Perhaps not as well as Dr. Doolittle, but probably a whole lot better than a lost tourist in Timbuktoo!

When you think of communicating with another person or an animal, you probably think in terms of spoken words. But a cat only understands a limited number of words, and unless conversation is directed specifically at him, he will probably not react. His name and words he knows for food elicit responses from him. Other than that, your language is of little interest to him.

The prime means of communication for cats is body language. Cats have a varied repertoire of body gestures and movements that signal his intentions and moods. His tail, eyes, ears, mouth, hair, stance, and body movement are all part of his communication system. Thus if you are observant you may be able to predict your cat's behavior to some degree.

Certain of these are innate, universal gestures; others are learned and become part of the repertoire as your cat discovers that they elicit certain responses from you. One cat we know has learned that if he lifts his paw as though waving he will receive a tidbit from the table. Another has found he can get the same thing by pulling on his owner's pants leg. Still another knows that by sitting up on his hind legs and batting out with his paws like a prizefighter he will get a reward.

Cats have a kind of subtlety in their everyday body language, but in general animal gestures should be taken quite literally.

Pets don't have huge brains and will usually take the direct approach. Simple communication is what they understand best. Complicated concepts, subtle implications, and abstract ideas belong to human communication. If your cat brings his empty bowl over to you, assume he wants either food or drink. There are no hidden meanings. One client couldn't understand why her cat was always licking at the faucet. Like so many people, she wanted to give it some deep psychological meaning. It turned out that all the cat wanted was to drink. He didn't like the taste of the water in his bowl. His owner sprayed around his feeding area with an air freshener, and the spray naturally settled in his water.

If your cat keeps bringing a ball or object over to your feet, it is probably simply because he wants you to throw it so he can retrieve. And if he closes his eyes and yawns, don't immediately jump to the conclusion that he's bored. You should think better of yourself—it's really a sign of contentment not boredom; he's just completely relaxed.

Body language carries over into the actual physical features of your cat. In this context, a male cat has thicker cheeks than a female, giving him a big-faced look. This is not only to make him look big and handsome for females, but also to make him seem larger and more threatening to other males. Nature gives him a big, impressive face that tells other males just how big and tough he is. Why do you think lions have manes? And conversely, why do you think a lion who is castrated too young will usually not develop a mane?

This first-impressions-are-important aspect of a cat's appearance also shows up in the actions of cats. Thus, when a really aggressive, confident male is threatened, he will attack frontally. A more cautious or timid cat, on the other hand, is likely to take a more defensive stance. He will turn sideways, arch his back, and fluff up the hair along his back from his head to the tip of his tail. Attached to the base of each hair follicle is a tiny muscle that allows the hair to stand straight up when the cat is angry or frightened. Thus he looks larger and is hopefully able to intimidate enemies or scare them away and thus avoid a conflict. If this tactic doesn't work, he can still approach or retreat while maintaining his sideways stance. This way he retains his affected largeness until he can either safely run away or, if he suddenly gets his confidence, chase the other cat away.

Even humans use body language much more extensively than you might think. Though frequently universal in both form and meaning, many of these actions are completely unconscious. Rubbing your nose, for example, in the old fighter's tradition is an unconscious sign of aggression and hostility—so if you are talking to someone and he starts rubbing his nose, watch out! We use our complicated vocal language to communicate philosophical and intellectual thoughts. However, gut emotional responses and intentions are frequently telegraphed by body language, including facial expressions, gestures, body shifts and eye movements. In fact, some researchers say that as much as eighty percent of human communication could be accomplished through body language.

Cats definitely don't have facial expressions as we would think of them in human terms. They don't smile, pout their lips, wink, frown or shed tears. But you can pick up clues to what they are thinking and feeling by watching their features. If a cat's eyes are wide open and his ears straight up and forward, he's in a good mood. Both ears back means he is probably a little angry or at least annoyed. And if his tail is flailing from side to side at the same time his ears are back, you'd better watch out because he's really angry.

Expressions of fear and anger in a cat are visually very similar and people frequently mistake them for each other. In both reactions, the cat's ears go straight back, his eyes open wide, and as a final warning, he shows his teeth and hisses. Both moods signal potential danger, since both can result in aggression—offensive or defensive. If you corner a scared cat, even one you know, he may well strike at you out of fear. Still, we'd rather cope with a scared cat than an angry one. A scared cat will usually not bother you if you don't do anything to threaten him, but an angry cat will frequently attack without apparent reason.

If you watch your cat you will also be able to tell how well he is feeling. Many owners jump straight to the conclusion that a sulking, mopey pet is skulking around because he did something wrong, or is reacting to something they, the owners, did. Actually the cat might be sick. If your cat is acting completely differently than he normally does or is moping around for a prolonged period, get him to a veterinarian. We're sure you know your cat well enough to see any drastic changes in his appearance or behavior that might point to his not feeling well. Watch him to see how he's feeling; but at the same time, try to be objective and be careful not to read your own thoughts into his behavior. Cats are certainly not averse to living off your sympathy. In fact, if moping around will get him special attention, he may well fake it. However, anything prolonged or outrageously unusual should be checked.

There are similarities between human and cat body language. Look carefully—you can see a little bit of your own reactions in your cat's. For example, a nervous person will scratch or adjust his hair and clothing, while a nervous cat will briefly groom himself. In order to look important, both human and cat stand up really erect and adopt a direct stare. A person inflates his chest, while a cat arches his back and fluffs out his hair. Both try to make themselves look bigger and more impressive. On the other hand, the avoidance of eye contact and a slight crouching or pulling in of the body to make a smaller, more humble appearance is a sign of submission in both human and cat.

Staring is an aggressive act among cats. Strange cats often stare each other down until one walks away or shows his submission by looking away and possibly crouching at the same time. Cats don't usually look for fights unless they really feel threatened. Stares may, however, elicit an aggressive response either out of fear or anger.

Submission in cats never seems to be absolute. A cat may go into a lowered crouch, but even in this position he still retains the option of rolling over on his back and slashing out with his claws. A cat who has really lost a fight usually runs away instead of meekly yielding.

Tickling a contented cat on the stomach can turn out differently than expected. In fact, if you tickle your cat on his stomach he may suddenly claw at you and run away. Don't worry or think he's lost his mind. Being on his back sometimes triggers a primordial defensive-aggressive reflex in your cat, which at times is as much of a surprise to him as it is to you. A cat lying on his back with his legs in the air is in a fighting posture, in which he is protecting his spine—his weak spot. From this position the cat flails out with all four paws and sometimes even uses his mouth.

Surprising little innate behaviors such as this show that you will never be able to understand completely or predict exactly your cat's action or his mood. In fact, there is one bit of cat language which seems to have many meanings and functions for the cat—the grooming habit. Cats lick themselves constantly. They have a well-justified reputation for cleanliness, but they often groom far more than necessary. We'd therefore speculate that it is rather their way of releasing many things that are pent up inside them. They lick to expend excess energy, work off nervous tension, to make you think there is nothing wrong, to cover up something, to mask that they are upset; in fact they even lick when they can't think of anything else to do.

Psychological transference is a fascinating aspect of behavior problems in animals. The cat, for various reasons, often starts to act like his owner. Perhaps he feels this is what is expected of him. More likely it's simply because so much of a cat's learning mechanism is based on imitation that over the years he learns to imitate certain things the owner does. In this way human emotional habits can be picked up by cats—a nervous person often has a nervous cat, and not necessarily because the cat was born with that tendency.

A cat brings with him many instinctive reflexes and actions that he can't control completely. These can manifest themselves variously, depending on the cat. Just observe your cat and you will get to know him and his ways. Certain actions have universal meaning and are common to all cats. These are generally confined to communication between cats and involve such matters as mating or fighting; humans are not really let in on the act. Such behavior springs from some internal, eternally lasting instinct that ensures a cat's survival and the survival of the species—not from any deliberate intention on the cat's part. However, you can try to understand some of these simple gestures, which a cat uses on a constant basis, to help you understand your cat.

3

SELECTING AND BASIC CARE

Perhaps the most important question to ask yourself when getting a kitten isn't "Do I love it now?" but rather "Do I love what it will be when it is a cat?" Many people buy a kitten or adopt one because they are taken by its cute, cuddly appearance. But what if they don't like what it turns out to be when grown?

Remember that cats are living creatures who need care. When you take one in you are taking on a commitment for the rest of its life. Be sure you really want a cat and not just a toy to be quickly discarded. In our society, where disposability is the order of the day, all too many people discard pets for newer or more original models, the way they do cars or appliances. This is not the way to treat a living creature. Just keep in mind that a cat is a responsibility and not a possession.

Cats, of course, come in all shapes and sizes and differ in temperament just like humans. Every kitten/cat is not the same to every owner.

It's up to you whether you want a registered purebred or an unregistered cat. Most people opt for an ordinary cat, but many are turning to purebreds.

Purebred cats are costly. Therefore, if you are buying a cat for show, be sure it lives up to the qualities set up by cat show organizations. There are requirements for cats at these events so it would be a good idea to check on the specifications before buying.

If you buy a registered cat, be sure to get his papers. You're paying for them and are entitled to them. They may come in handy and be of value later, especially if you want to breed your cat or show him. At the same time you can get a genealogy, or family tree, of your pet telling you about his background.

No matter what you opt for in a cat, chances are you'll end up with a cat with some kind of white markings, since white in cats is dominant. If you are getting a completely white cat, however, you should know that many white cats, especially those with blue eyes, are deaf. True albinos are not deaf (and Siamese are rarely). Test for deafness by standing behind the cat and clapping your hands. If there's no reaction whatsoever, you'll know something is wrong. Keep in mind that tortoise-shell cats are nearly always female, and if you find a male tortoiseshell he will probably be sterile. Ginger or marmalade cats are nearly always males.

Despite the fact that there are many different breeds of cats, there are really only two basic categories—shorthairs and long-hairs. Each of these categories is subdivided into breeds, which in turn are subdivided on the basis of color.

Long-haired cats must be brushed on a regular basis, whereas shorthairs need less attention. However, long-haired cats often tend to be more docile just because they do need so much brushing—which means they tend to lie around more than shorthairs and thus get into less mischief. To produce these gentle cats who will allow themselves to be brushed with no fuss, longhairs have been bred docile to docile. But you should still check the parents for their dispositions, since vicious streaks are hard to eliminate. If you're not willing to take care of grooming, don't get a longhair. Bad or neglected grooming can lead to problems. Short-haired cats, on the other hand, though easier to groom, have not been bred for docility, and some can be extremely active. But this makes them better for certain trick training.

You should have no trouble finding a nice Domestic Shorthair, or just plain cat, unless of course you have a specific color and perhaps even markings in mind. Just look for ads in your local newspapers, check the humane societies, or put the word out to friends.

Cats from a pound are almost always healthy because the animals are given a physical examination before being released to new owners. Most—and in some places all—will be young. They come from various sources: off the streets or from owners who have been forced or simply wanted to give them up. Some people genuinely can no longer care for pets, but more often it's simply that the owners tire of them or have to go away for a few weeks. This saves them the expense (minimal as it is) and the annoyance of putting the cat in a cattery or kennel, or having someone look after him. They know it's easy to get a new cat when they come back. All they have to do is look in the paper.

Unfortunately, this shameful way of looking at cats is widespread. There is no excuse for giving up an older cat other than dire circumstances, such as the original owner's death or a move to England, New Zealand, or Australia, where there are six- to nine-month quarantine periods which most cats can't withstand. In such a case we can see trying to get the cat a good home. Unfortunately, however, many people look on cats as possessions; they get cats because they think they don't have to worry about them or give them too much care. Then with the first problem, or even on a whim, they will dump him at the local pound or just out on the street.

If you have your heart set on a purebred registered cat, get in touch with one of the cat organizations, go to cat shows, look up breeds in cat magazines such as *Cat's Magazine* or *Cat*

Fancy in the U.S. and *Fur and Feather* in England, ask your veterinarian and friends. This way you can be sure you will be dealing with a reputable breeder. (You may even find pedigreed cats in the pound, alongside the mixed, but the papers to prove it will, of course, usually be lacking.)

If there are no cat shows in your area and you can't find a breeder, there are reputable pet shops where you can find a cat. Just be sure the store is clean and run by people who care for their pets. Never take a kitten from a dirty place, and never take an unhealthy kitten. You might feel sorry for it, but this is not worth the heartache you may have to go through. Look for the more obvious signs of health in selecting your cat. He should look alert, alive, active, and responsive. He should have clear bright eyes free of irritation. There should be no nasal or ocular discharge. Look under the tail to check for any pasting; this is a sign of diarrhea. Check that he has a sleek, glossy coat and not a dull, flaky one. Run your hand over the coat to be sure that the cat is free of any sores, bare patches, lumps or rashes. He should have a firm, muscular body, and his stomach should be firm, with rubber-ball give—if it is soft and flabby that's bad. If he gives off an odor something could be wrong. Check the ears to make sure they are odorless and clean, free of ear mites (these may seem harmless, but they can become quite a problem) or any foreign material. The cat should have firm pink gums free of sores, and his teeth should be sharp and white.

If the animal meets these requirements, chances are he will get a clean bill of health when you take him to your veterinarian. But no matter what, a veterinarian's checkup should be scheduled as soon as you get a kitten or cat.

When picking your pet, check out the entire litter. Look for a friendly, playful disposition, not frightened or nervous. Avoid choosing a very dominant and assertive kitten or a submissive and timid one; neither makes the ideal pet. Don't expect the kittens or cat to come running over to you, since they don't know you, but do expect a certain amount of animation and interest.

In looking for your new pet, don't fail to consider a mature cat. In fact, many people prefer a cat to a kitten. Older cats usually know when and how to make themselves scarce if kids start getting out of hand, whereas a kitten hasn't learned this little diplomatic maneuver. (Some humane societies will not release kittens to families with very young children, since they worry that youngsters may treat kittens as toys.) In addition, a mature cat usually needs less care than a kitten. If you're lucky, you may even find an adult cat who is already altered (and perhaps even declawed). And if you need a mouser for immediate duty, take an adult cat—this is one skill that gets better with practice.

A kitten has the advantage of adjusting more easily to a new owner and a new home, because the memory of his first home and owner is very brief. An older cat will probably find it harder to adjust, since he has grown accustomed to his previous environment. In fact, some have great difficulty. This may make for a little shyness when he is first brought into the home. If you are planning to adopt a second cat or already have other pets in the house, it might be best to get a kitten, as he will be less of a threat to the established residents. An older pet may even take charge and become surrogate parent to the new arrival.

In picking out an older cat—especially from a pound—don't judge a cat too harshly for a standoffish attitude. Remember he is confused and disoriented, and may even have been mistreated. Therefore he will be cautious. Go back several times to give him an opportunity to get used to you before making a decision. Even then don't expect too much of him. And if he looks a little thin or scrawny, keep his unfortunate background in mind and give him a chance.

In the final analysis the only things you can really check on in a kitten or cat are his physical health, looks and heredity. The rest is up to you, including his temperament. Just try to be sure he is alert, lively, friendly and full of pep.

After you choose your pet, be careful how you get him home. The way he is treated at this time can leave a lasting impression on him. What was a playful, happy kitten can become a different cat in transit if he has a bad time. The least traumatic way of transporting him is to use an enclosed carrier of the type you would use when traveling. The way he is introduced to his new home can make all the difference, so do it right.

The sex of a cat shouldn't be a prime consideration in your choice of a pet. However, you should know how to tell, so you don't end up with a cat called "Arthur" plus a litter of kittens. Altered male cats have a reputation for being very cuddly and friendly toward their owners, whereas females are said to be more standoffish; but we have found many exceptions to this rule, and when altered both make friendly pets.

Distinguishing the sex of many species is not as simple as you might assume, and cats can be obscure to many people—at least until they reach full maturity. If you pick up a cat's tail and look underneath you will always see two openings aligned vertically close together. The top one is the anus the other the genital area. Now look and feel. If the lower opening forms a slit rather than a circle and it is flat, then it is a female. The male has two bumps, the testicles, on either side of the lower hole which is circular. If you cannot see these, feel. There'll be at least one soft bunch and more likely and properly two. Check a few times, and try to get a good professional second opinion if possible. All cats have teats, so don't make these your criteria for determining the sex.

If you are still in doubt about your cat or kitten's sex, try this formula: the male cat has two small dots like a colon (:) beneath his tail; the female cat has an upside-down exclamation point (¡) or the letter i. This isn't foolproof by a long shot.

Lots of people think that it's inhumane to alter their cats. In fact, the operation disturbs the owner far more than it does the cat, who quickly recovers and becomes an even better pet. Such people think altering makes their pets only half a cat, but really it's the kindest thing you can do. If you don't have your cat altered, you're in for a few surprises: unfixed cats can be a source of aggravation to any owner.

Altering your cat—male or female—is not a major operation. In fact, it is relatively safe and simple, has good results, and is usually recommended by vets. Many cats have the surgery in the morning and are back home again in the afternoon or the next day. Of course, as with all operations, there is a risk, but it is really very slight. A good vet is of prime importance.

The physical aspects of the altering operations are not complicated, but they do require skillful surgical work. Of the two operations, castration is usually the simpler, since it normally isn't necessary to cut into the body as with spaying.

Vasectomies have been suggested as an alternative to castration. This way the objections of many owners, about the visibility of the removal, are eliminated. Unfortunately, though this would stop cats from reproducing, it wouldn't stop the sexual drive and all the annoying behaviors associated with it.

As you know, in males the reproductive glands, the testicles, are on the outside of the body. In castration the testicles are removed and thus all sexual activity is stopped. The operation requires anesthesia and perhaps an overnight stay in the hospital. If, however, your cat has an undescended testicle, your vet may have to look for it, which could mean going into the abdomen and thus a major operation—but it's worth it to avoid later problems.

Spaying a healthy cat—and only a vet can tell you whether she is or she isn't—involves going into the abdomen and removing the ovaries so that ova (eggs) no longer develop. This requires anesthesia and hospitalization for a day or so. For the first few days the cat is home, care should be taken that she does not break the incision.

It is very important that a cat be altered at the right age. If it is done too early it can cause problems in physical growth. This is especially true in the male, where too early castration can often lead to a stunting of the growth of the penis, causing many urinary tract problems including possibly cystitis. When spaying is done too young, it can disrupt the glandular development of a female.

The best age for a male to be altered is eight to nine months. By eleven months to a year he will have begun to form his sexual and territorial behavior patterns which, once started, are hard if not impossible to stop.

Many people say that the ideal age for spaying is about four to five months, before the female cat has her first heat cycle. If she is an outdoor cat—which we don't recommend—and comes into contact with unfixed males, this could be a good idea. However, this is generally considered to be too early since the cat hasn't had the opportunity to develop properly physically. The only way to tell if everything is normal with a cat is to see whether she goes through the normal growth functions or not. This would mean you should wait until she is seven to eight months old. But this is only feasible if your cat is an indoor animal who never comes in contact with uncastrated males. It is better to spay early than to have an unwanted pregnancy. No matter what, spaying should never be done earlier than three months.

If altering your cat changes your cat's personality at all, it will only be for the better. It'll probably make him/her less nervous, less noisy (an altered cat never caterwauls); and all those undesirable behaviors related to mating periods will, of course, be eliminated. And don't think that just because your cat is altered it won't be allowed to enter cat shows. When it comes to showing, alters are accepted—in special classes.

Some people claim that an altered cat tends to gain weight easily. This gaining is not due to the operation but to overeating. If you feed him/her properly and keep his/her diet under control, your cat won't get fat. Despite rumors to the contrary, a cat always thinks of food, especially if he smells something he likes. But his intake can be easily controlled by a little discipline on your part. Don't let your cat eat all he wants unless you want him to put on weight. A fat cat's life may be shorter, less active, and filled with more health problems than a normal one's. No cat climbs up to the cupboard and opens a can or package of cat food for himself, or cooks himself a meal. You should be able to tell whether your cat is in good shape by looking at him and feeling him.

Cats are fundamentally carnivorous in their wild state, meaning they can devour the entire carcass. They kill their prey and rip open the stomachs first, eating out the contents—the already partially digested greens—before they eat the meat. This way they get a well-balanced diet.

In your home a cat has to wait to be fed. How, when and what he eats are all up to you. Pets are dependent on us and we must feed them a balanced diet. Your cat will, if trained to do so, learn to eat whatever you pick out as his food.

Mice and rats are not the ideal diet for cats—even those kept primarily as mousers—table scraps, though great for snacks, don't measure up nutritionally. By and large, the best thing to do is to get your cat on a steady diet and stick to it. Commercial cat food is usually nutritionally balanced, since years of careful research have gone into developing it. However, your best bet is to have your veterinarian help you choose the right diet for your pet. And if you have any suspicion that your cat could be allergic to certain foods, please see a vet. A cat's diet is very important and deserves special attention.

If a cat doesn't immediately start eating a food and go absolutely wild over it, people assume he doesn't like it and go running out for something else. They try giving him more and more different foods or special tidbits, and some people even end up cooking for him.

Make sure not to feed your cat anything that contains bones, such as fish or chicken, unless it is pressure-cooked in a small amount of water until the bones are really soft. Even then, they should still be pulverized. Bones can get stuck in a cat's throat and possibly choke him. Large pieces of food can also do this, for as soon as a cat gets a manageable piece of meat into his mouth, he swallows it. Cats chew very little and are unable to grind large pieces of food or bones. A cat's jaw works only in two directions, up and down. To grind, the jaw must also be able to move sideways, like humans' and dogs'.

When buying food for your cat, you should read the label just the way you would on food for yourself. The words "complete and balanced" on the label mean that a cat food has been tested by the manufacturer and been found adequate for the growth of kittens and the maintenance of adult cats and pregnant and nursing females. If it doesn't say this on the label then the food is probably simply a treat. These should be reserved for special occasions or for use in training.

The way you schedule your cat's mealtimes may depend on the type of food used. Canned foods dry out and so should be eaten fairly rapidly, but most cats love them. Semimoist stays edible for a reasonable length of time and is becoming increasingly popular because cats like it and it is convenient. Dry food can be left out all the time, but some cats dislike it and people often forget to replace it but simply add to the stale food.

A cat will quickly fall in with whatever feeding schedule you set up for him. Cats do not know clock time, certainly, but they can catch on to regular schedules.

We feed our cat two times a day and give him treats to nibble on when he responds to training or performs between meals. This is the best schedule—two meals a day, which should be eaten on the spot.

Teach your cat to eat his meals at definite times. It's really not hard to get a cat to realize that he's only going to be fed at a few set times. Simply put the food down and leave it for twenty minutes, a long enough period of time for the cat to decide to eat it. If he doesn't, take it away and don't offer to feed him again until the next regular mealtime. If he refuses it again, you should follow the same procedure. Eventually the cat will learn that he must eat what you put out for him when it is offered, not at his own whim. Don't worry, he'll soon catch on. In the wild a cat doesn't get to eat all day long. Oftentimes he's lucky if he gets a kill every few days.

If you change your cat's diet and he doesn't eat for a couple of days, he's probably just being stubborn. Once a cat gets used to a diet, you have to work hard to get him to change. Cats love the familiar. (If a cat doesn't eat his regular food, there could be something wrong.)

One woman tried to change her cat's diet and the cat vehemently objected, refusing food for a good week. The woman was determined to stick it out, but she was naturally worried that the cat might be losing weight and would eventually get ill. She put him on the scales to check it out, and to her amazement the cat had gained weight.* Apparently her husband—a recalcitrant weight watcher—couldn't stand to see the cat go hungry and would feed him succulent tidbits whenever he got the urge to stuff himself at night. A diet and a taboo on the midnight raids on the refrigerator helped reduce both their

* To weigh your cat, stand on a scale holding your cat. Then stand on it without your cat. Subtract the second weight from the first: the result is the cat's weight. Some cats may even sit on the scale for a few seconds by themselves so you can check the weight. If your cat balks at either of these methods, weigh him in his carrier and deduct the weight of the carrier.

waistlines. Now they are both eating at regular times and are in good shape.

A kitten has a tiny stomach, and can eat only small quantities. Feed him more often, gradually increasing the size of each meal and cutting down on their number as he gets older. It is generally recommended that by nine or ten weeks a cat should be given four meals per day. Over the next few months the number of meals is reduced but the quantity of food is increased until at nine months he is on an adult feeding schedule. Unfortunately not everyone is in a position to be home to take care of these feedings. In that case, feed your kitten two or three meals a day and leave a little food out to allow him to eat when he wants. Avoid feeding your kitten too much meat. Meat is high in phosphorus, and an excess of this mineral in the diet can cause soft, easily broken bones.

Some people get really technical in the feeding of their cats. Other owners practice what we call common-sense feeding. Thus a friend of ours who owns two cats, both exactly the same size, feeds one fifty percent more than the other. He found that if they were both fed the same amount the male gained weight immediately and the female lost. He originally suspected that the fatter one had been stealing the other's food. But supervision of their eating for a couple of days showed that this was untrue. Apparently the cause was their different metabolisms. After a little experimentation he arrived at his special formula of amounts to feed the cats. This is the best approach.

Despite our friend's experience, in general if you live in a multi-cat or even multi-pet household and you see that one animal is very fat and the other very thin, chances are the fat one is eating the other's rations. The eating habits of the wild cats often preclude any particularly good manners at the dinner table; likewise, unless carefully supervised, the dominant cat in a multi-cat household may well eat the dinner of all the others, even the kittens. If there are two or more cats in your house, you may have to stand over them to make sure there are no squabbles. If one erupts, reprimand the aggressor. It is important you do this at the first sign of aggression, or you might have troubles later if the aggression spreads or continues.

Separate bowls should be used for each cat. These should be solid and heavy so they don't tip over easily or slide all over the place. The food bowl should be broad and flat, or at least very shallow, rather than narrow and deep. Both the food and water dishes should be easily washable and kept clean and spotless at all times.

It is important to make sure your cat doesn't eat anything that could be harmful. Always keep medicines safely out of reach. Many of our pills and capsules come with flavored coatings that emit tantalizing smells, and the contents can wreak havoc in a cat's stomach. In some fortunate cases the effects are minimal. These, however, are not usual. Many times the effects are fatal. Exercise extreme caution where medicines are concerned.

For narcotics or barbiturates, pain killers, tranquilizers, sleeping pills and the like, about all you can do is feed the cat coffee, with cream and sugar if needed, until you get him to a vet. It contains caffeine which acts as an immediate stimulant to the heart and muscles. Tea can also be used. To counteract the narcotic or barbiturate you'll need to use a fair amount.

We know an animal who ingested an hallucinogen. The cat started throwing himself at the massive windows of a penthouse in a luxury skyscraper. Cats just can't cope with such mind-altering drugs. They are instinctive, and if they suddenly feel they can fly they will try to do it. They have no real reasoning power to hold them back.

If your cat eats a depressant, a narcotic, or a poisonous medicine, you should rush him to the vet along with the package or bottle, or at least the name, of what he ingested if possible. This way proper treatment can be started immediately. For small amounts of "soft" drugs it's best just to let him sleep it off. Remember though that drugs (unless prescribed by a vet), have no place in a cat's life.

A bowl of clean, cool, fresh water should be left available to your cat at all times. He can't ask for it. Your cat's water intake will depend greatly on the nature of the food products you feed him. If he eats a dry cat food he will need greater amounts of water. Older cats need more water to keep their fluid balance correct. A cat won't usually drink more than is good for him. Excessive drinking can be a sign of medical problems—but it is really hard to tell if a cat is drinking too much. If he appears to be drinking an outrageous amount or he suddenly starts drinking more than usual, check it out.

Most cats have a real aversion to being bathed. Fortunately a house cat usually doesn't need washing. In fact, unless absolutely essential, bathing should be avoided. If, however, it is absolutely essential that you wash your cat, you should place a towel or something similar in the tub so that your cat can get a good footing. If he slips or does not feel secure he will jump out and you'll have a rough time getting him back in.

Close the door and keep it closed when bathing him or he may decide to leave the bathroom in the middle of his bath. Fill the towel-covered, flat-bottomed bathtub with three to four inches of lukewarm water. Gently grasp your cat by the nape of the neck with one hand; then, supporting his hindquarters with your other hand, lift him into the tub. Keep the cat's back to you and your arms extended so that if he does fuss he can claw the air or the opposite side of the tub but not you.

Use a plastic container and gently pour water over him. Don't splash the water around a lot; this will scare him. After his coat is dampened thoroughly apply a few drops of a mild shampoo or soap. No fancy-smelling ones. Don't dunk him in any soaps with harsh chemical additives, even if the labels say they're harmless. Use special solutions only on the advice of a vet and then follow his instructions for use closely and carefully.

Once the shampoo is on, work it into a lather. Then rinse thoroughly using warm water from the faucet. Don't put your cat directly under the water. Try not to let him get submerged in the water, for he may panic. If you feel up to it, soap him up a second time and rinse again. Don't use a spray nozzle unless you acclimatize him to it gently and slowly.

Be patient and gentle with your cat when bathing him; soothe and praise him often. Always make sure all the water is drained before taking him out. He'll then shake himself off a few times while still in the tub and the mess will be kept at a minimum. Just be sure to keep him away from the sucking of the drain as the water goes out; it can frighten him.

When he gets out, dry him and yourself off as best you can. Clean his ears with a cotton swab to remove excess water. Keep him in a warm dry place until he is thoroughly dry. Some cats don't mind if you use a hair dryer on them; just keep it on low, and get him used to it slowly.

For extremely difficult cats or ones whose nature you're not sure of, there is an alternative way of bathing. Get a good strong pillow case or a heavy cotton laundry bag with a drawstring. Throw some of your favorite shampoo or the medication your vet has recommended for bathing into the bag. Put your cat in it with his head sticking out. Dunk the bag with the cat in it into lukewarm water. When it's thoroughly wet, scrub the cat with the folds of the bag. Then rinse and keep rinsing until the water runs clear. Try to be as gentle as possible. With luck, his claws won't come through. (If they do, try a sack of heavy canvas.) This might sound a little rough, but in an emergency it is often the best and safest procedure. (You can also wrap the cat in a thoroughly soaked towel which has a lot of shampoo in it and then rinse.)

If your cat is ill, bathe or groom him with a damp cloth. Simply rub it over him. If his condition is bad enough to require a real scrubbing bath, or if he objects violently to being washed, a trip to the vet might be the best thing. Here they can do a thorough job because if necessary they can give him anesthesia while they are scrubbing him.

If your cat desperately needs to be bathed but you can't get him to a vet and won't go through another wet bath with him, a dry shampoo might help a little. Use a dry shampoo, cornstarch, fuller's earth, or even a coarse dry oatmeal. Cornstarch is the most popular choice. As a matter of fact, many people dip a comb in cornstarch routinely when brushing their cats. Apparently this cleans a bit, helps to get out the tangles, and coats and conditions the hairs so they don't mat so easily.

Sprinkle whatever dry shampoo you are using into the cat's coat. Leave it on long enough to absorb the oil, grease and dirt. Then brush it out as best you can.

Dry shampoo is also the ideal solution for tar or grease spots your cat may get on him. Sprinkle the shampoo on the spot the way you would for a complete cleaning. This method will only work on a small spot. Anything big is best taken care of by a vet—your shampoo won't be strong enough to cut it.

If your cat gets an oil-based paint in his hair and the paint has not yet dried, remove it with turpentine. Then wash it off immediately. Unremoved solvents on your cat can be a problem, since cats tend to lick them off. If he gets into an acrylic-based paint, remove it with soap and water. If the paint has already dried you'll have to cut it out.*

If he gets tar on his paws, dip them in mineral oil and confine him to a small area with newspapers spread under him. The tar should come off. But if you kept him inside the way you should, you would not have this problem. What if a car had

---

* Ingestion of paints and cleaning solvents or inhalation of their fumes can be extremely serious.

been coming down that road where he picked up the tar as he was crossing?

If your cat chances to get sprayed by a skunk or runs into some other foul smelling thing, first neutralize the smell by pouring tomato juice on him and then bathe him.

All cats need grooming, even the hairless variety. One friend bought a hairless Sphynx cat to save herself the bother of brushing. About a week later she noticed that the cat's skin was getting coated with a brown substance which was becoming crusty. She assumed something was wrong and rushed him to the vet. The treatment turned out to be simply wiping the cat down with a wet or damp cloth every few days. Sphynx cats excrete a very small amount of a brown liquid consisting of wax and other skin secretions which would normally be absorbed into or coat the hairs of a cat's fur.

Most cats have hair, and for them regular brushing and combing is an important aspect of grooming. All varieties of cat coats—long-haired and short-haired—shed (with the possible exception of the Japanese Bobtail, which is reputed not to shed or to shed very little). If your cat seems to be shedding excessively and persistently, consult your veterinarian to see if anything is wrong. Fleas, external parasites, allergies, ringworm, and any number of other complaints could be the cause.

A cat's coat sheds noticeably in the spring and the autumn and is then regrown—or at least that was nature's scheme. The shedding mechanism is triggered by the changing lengths of the days, the amount of light and darkness. But now that cats spend most of their time indoors under artificial lighting, they shed heavily constantly. Hence the perennial complaint about cat hairs.

You should start a cat on his grooming routine when he is as young as possible. You will be able to control him more easily at that time. But no matter when you start, any attempts to play, run off, or claw and bite should be stopped immediately.

If he makes a fuss don't let him get away with it; place him back where you were originally grooming him and resume the routine. You must be firm. It's essential that your cat be brushed. Lay down the law at the outset and stop any later problems.

For long-haired cats first use a wide-toothed comb to remove all the mats and then brush with a good stiff bristle brush. Try to manipulate the fur against the way it grows so that it will be fluffy when you are finished. Groom all of your cat. Don't forget the stomach area and under the legs. If the hair is matted badly, first pull the mats apart by hand and then comb it. Nip out any mats and excess hair from between the toes and pads— it's more comfortable for the cat—but be careful that you don't cut him.

A short-haired cat does not require as much grooming. First run the comb over him, then brush him—using the same currying type action you would with a horse—and finally take a piece of chamois or a soft cloth and rub it over him to make his fur gleam. Always work a short-haired cat's coat in the direction in which it grows. If your cat absolutely refuses to let you groom him this way, wet down the palms of your hands and stroke him firmly. This will remove some of the excess hairs.

Whether you groom your cat or not, he will certainly engage in constant self-grooming. The papilae (sharp raspy little bumps) on his tongue act like the teeth of a comb or the bristles of a brush to pull out loose hair and remove flaky skin, which he then swallows. Unfortunately this hair remains undigested, and unless passed through the cat's system frequently, it accumulates in the stomach to form potentially dangerous hair balls.

Feed your cat about a teaspoon of mineral oil,* sardine oil, castor oil, or commercial lubricant once a week—twice, at most.

---

* If you use a mineral oil or one of the commercial lubricants that contain it, be sure to feed the cat only the limited amounts recommended, since it has a tendency to absorb certain oil-soluble vitamins (A, D, K, and E) from the food, preventing them from being digested.

(Some people suggest using butter or Vaseline, but these are not as effective as oils.) This will act as a cathartic to move the hair through the digestive tract. The oil picks up the hair and then passes straight through without being digested, carrying the hair with it.

The best way to feed this oil to your cat is straight. Use a plastic eyedropper or empty syringe—never glass, since that can break. Back behind the cat's canines there's an open spot where you can push the eyedropper into his mouth. Hold his head with the mouth shut, put in the eyedropper, and squeeze. If he squirms, get someone to help hold him while you do it. If he absolutely refuses, you'll just have to try adding it to his food or smearing it on the pads of his feet for him to lick off (this is also the way to administer liquid vitamins or medicines prescribed by your vet).

If your cat starts retching up hair and/or seems to be constipated, it could be a sign of excessively large hair balls. Feed him the oil, and if you see no relief within a day, get him to a vet. These balls can get really big and, when they do, expert veterinary attention is the only answer.

If your cat is not declawed you might want to trim his claws regularly. Just as your nails need clipping so do your cat's. Clipping is a simple matter and could help protect you, your family, your friends, and your furniture and belongings. In play, cats often unsheath their sharp, hook-shaped claws and attempt to catch the object of their attention. In addition, ragged edges may inadvertently dig into furniture.

To clip your cat's nails, use either human nail clippers or the special cat nail clippers available in pet stores. Press each of the outer pads on your cat's paws, one at a time, to unsheath the nail. (And don't forget the dew claws up farther on the inner side of your cat's legs.) Look for the pink blood vein, or "quick," running down the center of the claw, and clip the nail, being sure not to cut within one-eighth inch of the vein. If there are any ragged edges remaining, use sandpaper to smooth them out; otherwise the cat may finish the job himself on your furniture.

If you can't see the quick, take your cat to the vet. Trying to guess where it is is not a good idea. If you must clip, snip off just a very small bit at a time. (If you do cut into the quick by accident, take a bar of soap and press the nail into it. This will effectively block off the end of the nail and stop the bleeding.)

If you have any doubts about being able to do this job properly, take your cat to your veterinarian and have him do it. At the same time he can show you how it's done.

To clean your cat's ears, take a cotton swab and dunk it in some light oil, such as mineral oil, or even just in some warm water. Squeeze it out and then wipe out any dirt and excess wax in the cat's ears. Confine yourself to cleaning the flaps of the ears—don't dig into them. If you see something down in the ear that looks abnormal, get the cat to a vet. Potentially dangerous ear mites can hide in dirty ears, and ears are delicate instruments that should be cared for properly or problems may arise.

Another chore you might have to do one day is to take your cat's temperature. A cat's temperature is normally 101 to 101.5 degrees F. If it goes outside the 100 to 102 range, whether up or down, you probably should get in touch with a vet. Once a cat's temperature goes up to 104 degrees it's really serious, so get treatment before it gets that high. The same is true of a temperature as low as 99 degrees.

To take his temperature, use a heavy-duty complete glass rectal thermometer. (A thin, human, oral one may break inside the cat.) Dip the tip and about half of the thermometer in Vaseline before using it. If you are really friendly with your cat, you may be able to handle taking your cat's temperature by yourself. Usually, however, two people are needed—even a vet uses two. One person holds the front end steady and in place while the other supports the abdomen and inserts the greased thermometer. Don't push the thermometer, but rather rotate it gently and it will slide in. And be sure to insert it only halfway.

Check your cat periodically for fleas and ticks, whether he goes outside or not. Fleas are little black things that run fast and jump high. They leave flea dirt. Ticks start out small but can become huge depending on how long you allow them to live on and feed off your cat. Pull them off, making sure you get the head. Drown or burn them. Don't just throw them away to get on another animal or even back on your own. If your cat is really infested, take him to a vet for treatment. He may recommend that you use a flea and tick collar to keep them away in the future. Make sure this is loose enough to be slipped but not so loose that it hooks onto things easily. If your cat has any adverse reaction to the collar, get it off. If you use one, remember to replace it when necessary.

We don't recommend using any grooming aids, powders, or coat dressings unless you check with your vet to see if they're okay. In general it's best to use only the mildest hypoallergenic stuff such as you would use on yourself. As for medicated products, use these only as recommended by your veterinarian.

Since cats have basically very little body odor, skin odor could be a warning sign that your cat has contracted some skin problem, needs a bath for some reason, or is sick. Trying to camouflage the smell with another one might well only aggravate the problem.

The only smell about a cat which you might try to camouflage is his urine. Some breeders say you can do this by adding one-quarter teaspoon of apple cider vinegar to his food or water daily. Do *not* use distilled vinegar. Cats won't touch it, and besides, we use that kind for housebreaking. The vinegar apparently somehow counteracts the odor of the urine.

Additionally, this vinegar may offer some protection against cystitis. The evidence is far from conclusive, but one major breeder claims to have eliminated the cystitis problem in her cattery for over ten years.

Another breeder's trick that they claim works is for the treatment of acute cystitis. It is not a medical solution. However, in cases of extreme emergency, when the cat cannot urinate, is in obvious pain, and you can't get him to a vet, it is the best you can do. Besides, you have nothing to lose; it is harmless and may well work for you, since it has been successful for many people. Get some empty gelatin-type capsules like the ones your capsuled medicines come in from the drugstore. If you can't get any, empty some of yours and replace the contents with freeze-dried coffee. Feed your cat a couple of these, then put the cat in a warm-to-hot bath for about ten minutes. After this the cat should relieve himself. As every coffee drinker knows, coffee speeds up digestive functions. And everyone knows what sitting in water does—especially warm water.

4

WHEN TO CONSULT YOUR VETERINARIAN
by Martin DeAngelis, D.V.M.

Dear Cat Owners:

Your new kitten should be examined by a veterinarian as soon as possible, preferably within twenty-four hours after taking him home. This means you won't have much time to find a veterinarian, so you should try to make your choice beforehand. Most people seem to choose a veterinarian by the trial and error method. If you have no previous experience with a veterinarian, it's a good practice to talk to pet owners in your neighborhood and find out whom they recommend. Local cat breeders and the members of cat organizations invariably have strong opinions on which veterinarian to consult.

No matter how you choose your kitten's doctor, when you go to the office you should look for certain things. The office should be clean and efficient, and you and your animal should be approached with consideration and courtesy. You also should inquire about emergency coverage during non-office hours.

On your first visit bring vaccination certificates and any other pertinent medical information. If your kitten is brand new, take along your bill of sale and any agreements you may have signed. This way if anything is wrong with your kitten the veterinarian may be able to advise you on any recourse you may have. Be prepared to tell the doctor all you can about your pet's diet, behavior, and bowel and bladder functions. Routinely the veterinarian will examine the animal and check for the presence of internal parasites. This is done by examination of a fresh stool specimen, so bring one with you.

If found to be healthy, your cat will be vaccinated against feline distemper (panleukopenia, feline enteritis), a highly contagious disease caused by a virus and sometimes serious enough to be fatal. The usual early signs are fever, loss of appetite, vomiting, and lethargy. Another contagious disease your cat may be vaccinated against is feline rhinotracheitis. This is another viral disease, which primarily affects the upper respiratory tract. It causes sneezing and runny eyes as well as depression, loss of appetite, and fever. There are other viral respiratory diseases in cats but rhinotracheitis vaccine seems to offer some degree of protection. The pattern of giving vaccinations varies somewhat, but usually the injections are given first at about seven or eight weeks of age and then repeated one to three times at two-week intervals. Vaccinations against rabies are given after six months of age and are highly recommended for cats allowed to roam out of doors.

Once your cat has all his basic vaccinations you should continue to take him in for health care on a regular basis. Routine checkups are the only reliable way of keeping tabs on your cat's health. For one thing, yearly boosters are recommended for innoculations. For another, a health problem that is neglected can become serious. For example, a heavy parasite infestation can drain nutrition from your kitten or cat faster than the diet can provide it. Regular examinations and stool analyses (remember to bring a sample with you) are generally reliable methods of diagnosing parasite problems.

Cystitis is another commonly encountered disease in cats. It is an inflammation of the urinary bladder. This disease occurs in both sexes and at all ages. It is quite rare in those less than six months old, and is most frequently seen in the adult castrated male. The usual signs are increased frequency of urination, often accompanied by straining and blood in the urine. Eventually the animal may have a complete blockage of the urethra and be in extreme distress. The blockage material may be sandlike clumps of crystals or a plug of mucous debris.

The cause of feline cystitis—urethral obstruction complex— is not known. However, a virus may be involved and bacteria are also suspected in many cases. Additionally, injury, tumors, and the presence of calculi or stones can also cause cystitis. Alkaline urine, dry cat foods, and diets high in ash content are also possible factors. Castration has been incriminated widely. However, there is no proven cause and effect relationship. Treatment involves relieving the obstruction, administering antibiotics and urinary acidifiers, proper diet, and encouraging increased water consumption by salting the food. Cats who suffer repeated episodes may need long-term or continuous medications and special diets. Surgery to remove bladder stones or to create a larger urethral opening in the male may be required. Any time your cat is straining to urinate and is unable to produce a stream of urine, your veterinarian should be consulted without delay.

Emergencies may be truly life-threatening situations or just exasperating occurrences that make it difficult to keep your cat at home. Some of the problems that can require an emergency visit are accidents resulting in lacerations, fractures, unconsciousness, difficulty in breathing, or pale gums. A cat that constantly breathes with its mouth open even when at rest should probably be examined without delay. Drooling or panting, on the other hand, may only be signs of nervousness and do not in themselves constitute an emergency. Vomiting and diarrhea are fairly common occurrences, and if prolonged can be quite serious. Initially one can apply first aid to treat the problem at home. For vomiting it is usually recommended that you withhold food and water for twelve to twenty-four hours and administer a teaspoon or two of a coating agent such as Pepto-Bismol or Maalox to soothe the cat's stomach. For diarrhea use an intestinal binding agent such as Kaopectate and add boiled rice to a bland diet until the condition subsides. If it worsens or does not improve within twelve to twenty-four hours, your veterinarian should be consulted. You should also take your cat to a veterinarian if it eats any foreign materials. Needles and thread, strings, baby bottle nipples and tinsel are fairly common items eaten by house cats. These materials once ingested can cause serious problems.

If your cat should suffer a severe injury there are certain measures you can take until you can bring your pet to the veterinarian. Be careful when handling your animal, for in a state of excitement it may scratch or bite you. You should not offer food or water unless instructed to do so by the doctor. If there is to be some delay between the time of injury and a veterinarian's examination, keep your cat warm and quiet, and if there is an open wound you may bandage it with a clean dressing. Unnecessary handling of your pet at a time of stress should be avoided.

Common surgical procedures such as spaying, castration, and declawing should be discussed with your veterinarian. Castration of male cats and spaying of females (removal of the uterus and ovaries) are usually desirable for those animals not intended for breeding. Altering usually decreases any tendency to wander and the spraying of urine by males, and particularly important—eliminates unwanted kittens. Many pet owners and their neighbors welcome relief from the feline love calls too. Castration and spaying are usually done after puberty, at approximately six to nine months of age. Declawing is usually indicated for cats that destroy household items in spite of scratching posts and for cats that hurt people with their claws. In homes with small children it is sometimes done to prevent injury in play. Declawing can be done as early as three months of age and usually only the forepaws are done. Due to the nature of the nailbed tissue an occa-

69

sional nail may regrow, but this is uncommon. Declawing does lessen a cat's ability to defend itself, so cats that are outdoor animals should probably be left intact. Oftentimes details about your and/or your cat's lifestyle can be important in determining the procedures to be followed.

Your veterinarian is one of the best friends your cat can have, so pick one carefully and keep in touch about your cat's health.

Martin DeAngelis, D.V.M.

5

CAT BREEDS: A Chart

SHORT-HAIRED CATS

BREED	ORIGINS
ABYSSINIAN	Abyssinia—Ethiopia
AMERICAN SHORTHAIR OR DOMESTIC SHORTHAIR *(Commonly called "Alley Cat")*	Not native to America but brought on ships as far back as the Mayflower. The oldest short-haired breed in America and also the most numerous. If you own a cat and live in America, this is probably the type you have.
AMERICAN WIREHAIR	A spontaneous mutation of the American Domestic Shorthair
BOMBAY	United States Bred from cross matings of Burmese and Black Domestic
BRITISH BLUE *(Often listed under British Shorthair)*	England
BRITISH SHORTHAIR	England

72

COLORS
Ruddy, red, blue, cream

Solid colors: white (blue, copper, and odd–eyed), black (amber-eyed), blue, red, cream, chinchilla, shaded silver, black smoke, and blue smoke
The standard five tabbies, all in classic or mackerel form: silver, red, brown, blue, and cream
Tortoiseshell (covered in patches of black, red, and cream), calico (tortoiseshell and white), blue-cream, and bi-colors
All the colors of the American Shorthair

Glossy black

Lavender to plum blue with copper, orange or yellow eyes

Tabbies: brown, red, and silver
Solid colors: black (amber-eyed), white (blue, orange, and odd–eyed)
Bi-colored, blue-cream, spotted, and tortoiseshell

CHARACTERISTICS
Close-cropped ticked fur, big almond-shaped eyes, large ears, svelte body type, long tail. Active, intelligent and friendly.
Basically a product of natural selection, this breed is tough and hardy. Show standards call for a powerfully built, muscular, medium to large body, not too rangy or cobby. Short, thick, hard-textured fur. Large head, slightly oblong and longer than wide, with rounded tips on the ears and large round eyes.

Identical to the American Shorthair but with a stiff, coarse, wiry, resilient, medium-length, fairly dense coat, which is even coarser than that of a wirehaired terrier dog.
A combination of both ancestors' characteristics.

The same specifications as for the British Shorthair, but with hair short and plush-like rather than sleek and flat, and extra-large eyes. Quiet homebody.
Well-knit, powerfully built body. Slightly smaller than the American Shorthair, and somewhat like the Exotic Shorthair but with softer short, fine hair. Short nose and face, small

BREED	ORIGINS
BURMESE	A brown cat from Burma was brought to the U.S. and bred to a seal-point Siamese.
CHARTREUSE	France
COLORPOINT SHORTHAIR	United States and England Developed as new colors of Siamese bred to tabbies or Abyssinians
EGYPTIAN MAU *(American)*	Egypt Reputedly bred in the U.S. from two cats brought from Egypt
EXOTIC SHORTHAIR	America Product of an American Shorthair bred to a Persian

COLORS

Often also includes the British blue

Sable (brown), champagne, blue, and platinum

Plus, in England: cream, blue-cream, red, chocolate, and tortoiseshell

Slate blue to clear gray-blue

Lynx-point: seal, blue, lilac, and chocolate

Tortie-point: seal, blue, lilac, and chocolate

Red-point

Tabby markings of silver, bronze, and smoke

Solid colors: white (blue, copper, and odd–eyed), black, blue, cream, red, chinchilla, shaded silver, shell-cameo, black smoke, blue smoke, cameo (red)

Tabbies: silver, red, brown, blue, cream, and cameo

Tortie, calico, blue-cream

Bi-colors: black and white, blue and white, red and white, and cream and white

CHARACTERISTICS

rounded ears and round eyes.

In the U.S. a stockier and sturdier body type than the Siamese and rounded eyes are desirable. In England the trend is more toward the oriental type, with almond-shaped eyes. But neither wants a real Siamese type, since the face is shorter and wider with large rounded ears.

Massive solid cats with broad chests and round heads and eyes. Thick, short, plush-like coats rather than flat sleek ones. Bodies like mini-lions and similar to the British Blue.

New and varying colors or markings on the points of Siamese not categorized with the normally recognized ones.

Markings of a spotted tabby and a body type midway between a Domestic Shorthair and Siamese, with the pointed ears of the Siamese but a quieter voice.

A Persian-type cat with a short, thick coat. Fur is the texture and quality of a Persian's and stands out from the body, but is short.

BREED	ORIGINS
HAVANA BROWN OR **HAVANA (ENGLAND)**	Continental Europe and England Bred from crossings of black Domestic, chocolate-point Siamese, and Russian Blue
JAPANESE BOBTAIL (Mi-ke)	Japan
KORAT	Thailand The good-luck cat of Thailand and one of the few natural breeds left
MANX	Isle of Man The tailless cat
OCICAT OR **EGYPTIAN MAU (ENGLAND)**	United States and England Cross-breedings of Abyssinians, Siamese, and American Shorthairs

76

COLORS

Chestnut brown

Solid colors: black, red and white
Bi-colors: black and white, red and white
Tri-colors: black, red, and white
Tortoiseshell

Silver-blue

Any color: tabby, bi-color, tortie, and any solid color

Spotted cats: silver, bronze, and smoke (U.S.)
Tabbies: silver, bronze, and smoke (England)

CHARACTERISTICS

An extreme foreign type with almond eyes, a long slender body, pointed ears. Looks like a solid chocolate-colored Siamese with green eyes.

Medium-sized cat with a bobbed tail and slanty eyes set in a triangular head. Soft, silky hair which is slightly longer than most shorthairs and said to be practically non-shedding. Quiet with strong family and social ties.

Semi-cobby body. A definite heart-shaped face with extra-large eyes which are either green or gold. His ears are large and round tipped. Affectionate.

A cat which ideally has no tail but usually has some. Extra-long hind legs like a rabbit give this cat a hopping gait. Not prolific breeders and often have deformities in the hinds, so pick carefully. Quiet, friendly cats.

In the U.S., a cat with the same standards as the American Egyptian Mau, with pointed ears and oval but not oriental eyes. In England, a cat with all the Siamese traits but with spotted or mackerel tabby markings and a "scarab" mark between the ears on the forehead. Both types have the doglike quality of the Siamese but with a slightly quieter voice.

BREED	ORIGINS
ORIENTALS OR FOREIGN SHORTHAIRS (ENGLAND)	England Hybrid Siamese
REX OR CORNISH OR DEVON (ENGLAND)	England, Germany, and the United States Spontaneous genetic mutation
SCOTTISH FOLD	Scotland and Belgium Now bred mainly in the United States
SIAMESE	Thailand
SPHYNX *(Canadian Hairless)*	Canada Spontaneous mutation of American Shorthair
TONKINESE	United States Product of Burmese and Siamese crossings

78

COLORS

All solid colors, with lilac and white the major ones

All colors and combinations

Any color and coat pattern normally recognized for championship showing

Seal-point, chocolate-point, blue-point, lilac-point, and albino

All colors

Solid colors: honey and mink

CHARACTERISTICS

Exactly the same as Siamese but of a solid color and with a quiet voice.

Cats with curly coats the texture of a soft Persian lamb. Long, extremely slender bodies of the foreign or Siamese type. Wedge-shaped head, flat skull, and over-sized ears.

A short-haired Persian with a plush coat and ears that fold forward from the base in back. Always keep their baby kitten look. Sweet homebody type.

A white body of varying shades with points—around the muzzle, ears, tail, and feet—of a different color. Slim, longish bodies with a tapering wedge-shaped face, large, pointed ears, almond-shaped eyes, a long tapering tail (with or without a kink near the tip), and a definite Far Eastern look. High pitched voice; doglike qualities and devotion.

A basically hairless cat with short plush fur found as a mask on the face, on the ears, and on the feet. No whiskers, and only microscopic hairs on the back. The body type and characteristics are those of the American Shorthair.

A cross of Burmese and Siamese characteristics, but always a solid color.

79

LONG-HAIRED CATS

BREED	ORIGINS
ANGORA	Ankara, Turkey Bred at the Ankara Zoo
BALINESE	United States Spontaneous mutation of Siamese
BI-COLORED PERSIANS	Persia (Iran)
BIRMAN	Burma The sacred cat of Burma was exported to France and bred there
HIMALAYAN OR COLORPOINT LONGHAIR (ENGLAND)	Britain Cross between Siamese and Persian

COLORS
White-blue, copper, or odd–eyed–
  best quality
Black, blue, or smoke

Blue-point, seal-point, lilac-point,
  and chocolate-point

Black and white, blue and white,
  orange and white, cream and
  white, red and white, or tortoiseshell and white.
Seal-point, chocolate-point, lilac-
  point, and blue-point

All the colors of the Colorpoint
  Shorthair and seal-point, chocolate-point, lilac-point, blue-
  point, blue-cream-point, and
  flame-point

CHARACTERISTICS
Fine, silky, medium-length coat
  that tends to wave. Longish,
  fine-boned, slim body; smallish
  head tapering to a rounded chin;
  large, pointed, tufted ears; large
  almond-to-round-shaped eyes.
  Smart and affectionate.
Body of varying shades of white,
  with all the color combinations
  on the points and the same body
  characteristics as a Siamese; but
  with silky, medium-long hair
  and a bushy tail.
All the characteristics of a Persian
  except for coloration. Attempt
  to get "Dutch Rabbit"
  markings.
All creamy gold with points of another color, like a Siamese, but
  with long hair. The most out-
  standing characteristic is the
  white paws, which ideally should
  end in front in an even line at
  the third joint, and in back
  should cover the entire paw and
  go up the back of the leg to end
  in a point. A heavier body type
  than a Siamese, with stocky legs,
  rounded head, medium-length
  nose, blue eyes, and largish ears.
  Long bushy tail and a ruff
  around the neck. Small-voiced
  and gentle.
Coat, face, and body type of a
  Persian with the coloring of a
  Siamese. There should be *no*
  similarity to the Siamese other

BREED	ORIGINS
MAINE COON	Maine, United States Long-haired cats brought on ships and let off on the coast of Maine bred with short-haired cats brought over in the same way. (The rumor is that this cat is a product of the interbreeding of a cat with a raccoon, but this is untrue.)
MANX (LONGHAIR)	United States Spontaneous mutation of the short-haired Manx
PEKE-FACED PERSIAN	United States
PERSIAN	Persia (Iran)
RAG-DOLL	California, U.S.A.

COLORS

CHARACTERISTICS

than color; everything else
should be Persian.

All colors and combinations of
colors

A large, big-boned cat ranging
from 16 to 25 and even 30
pounds, with the hind legs
slightly shorter than the front,
and medium-length silky hair.
Wide head with a medium-long
face and nose, squarish muzzle,
large round eyes, and big tufted
ears. Tends to be shy and quiet
but also intelligent.

All the colors and combinations of
colors of the short-hair type

All the characteristics of the short-
haired Manx but with long hair.

Red and red tabby

Same qualities as a Persian except
for the Pekinese-dog-type face,
for which the breed is named. A
depressed or pushed-in nose, in-
dentation between the eyes, and
a wrinkled muzzle distinguish
him.

Solid colors: black, blue, cameo,
chinchilla, cream, red self (solid
red), shaded silver, smoke,
golden, and white (blue, copper,
and odd–eyed)
Tabbies: blue, brown, red, cream,
and silver
Tortoiseshell, blue-cream, calico
(tortoiseshell and white)

Short, cobby, solid, massive body.
A big round head, large round
eyes, a short face, a snub pushed-
in nose, plus small, neat, heavily
tufted ears. Thick hair of varying
lengths on different parts of the
body stands out from the body,
giving an even bigger appearance. A heavy ruff around the
neck and back of the head makes
the cat resemble a lion. The tail
is short and bushy, and the legs
short and thick, keeping the cat
low to the ground.

Seal-point, chocolate-point, blue-
point, and lilac-point

Fifteen to 20 pounds and 3 feet
long. Long silky hair on a cat

BREED	ORIGINS
SOMALI	United States and Canada Spontaneous mutation of Abyssinian
TURKISH VAN	Turkey (Lake Van area) Bred only in Britain The swimming cat Domesticated as long ago as the saluki of ancient Egypt

COLORS

Ruddy, red, and blue

Chalk-white (no yellow), auburn
markings on the face, with a
white blaze, and an auburn tail
with slightly darker auburn rings

CHARACTERISTICS

of Siamese coloration. A huge
friendly cat.

Long-haired Abyssinian. Medium-
length hair with a ruff around
the neck, a bushy tail, and large
tufted ears.

Long, sturdy body covered with
soft silky fur which has no undercoat. Short, wedge-shaped
face with a longish nose, a ruff
around the neck, large well-
tufted ears, amber eyes, and a
medium-long bushy tail. Reputed to love water.

PART TWO

TRAINING
YOUR CAT

6

OUR BASIC TRAINING METHODS

A client had a cat who wouldn't listen to a thing she said. Not only that, but the cat had recently become so alienated that he refused to go near her. A demonstration of her training techniques soon showed the problem. She got her cat and placed him on the table. She pushed him into a sitting position and said "sit." The cat got up and tried to get away. She grabbed the cat, hit him, and pushed him down again, but much harder this time. The cat tried to bite her and she hit him again, but this time also threw him out of the room—and she wondered why he wouldn't listen!

It wasn't that she intended to be cruel, but rather that she was ignorant about cats and how they should be handled. After a lecture on the proper treatment of animals, we showed her the correct way to work with a cat.

In training, never reprimand your cat for doing something improperly or he'll never do it again at all. Attach an unpleasant association to something and a cat won't touch it. Cats learn fast, so one bad experience can be enough.

The word "no" is *not* a command but a reprimand, and should be used only as such. In addition, it must be applied correctly. If it is used improperly—for example, without being clearly connected to your cat's wrongdoings, or too close to a training command—you could ruin any chance of ever getting your cat to listen to you. "No" should be reserved strictly for reprimands. If you confuse it with commands it could cause problems.

A classic case is a friend of ours whose cat suddenly started messing all over the house. Apparently the man would reprimand his cat for jumping on his lap every time he sat on the toilet. He would spank the cat, then put him in the litter box, which was right next to the toilet. The cat thought he shouldn't be in the bathroom at all, so he started to mess on a prized couch instead.

Just verbally reprimanding your cat is not enough. As a matter of fact, if not enforced, the "no" means nothing. The "no" must be associated in an unpleasant way with the action you want stopped. A slight tap on the cat's rump or a slight shake as you say "no" will put some meaning into it and establish a convincing reprimand. Once you give the word "no" a meaning the cat can understand, you should be able to control your cat's bad habits and stop him from doing the wrong thing. In correcting your cat, the more you combine actions with words the quicker he'll learn and the longer he'll remember.

A mother cat has no problem teaching her kittens right from wrong. Just a smack of the paw, or picking them up by the neck and shaking them and taking them away from danger gets the message across. She doesn't say a word. Their survival depends on learning right from wrong—or safety from danger. Therefore it's up to you to follow her example in teaching your kitten right from wrong.

You must be utterly calm and methodical in correcting your cat. Never lose your temper. Use the name of the cat, then "no." If he has been taught the meaning of "no" properly, a firm "no" whenever he does something you don't want should bring about the proper response. But first he must know that "no" means something.

To instill the "no" properly you may have to employ our "rubber-arm" technique. This teaches the cat that you can reach him no matter how far away you are. Toss a magazine in his direction, not necessarily to hit but near enough so the sound startles him, and say "no" sharply as it lands. Reprimands don't have to be painful; they can simply be startling or unpleasant for your cat. A glass of water poured on a really recalcitrant cat will also stop an undesirable action fast. Of course, there are only certain places where this method is practical—but it is very effective. Keys used instead of a magazine and later shaken as a reminder also work.

Another reprimand technique that makes use of your cat's innate behavior is the *White Distilled Vinegar Method*. This is generally reserved for a cat who messes up somewhere other than in his litter box or in the toilet. When you see the mess, ignore your cat and simply go into the kitchen and get a bottle of white vinegar and a roll of paper towels. Uncap the bottle and put it and the towel down next to the spot. Then go get your culprit, but *without* calling him. Bring him over to the spot. Put him close enough to the urine and/or feces so he can see and smell it. This way he'll associate what is to come with his dirt. Stick the open bottle of vinegar under his nose or put some on a towel and touch his nose, and let him have a good sniff of it. Then let him go. Now put a drop of vinegar on the spot after you've cleaned it up.

The smell of white vinegar is harmless to cats and will not stain rugs or furniture, but it will add a smell to the spot that will remind him of your punishment, and his bad act. Thus when he smells the place he will tend to stay away. His sense of smell is not terribly acute, as you know, but an acid smell is quickly recognizable.

No matter what, "no" should be the only word ever used when you correct your cat. The word "no" literally covers a multitude of sins. It's the one word, really the *only* word, an owner ever needs in the way of a reprimand. And remind yourself not to be mean after the cat has been reprimanded. There's no point in "punishing" your cat by locking him in the bathroom for three or four hours—after a few minutes he probably won't remember what he was being punished for, and all you'll accomplish will be to teach the cat to stay in the bathroom. Instead, after saying the harsh "no" and/or giving him a slight physical reprimand such as a slap or shake, turn around and walk away. Then just leave him alone—ignore him—for five to ten minutes.

We can't overstress the need for *simplicity* in letting your cat know what you require of him. Your cat should be corrected immediately for bad actions whenever possible—catching a cat in the act and stopping him is the best way. If you haven't got time to scold him right then and decide to forget it just this once, congratulations! You have just won yourself a cat who won't listen to a word you say. It's the "just onces" that ruin the owner/cat relationship. If you aren't consistent with your cat, he won't know when you are serious. Cats are very much like children in this respect. If you tell them "no" in no uncertain terms they will listen. If you ignore their bad behavior they will become obstreperous.

We often find it difficult to get owners to reprimand their cats because they don't like to be "unpleasant." Additionally, "discipline" seems like a dirty word to many people because it makes them think of all the things they should be doing themselves. Make it as simple as possible for yourself by leaving as little room as possible for the cat to make a mistake. Try to maintain a standard mood and set of rules for your cat.

Teach your cat the difference between right and wrong. Show him what he is allowed and what he isn't, make it very plain and take all the confusion out of it. If you chase him from the table, a few minutes later take him to where he normally eats and give him a treat. This way he will have been punished for unwanted actions and rewarded for desirable ones. In the same context, if he isn't allowed in or on certain places, chase him away, wait a bit, and then take him to one of the spots where he is allowed and pet him or give him a treat to show him it is okay to be there. Thus whenever you take a bad habit away from a cat you should try to replace it with a good one. This small point can be the difference in whether or not your cat is trained and properly behaved.

Reprimands mean more if you show the difference between reward and/or praise for good behavior and punishment for bad. But be very careful about doing this correctly so that the cat really does get the distinction. One woman, after lecturing her cat about scratching the furniture, gave the cat a treat to reinforce the lecture. But the only thing it reinforced was the cat's clawing at the couches. He thought the reward was for doing this, not for staying away. When his owner came home to see his handiwork, she couldn't understand and fumed furiously at her cat.

It's all communication. You must let your cat know exactly what you want through the use of the word "no" or even a mild slap. This is far better communication than the anger the woman let loose on her poor cat when she saw the mess. She kicked him and screamed hysterically.

We told her to take the cat over to the couches and not do anything until the cat began to scratch them. As soon as he did, she was to slap him and say "no" emphatically.

For those times when we are not around to say "no," we believe in harmless booby traps that communicate with a cat through "body language." One aquarium makes sure its cats stay out of the fish tanks by leaving a small electric eel in an open tank. The cat goes for the eel. After the first shock he never goes into another tank! The shock is strong enough to leave a lasting impression but not strong enough to injure or harm the cat in any way. The idea of the booby trap is to surprise, not to hurt. In fact, this is true of all reprimands we suggest for controlling bad habits. Generally a cat will react, or even overreact, to anything he feels is different from the norm.

We used the booby-trap method in one case where the cat had learned to turn on the faucet to drink. The owners thought it was cute and never corrected it. The only problem was that the cat never turned the water off and one day flooded the kitchen. To break the habit, we had the handles changed to the round type rather than the long ones. We then took a chopstick and used it as a prop to hold up a plastic plate, wedging it between the sink's handle and the lip of the plate. When the cat tried to turn on the water he released the plate and it came falling down. The surprise of this booby trap soon ended the problem.

Some cats love to get outdoors and wander. They are curious to see what's going on out there. If your cat wants out he will sit by that door and wait and wait. He may well even feign disinterest; but when it opens he will woosh out at the slightest opportunity—often unnoticed by you, the owner. Cats have mixed emotions about going out: they crave it but at the same time fear it.

Once outside, some cats panic and try frantically to get back indoors; they are scared of their strange new surroundings. However, it is not always easy for them to find their way home. One night friends were awakened about midnight by wild scratching on their door. They thought they were being burglarized and called the police, who arrived promptly to find two cats frantically scratching on the door. It turned out that the cats belonged in the corresponding apartment three floors below. They recognized the door from the outside layout, but definitely not the floor.

Cats get lost really easily. One Milwaukee cat owner called the local station about a black cat she had seen in a T.V. commercial. Her cat had run away about a month before, and she was positive that the one in the commercial was hers. She said that she could tell this by the way his nose twitched. The fact that the commercial was shot in New York was unimportant to her. She was convinced that some smart producer had seen her cat, spotted him as definite star material, and had somehow lured him away from home with the promise of riches and fame and stardom. It was not her cat, but this did not stop her persistent attempts to locate him. She even contacted the product company. If this woman had simply taught her cat not to run away, or rather had not allowed him to roam, she wouldn't have had to worry, and there would be one less stray wandering around the streets. People are often being cruel when they think they are being kind.

No matter how much cats like to roam, for their sake it is better if they don't. Life is much safer and in the end happier for your cat—even though he may seem to be pining away for the great outdoors—if you keep him at home. It is in his and your best interests: no traffic, no dogs, no malicious cat-haters, no possible unintentional poisoning, no fights.

Most cats who like to wander and try their luck outside are unaltered adult animals or as-yet-unaltered kittens. In a vast majority of cases, simply altering the cat is one of the easiest ways of encouraging him to stay home. Other cats need more forceful persuasion. Generally after a long period of forced confinement indoors a cat will be more reluctant to leave, since the outdoors will have become a strange new place that needs very careful exploration. But for cats that really like to wander constant vigilance is required.

Another way of stopping the running-away habit is simply to leave the door slightly ajar (not wide open so the cat can come rushing straight out), stand outside the door, and have someone inside shout when your cat is heading toward it. As his head comes through the door, throw a magazine down hard without hesitation right in front of him. After this happens a few times, the cat won't be so eager to go out—he'll be scared of what's out there. Use this same method when your cat tries escaping through an open window. (You could add screens as further insurance.)

Even if your cat is not a big rover, it is best to set up the situation and thus ensure that he never develops the habit. Make the outdoors a fearful or unpleasant place to wander into unaccompanied by you.

It is easy to stop a cat from jumping out of windows and/or running through doors if you catch him in the act. Stand outside the door or window and induce him to run out. Get his attention, dangle a toy, do something to entice him out without using the command "come" or anything like it. You must *not* call him, because he's going to be reprimanded and if you ever want him to come to you later he won't. "Come" should never be followed by anything but praise. Excite him, lure him, tempt him. And as he comes through the window or door, throw a pail or at least a glass of water at him. This will surprise him and bring him up short. It does wet the floors, but you won't have to be out searching for him all night.

You need not worry that the bucket technique will give your cat an aversion to water—he already has one. And if you're worried about the cat getting hurt, don't. It's the surprise, the sudden wetness, the drastic change in temperature that bothers him, not the water itself. Even Esther Williams would be put off by an unexpected drenching. Nor should your cat become afraid of buckets or glasses because he'll feel the water before he realizes where or even whom it comes from. The first splash will usually cure him of his annoying pastime. If not, the second one will. (Bring possible problems such as this out in the open—deliberately set up situations.)

A bucket, or more likely a glass, full of water is also one way to break your cat of rifling the garbage can. The secret is to sneak up on the cat and catch him in the act, so as to preserve the element of surprise. But because your cat can often see you coming, and it does take a while to locate and fill a glass, it is probably far easier to use your set of house keys in the rubber-arm technique. Simply fling them near the errant animal, and when the keys land with a clatter, startling him, tell him "no" loud enough so he hears you (but not screaming hysterically— just one word, "no"). Squirting water guns is really useless and has never stopped a cat we know of, except at the moment of the squirt and on a temporary basis.

Unaltered cats will cry constantly and piercingly when in heat or when looking for a female in heat. The only way to stop this kind of crying is to have your cat spayed or castrated. There is, however, another type of plaintive meowing that is just an annoying habit. Siamese and their relatives are quite vocal with their higher-pitched voices, while some other breeds have softer voices. But no matter what the quality of the voice, a plaintive, begging cat can grate on your nerves. Initially a kitten meows because he feels that he's very small and alone—it's like a baby's cry. Your kitten will meow when he's unhappy but also, just like a baby, when he wants something. When you first got your kitten, you cuddled him and kissed him. Then you put him to bed in another room. First he whined to get your attention, and then, when you didn't come to him, he started to cry louder and louder. You probably thought you were being cruel to lock him up all by himself, so you went in to soothe him and he probably ended up in your bed. Thus he discovered that you would come in and comfort him if he cried—and the habit was off and running.

A cat will meow with excitement when he suspects he might get a tidbit or a toy. It's the rough equivalent of a pleased giggle, but at the same time it is a pleading noise, a means of making you feel sorry for him, a manipulative gesture. He may even extend his meows into a more physical gesture, such as grabbing food out of your hand with his paw or even grabbing with his teeth.

Therefore, even if your cat's request seems to be reasonable, stop him with a firm "no," and back it up. Make it clear you don't want him to cry.

Crying is definitely a habit that should be curtailed immediately; otherwise your cat may well grow up to be constantly meowing for everything he wants. Once he finds that crying will get him what he wants he'll start meowing to beg for food, especially when you have visitors over to dinner. He may also come to enjoy meowing for its own sake, with no other purpose in mind. If you let this habit become ingrained you'll soon have a full-fidelity meower. He'll do it automatically just for the fun of it or because he's learned he can get attention or rewards for crying. Don't let it develop; stop it before it starts.

If, of course, your cat suddenly starts meowing and he never has before, he may be in trouble. Check to see if everything is all right—no physical things wrong with him, nothing like a fire or other danger he could be warning you of. But in general you should look at your cat's every act as an embryonic habit and act accordingly.

People tend to figure out too many ways not to do things right. One hairdresser taped his Persian cat's mouth shut to soothe a nervous neighbor's nerves, and at the same time to give himself relief from a reminder of what he said his clients sounded like all day long. "It doesn't hurt him," he claimed. "I use the tape with air holes in it!" He must have assumed it wouldn't pull the cat's hair out, though given his business we couldn't figure out how. Fortunately he kept the cat for only a little while and then passed it on to a more caring owner. Never do this with your cat—it does no good and can only cause harm.

When you have company, stop to consider whose company it is, yours or your cat's. Visitors provide new smells, new sounds, new sights and, if cat lovers, enough affection to make any cat overexcited. Cats love new things, and though most may be a little reticent to come out at first, the prospect of a good back rub or a tidbit treat or even plain old curiosity will bring them around. Pretty soon they'll be walking all over the visitors. The cat is not necessarily being friendly: it could all be part of that aggressive territorial behavior described in Chapter 10, and it can be extremely annoying. Stop it. Chase him from visitors if he displays this type of behavior. A firm, calm "no" will generally soon put an end to it.

Another habit that many people object to is suckling. Many cats love to suckle. They make a suckling movement with their mouths and knead by pushing their front paws alternately against the object they are suckling—usually a person—as though they were nursing, and they often salivate at the same time. Some people enjoy this, but to others it is annoying, especially when the cat has claws, which he inadvertently brings out. To stop this habit, gently push the cat off whenever he starts to suckle. Since this is an annoying habit rather than a destructive one, you shouldn't punish your cat but simply work to discourage the habit. If you reprimand him, he may feel it's for being with you and thus learn to shun you.

Suckling means a cat is contented. It is a natural reaction, though not all cats do it. Some people speculate that the habit develops only if a cat is weaned too early. However, we've found that it depends on the individual cat. A friend has two cats who are brothers from the same litter. One is a big suckler and even suckles a pillow, whereas the other has never shown any inclination. Therefore it would seem that suckling has more of a security-blanket or thumb-sucking connotation.

Many people really enjoy their cats' suckling and wouldn't stop it for anything. But some of these owners would still like to stop the drooling some cats do when kneading on an arm or whatever. The kneading movement triggers memories of nursing, and the cat may inadvertently start drooling in anticipation of food. Even though he is not actually trying to suckle for food, the response is imprinted. When it happens, the cure for drooling (not necessarily to deter kneading), is to take a piece of cotton wool and wipe off the outside of the cat's mouth and then inside around the gums. Your cat won't like this, and the drooling will stop. It will take a few weeks at least, but it should eventually be Pavloved in. The cat will stop drooling simply because he will get so used to the drying.

Realistically, however, it is best to stop the habit completely. Don't make the mistake most people do of encouraging their pets. At first suckling seems like such a cute habit, a sign of affection. People therefore encourage their cats by stroking them. But it can become annoying if he keeps it up, especially if the cat decides to suckle at your throat in the middle of the night. One client had this very problem with her cat, and was eventually forced to wear a neck brace to bed. However, the brace was no solution, as the cat simply transferred his suckling to her arm. The only real solution is to push him off. There is no way you can place a booby trap on your own body. The one person we know who did this ended up taking the brunt of the trap herself.

Suckling can also be a problem when it develops into a form of self-suckling. A cat may lick his flanks raw or suckle on his tail, hind nipples, or paw. It is best to discourage this by discipline since it is a self-destructive habit for the cat. A good slap across the snoot or the behind, along with a "no" every time he starts, is the answer here.

The habit of self-grooming can also become so excessive that it may lead to the cat's pulling out his hair or even mutilating himself. This is not uncommon in cats confined for a period for boarding. It is also observed in zoos. Boredom may be a cause. And nervous owners can transfer their habits to their cats, who in turn groom excessively because they are so nervous and up-tight that they need an outlet.

When self-suckling and grooming become so excessive that the cat starts to injure himself and can't be stopped, a "Queen Anne Collar" may be required. This is a large circular collar that stands out from the neck and prevents the cat from twisting his head around to get at wounds or other skin problems. Your cat may look strange for a while in his new collar, and some cats may object and try to get it off or simply try sheepishly to hide. But this is better than having your cat chew himself to pieces. After a while the habit will subside, and then you can take the collar off. If you can't get a real one you could try making one like we saw recently on a friend's cat. She took a plastic container, cut a hole in the bottom, and put it on her cat.

TRAINING SESSIONS

In all our years of working with cats we have found that, while each cat is unique, certain behavior patterns are predictable. Thus we have been able to develop specialized methods that have proven reliable when training cats.

At first don't try to train your cat where there are too many distractions. Make sure there aren't any unpleasant noises around when he is first learning a new command or trick. We don't mean complete silence, but try to avoid sudden loud noises that could scare him. If when a cat is first learning a command he has a bad experience, such as being subjected to a loud noise, he may never learn that command. Therefore you should be careful about what happens during training, at least until your pet is really comfortable with the command. Once the cat has begun to respond, however, you must start to introduce outside distractions. This will help reinforce the training, and the cat will learn to listen to you even in the face of a hurricane if need be.

Gear the length of a lesson to the cat's attention span. If the lessons are too long they will exhaust your cat. It's like teaching a very young child—everything has to be made plain and simple, but still interesting. This is doubly true with a cat. The shorter the time you spend on lessons, the quicker and better your kitten or cat will respond. Three to five minutes of training three or four times a day is a reasonable schedule. For maintenance, once a day should do it. If your cat doesn't complete the command within the time allotted for his lesson, walk him through it. You *must* make him complete every command before treating him and letting him go.

If he won't work, walk him through the command or even carry him through it if necessary. Then stop immediately and resume another time. If you let your cat get away with not carrying out a command, you will have difficulties the next time. And if you continue to push him and try to work with him too much at one time, he will get bored and tired and will come to think of the training sessions as punishment. Then nothing will be accomplished. He won't want to work with you, and you'll have a hard time getting him to respond to any of your commands. You wouldn't like to do things that are continually boring or unpleasant. Neither does a cat, and if you push him beyond his limits you may undo all the work you've already accomplished. Attention spans vary from cat to cat, but most have short ones, whether kitten or cat. Of course, the more training you put in with your cat, the more readily and longer he will concentrate on commands, simply because he is conditioned to do so. But in general the rule is to keep the lessons short and well spaced out. Work until your cat obeys a command a couple of times, and if he refuses to obey within three to five minutes, walk him through it.

OUR BASIC TRAINING METHODS

The use of positive reinforcement is extremely important when training your cat. He must be given a reward for working—and he must know that the reward is being given as a result of his work. This means that, at least in the early stages of training, rewards should be as simultaneous with the action as possible if they are to be really effective. The reward and the action must be connected in the cat's mind. If you wait too long, your cat might forget why he is getting rewarded.

This is exactly how cats learn in the wild: If an action is rewarding, they will repeat that action over and over. Cats have extremely retentive memories. If when hunting your cat sees a certain quarry, follows a specific action plan, and thereby captures the prey, the next time he hunts that quarry he will repeat the same action plan. Additionally, if he once catches something in a certain spot, he will keep on checking that spot in the future to see if there is any more of that good stuff around.

This is the basis of our training. Get your cat to do something and follow it with a reward, and he will tend to do it again in order to get the reward. After a while he will do it simply because it has become a habit.

Food treats are one of the best rewards you can use. Praise is nice, but food is more enticing—especially in the early stages of training. Thus, when first starting to train your cat it is often a good idea to have a training session just before feeding him. But this can also be a tricky maneuver, since you must never let your cat get away with not completing a command and yet, at the same time, you cannot punish him by not feeding him if he doesn't work for you. This means that if he refuses to do it by himself you must carry him through it before feeding him.

Once your cat has the basic idea of training, start varying the times of the day you give the commands and reward him with one of his special treats. If you only work with him at mealtimes you may eventually find you have to wait around until it's time to feed him in order to get your cat to perform.

After he has a trick or command down pat and is obeying regularly start to reward him on a random basis. But remember that it is really important to give him a special treat once in a while as reinforcement to keep him interested. He must feel at all times that there is a possibility of reward. Give him treats two, three, or even four times in a row, then space them out. This will serve to reinforce his obeying the command. Be sure you don't make the common mistake of setting up a regular pattern of treating, such as rewarding him every other time or every third time. Cats are smart enough to catch on to such patterns and to obey only at times they feel they will be rewarded.

Reward to a cat can mean things other than food. It can mean avoiding unpleasantness, returning to a security spot, or anything that gives some physical pleasure. You can't force cats to do anything: you must encourage by reward or discourage with something they don't like. It is important to do one or the other. However, for teaching commands and tricks it's the food reward that in the final analysis makes the training permanent. Cats don't tire of special tidbits, though sometimes they need an added incentive in combination with them.

When using treats of any kind as an incentive, remember to give them only *after* an exercise has been completed. If you treat your cat during the exercise, the anticipation will often be so great that his mind will be on the treat and not on the exercise. If you treat him before he does anything, why should your cat bother to obey you or do tricks? He's smart enough to know in advance that you'll give him the treat anyway. Therefore it is important that you give your cat the treat only after he has done something for you. This means making sure he completes every command you give him, even if you have to carry him through it, before rewarding him.

When a family is participating in the training exercises, remember that only one member should work an exercise at a time, and that no one else must interfere. If too many people get involved, the cat will get completely confused. If you don't want to put in the effort, let another member of the family work the exercise. Otherwise you probably won't be consistent and may consequently do the exercise wrong.

As you proceed through the following training chapters you will notice that we invariably give you a gesture or motion to associate with your verbal commands. You should use hand commands along with words from the very start. A kitten will often respond to hand commands faster than to words, because body language is a cat's own way of communicating. If you watch a mother with her kittens, you will see that she doesn't attempt to meow commands but instead uses direct physical means. She pushes, points, nudges and pulls. This is what the kittens understand. Therefore hand commands are the best, simplest, and most direct way for a human to work at a cat's level of understanding. The more you combine actions with words, the quicker he'll remember. "Action words," as we call them, can really help in training.

One of the most important aids we use is a dowel stick about three feet long. With this we nudge and point the way for cats during training. Get yourself one of these before you start working your cat. But remember this is *not* for reprimands. It is simply to assist you to push, nudge, and encourage your cat into position during training.

If your cat seems to be having difficulty learning any particular exercise, examine your training procedure. Are you rushing him? Are you skipping any of the steps? Are his treats rewarding enough and different enough from his regular food to make it worthwhile for him? Are you rewarding him immediately when he does the right thing? Are you training him amid too many distractions?

When you find out what you've been doing wrong, correct your mistake and work the command again. If you can't find any faults in your training, walk him through the command completely and then let him go. For the next week or so try concentrating on another trick or command. After this go back to the command he is having difficulty with and try again. With cats you have to be slow and methodical, working one step at a time. Pushing a cat too hard to do something he feels uncomfortable with can mess up training.

7

BASIC LITTER BOX TRAINING

There are many people with cats who assure us that they just showed their cat a litter box and that was it. But there are many others who have untold problems. The humane societies and pounds are full of "dirty" cats.

You can get both fancy and plain litter boxes. Most boxes are simply a tublike affair, but there are others specially constructed so the cat has to jump through a hole or onto a ledge, thus dislodging the kitty litter from his feet to prevent his tracking it into the house. One friend even has a special one where the cat enters from the top of a boxlike structure and jumps down a few steps to reach the actual litter. To get out, he climbs up the stairs, thus shaking the litter off his feet. Another friend has a special "doll's" house built to contain the box. This has a front door with a "porch" ledge in front, which the cat jumps onto before entering and leaving. Inside the house the box is situated just a little lower than the entrance, and the roof lifts off so the box can be cleaned.

You don't need anything as fancy as these, however. A plain box is adequate for any cat. A square or slightly rectangular plastic washbasin type is best, with galvanized metal a second. Don't use plain metal—it rusts—and wood rots, while cardboard falls apart. Moreover, both of the latter absorb the urine and thus the odor.

Whatever type of box you choose—plain or fancy—make sure it is accessible to your cat. If the sides are too high or if the box is hard to get into, a cat, and more especially a young kitten, will not use it. It should be a stable, secure box, not one that can tip over or move around. If it tips over just once, your cat may be reluctant to use it again. If it seems the least bit unstable, wedge it into an area where it can't move, and put some foam or other material under it to give it traction.

Use any of the commercial kitty litter materials available or even plain sawdust, which is about the cheapest litter available. (Sawdust can be obtained from any carpenter's shop or lumber yard.) If you live near a beach or sandy area, sand can be used also. Even earth will do in an emergency. Don't use ripped-up newspaper—it gets stuck on the feet when wet, is not absorbent enough, and cats can't kick it to cover their feces.

The most common material used in commercial litter is clay, but ground-up corn cobs and some new synthetic substances are also used. Chlorophyll is frequently added as a deodorizer. In this context, some people sprinkle a little baking soda under the litter to help stop the "cat-lives-here" smell. But watch out, because some cats won't use their litter if it has a strange, unnatural smell.

Fill the litter box with one or two inches of litter, enough to allow the urine to soak in and also to permit your cat to kick back and cover his feces. Don't fill the box up to the top. If you do, the litter will get kicked all over the place. Additionally, changing the litter constantly will be a very expensive proposition. On the other hand, if there is not enough litter, the cat may scratch up the box or, worse, refuse to use it because his urine won't be absorbed. He would probably much rather use the carpet, as it's much more absorbent than a sprinkling of litter barely covering the bottom of his box. In fact, this is the very reason one client's kitten never seemed to get housebroken. There simply wasn't enough litter in the box, and the kitten, not wanting to stand in the wet litter, decided the carpet was a much better place. So, for all her economy, the woman ended up having to buy a new rug.

The litter box should be kept far away from the cat's food and water, since most cats don't like and often will refuse to relieve themselves near where they eat. If you were furnishing your house, would you put your toilet near your bed, or put your food in the bathroom? Try to keep the box in a well-ventilated area (but if the window is open be sure it has a screen to prevent unwanted departures by your cat), and make sure it is in a place where it is constantly available—in other words, the doors should always be open for easy accessibility.

Some people like to keep the box in the bathtub so the litter doesn't get all over. Most people, however, place it near their own toilet. This setup is ideal, especially if you are eventually planning to toilet train your cat. But if you do put your cat's litter box next to the toilet, push it as far back as possible. One man visiting a friend's house stepped right into the litter box as he was using the toilet, getting dirt all over his shoes and litter all over the floor.

If you live in a large house or apartment, don't expect a tiny kitten to run all the way to one box; set up a couple and spread them around. If there are two cats of the same sex you may have to set up two boxes at opposite ends of the house or apartment. A second box is not always needed when two or more cats live in the same house—in fact many cats will use the same box, and of course kittens always share with their mother since she usually teaches them how to use the box. But some cats absolutely refuse to share, so if you have a multi-cat household, it's a good idea to set up several litter boxes spaced apart. This way the cats can set up their own individual territories, and if they both get the urge to use the box at the same time there'll be no squabbling over who goes first. Besides, cats don't urinate over another cat's marker, or urine, to leave a "calling card" the way dogs do. They respect another cat's territory.

A cat cannot be expected to learn to go outside like a dog. In fact, people get cats just because they don't need to be walked and thus are far less bother. We don't recommend allowing your cat to roam outside alone to do his duty, but if you absolutely must, make sure he is fixed and that he is able to get in and out at will. Put in a small swinging door just big enough for him to go through. Push him back and forth a few times and he'll get the idea. Never let him out too young, however, since a tiny kitten can contract various diseases, some fatal, if let outside before receiving the proper shots. Therefore litter box training is a must. Otherwise your kitten may not get the chance to grow up.

If you have a terrace or enclosed outside area, this could be a good place to keep your cat's litter box. If outside, the box must be covered; otherwise it will get wet and the cat won't use it. A friend keeps her cat's on her terrace. There is a tiny swing door for her cat to go through to get in and out of the apartment. The litter box itself is kept inside a special, oversized doll's house nestled amidst the plants.

For a cat to learn to use a box outside, first he must learn to use it one hundred percent in the house. Then show him where you are moving it by putting him in the box in its new location. If possible, it's a good idea to use the same box. But keep one in the original spot for a few days, until you are sure he is using the other; then remove the first.

Remember, cats are creatures of habit and tend to relieve themselves in favorite spots. If you move his box, be sure he knows exactly where his new one is. Otherwise he's likely to go in the original spot where the box was anyway. One lady brought her cat to her summer beach house as usual and was flabbergasted when the cat wouldn't use the litter box. He kept running to the upstairs bathroom and using that rather than going to the downstairs one, where she now had the box. It turned out that for the past few years her cat's box had been upstairs, but over the winter she had had the place remodeled and a new bathroom had been added downstairs. It's all a question of habit. She should have kept him confined in the new area where she had placed his box until he had used it a few times and knew it.

The basics of litter box training are simple but should be followed carefully. When you bring your kitten home, confine him to a small enclosed area, the place where you plan to keep the litter box. (This will be where he will live until he is trained to use his litter box.) Again, be sure his litter box is as far as possible from his food and bed, because cats don't like to relieve themselves where they sleep and eat. Right beside a toilet is ideal. Make sure that the box is in its permanent position so there is no confusion later about placement. The cat must know where the box is at all times. If you move it later, you may have to retrain the cat.

Many people feel the kitten will not like the corner they pick out. Not so. Within a very short period your kitten or cat will relieve himself in the box. All cats, from lions to domestics, dig holes and cover their droppings afterward. Take a kitten to the box. Pick up his paws and make a scratching motion with them. This sets the pattern for him to follow. Keep the kitten confined to his enclosed area whenever you are not actually with him—that is, when you're sleeping, working, going out. This will prevent him from relieving himself anywhere else in the house. You must be firm no matter how sorry you feel for him or how much he meows. Let him stay in there for a day or so until he knows exactly where his box is, and don't allow him the freedom of your house until you are sure he is using it. While he is confined, you should go in and spend time with him. Hold him and bring him out when you can. Show him around the house. But don't push him; cats like to be alone to explore at their own pace.

Once he is using his box regularly he can come out. But you should still help him by placing him in his litter box after meals, after periods of energetic play, and first thing in the morning and last thing at night.

A cat will definitely use the litter box you provide. We once used ten very small kittens in a commercial. They were all kept in a small room with three litter boxes. By the end of the day all the boxes had been used, and nothing was on the floor.

There is usually little if anything involved in litter training your cat. Cats are by nature meticulously clean animals, so housebreaking is less of a problem than with other household pets. In fact, most cats are trained before you ever get them. Your cat's mother usually takes care of all his training while he is a tiny kitten, so in most cases all you have to do is show him the box and that's it. However, when he first comes into your home you must realize that your cat won't know where his box is. If he doesn't know where it is, he can't use it. Therefore you have to show him and make sure he knows exactly where it is in relation to the rest of the house. For this reason, you should always confine a new kitten, litter trained or not, so he is not confused in his new surroundings.

The fact that the mother usually teaches her kittens about using a litter box makes your job a lot easier, especially as compared with the torture so many dog owners go through. However, your cat or kitten still needs training when he comes into your house. If the cat doesn't know where his box is and goes elsewhere just once without your catching him to stop it, then you may well have a cat who finds his own toilet. Remember, once a pattern or habit is established it's hard to break in cats.

Despite the fact that the majority of cats are instinctively sanitary and litter training is really simple, some cats remain untrained. Obviously, very few people want a cat past the kitten stage who is not trained, not in control of his bladder or bowels. People often ask us to try to give their "dirty" cat to someone else. But, unless they're trained, the inevitable fate of such cats is to get dumped by their owners in a humane society, for the lucky ones, or in a public pound or the streets, for the unlucky. It's almost inconceivable how many people say they can't train their cats. If they were really insistent that their cats do the right thing there would be nowhere near as many problems. Untrained cats are usually the fault of the owners, not the cats.

For an older cat or for one who has previously gone outside, litter training is the same as for a kitten. They must all go through the confinement process. It will probably take longer for cats who are well set in their ways, but it can be done. Only after the cat has used the box one hundred percent for a day or so should he be allowed out.

In one Fifth Avenue household, the family pet—a one-year-old tabby—could not be housebroken. No one could understand or get to the root of the problem. It turned out that the daughter, a four-year-old, always closed the door tightly behind her when she was finished in the bathroom. She'd been taught in her nursery school class to keep the bathroom door closed, so she followed the same advice at home—and the cat couldn't get to his box.

In another household the cat wouldn't use the box unless his mistress used the toilet at the same time. Now they sit side by side.

No matter what the reason, reprimand your cat for mistakes. This means even when you feel you are to blame. With cats, one mistake can turn into a dirty habit, and favorite spots evolve easily. He has to be taught he can go nowhere but where you want. Don't allow yourself to feel sorry for him.

A cat quickly learns he gets reprimanded if he misbehaves in front of you. So the first "lesson" he learns is to be sneaky. You'll have to watch very carefully to catch him in the act. The cat will relieve himself only when your attention is elsewhere, so never let a cat/kitten out of your sight or out of his enclosure until you are sure he's litter trained.

If he gets out of his confined area by mistake or design and does relieve himself in another part of the house, or if he simply doesn't get back to the box in time, you must reprimand him using the *White Distilled Vinegar Method* outlined on page 91.

If by any chance you happen to catch him in the act, try one of the other reprimand techniques, especially the rubber-arm type. Cats catch on very fast. Be sure to say "no" every time you reprimand him for missing his box. He must understand what "no" means. And "no" only becomes meaningful when associated with something unpleasant for the cat.

Unfortunately many cat households are identifiable immediately upon entry because of their "cat-lives-here" odor. If you follow our trick of feeding your cat a quarter teaspoon of apple cider vinegar in his water each day, you might help relieve the problem. And don't worry, this won't interfere with your "vinegar for punishment" technique. There is no conflict between feeding your cat apple cider vinegar to stop the urine smell and using distilled white vinegar for punishment and to mask the urine smell on the floor. Their odors are entirely different: the apple cider vinegar is mild, less tart; the distilled vinegar is harsh and repulsive to cats. Try the difference just once on your salad and you'll see why. Additionally, the vinegar mixed in food or water to neutralize the urine is a very small amount; When you are punishing your cat you use larger, undiluted quantities. The relative strength of the white vinegar makes all the difference.

Changing your cat's litter regularly and keeping his box spotlessly clean are the best ways to handle the smell problem. Clean it out daily or at least every other day. Either change the litter completely, which can be expensive, or use a strainer to remove feces so that the box is relatively clean. (Use a wide mesh strainer or one of the special kitty litter ones, which should be kept near his box.) Then every three or four days change it completely.

When emptying the box, rinse it out and dry it thoroughly before putting in the new litter. It may become moldy if it is too wet, and the litter will stick to the sides. If you use a disinfectant, make it a mild one with little odor. Too strong an odor is as unpleasant to cats as it is to us. Don't try masking the smell with sweet-smelling perfumes or disinfectants; this may well alienate the cat from the box. You can spray it around but not directly on his box.

Litter boxes, especially soiled ones, are a favorite hangout of dogs and children, so the presence of canine pets or children in the household provides an additional reason for keeping the litter box clean. One dog we know never ate, but got fatter and fatter; the source of her weight was discovered when she was found in the litter box.

If the box remains dirty, parasites and worm larvae may develop or hatch which in turn may infest the cat. Larvae of certain worms can't hatch in the body but, once hatched, the worms can invade and live in your cat's body. These same worms can infest children or adults and any other pets in your family. Therefore it is better to keep a clean box at all times. This is of course not the most pleasant of chores, but like changing a baby's diapers it must be done.

Since the litter box is an integral part of your cat's life and environment, it must receive a lot of attention. If you don't want to do it, either toilet train him (see Chapter 15) or don't bother to get a cat. Don't expect your cat to have anything but an absolute disdain for dirty or smelly places if his box isn't kept clean, he'll quickly turn his nose up at it. Even though he buries his feces in a box, it accumulates fast. Many a person has untrained a perfectly litter-trained cat by forgetting or not knowing to change the litter box regularly. But things other than a dirty box can cause problems in training. For instance, if there is a strange smell in the box because it has been used by a visiting cat, your cat may refuse to use it. He may do this even if a stranger—human or cat—comes visiting your home. And when a cat reaches maturity, don't think for a second that an unaltered male (and perhaps even a female) won't start spraying around the house to mark off his territory—he definitely will.

Keeping an uncastrated male litter box trained is really difficult. We only know of one or two cases where it has happened. Some males never spray and others spray in the box, but it is really not worth the effort. You'd be better off saving yourself the trouble from the beginning and have him castrated.

Some owners insist on using toilet paper on their cats' behinds. Certain cats seem to require it for the sake of appearance, as they have long hair that doesn't look good when soiled. Obviously they have to be cleaned with something. If not, they may rub themselves clean on the furniture. We don't suggest shaving them—cats' shaved behinds look like targets—but some people do it anyway. If there is a continual problem with soiling from loose stools, perhaps you should try a different diet—usually one not so rich in meat—or better yet, see your vet and let him advise you.

8

BREAKING LITTER BOX TRAINING AND HOW TO CORRECT IT

Even the cleanest and best trained cat will break training under special circumstances. Usually there is a good reason for things so, if your cat breaks, look for the obvious. If he breaks training once in a while, it's no real cause for worry. Possibly he's a little under the weather. (If he's sick you should be able to detect some change in his other habits or behavior.) But if your aging cat has a sudden or even occasional housebreaking problem, check with your vet promptly. Never wait for such a problem to die away. Your cat may, instead.

The reason for breaking training is likely to be something as simple as someone's forgetting to leave the door open, thus closing the cat out of the bathroom so he couldn't get at his box or the toilet. Or perhaps you aren't changing the litter often enough. Most cats will not go anywhere near a dirty box. Some are fussier than others but all like to be clean. Possibly your cat broke because his food and water are too close to his litter box. And keep in mind that after boarding or traveling, a cat can get loose stools for a few days from excitement.

But, whatever the reason for breaking, reprimand him as if he had planned to do it. He should be punished for any transgressions, or it could become a habit. Oftentimes one mistake leads

117

to many, and thus a habit is formed fast. Stop it immediately, and don't let a "dirty" habit become ingrained.

A cat may deliberately defecate or urinate shortly after he has been disciplined. He may also do it as a sign of unhappiness or even defiance. And he will definitely use it as a sign of aggression. Oftentimes it is a cat's one means of self-expression. In fact, ceasing to be housebroken and refusing to eat are two of the cardinal signs of emotional disturbance in cats. These can occur, for instance, when the owners leave the cat at home alone. Instances of breaking for these reasons are rare, but if they do occur the cat should always be reprimanded for this kind of behavior—no matter how sorry you feel for him. Try to find the reason for his behavior but, at the same time, let your cat know that he can't get away with it, no matter what.

In the wild cats use their urine and sometimes their feces to mark off the perimeters of their territory, thus warning strangers to keep off. *Both* male and female cats indulge in the same marking procedure, since they often have separate hunting ranges. In your home female cats have less of a tendency to spray since the walls become effective markers or barriers to keep strangers out. However, since an uncastrated male cat urinates by spraying back against an object, it is almost impossible to get him to confine himself to his box. In fact, a mature male cat backs up in a standing position near the object to be sprayed and turns on a forceful stream of urine straight back. This spray can be ruinous to home furnishings and the odor is obnoxious to humans. You just can't keep a full male cat as a pet and still maintain a pleasant home.

If you have an uncastrated male, you may well find that he will try to get out of the house to expand his territory and establish himself in the hierarchy of the local neighborhood group. Neighborhood toms might even come around, taunting him to come out and prove himself a "man." Sometimes this can lead to problems and, like parents, owners are often drawn into it in one way or another. In fact, one of our clients had a very friendly young but uncastrated male who involuntarily became embroiled in just such a problem when he became completely intimidated by the neighborhood toms. His owners didn't know this one basic fact about their cat's innate social behavior, and inadvertently set him up for problems. They set his litter box near a screened but slightly open window. This was intended to let the smell out and keep the place clean; unfortunately, his smell was like a magnet, drawing all the local males who came and urinated all around the window, calling and taunting him for hours on end. He was still so immature that he hadn't even started spraying. Therefore he was easily intimidated and, rather than answering their call, beat a hasty retreat deeper into his lair for security. He refused to go near the window, and to the chagrin of his owners moved his business elsewhere. Once the problem was understood, the solution was simple. The box was moved to another position deeper into the house, the area around the window was cleaned thoroughly, and the window was closed for a few days.

Oftentimes you will find that, like this example, there is a perfectly logical explanation for and solution to why a cat breaks training.

An unfixed male will forever test you to see if this silly business about relieving himself only in his box is for real. Long after you've gotten him officially trained, he will continue to try you, so be alert. Remember a cat uses his spraying as one means of proving who's boss. The only way you might possibly be able to curb it is to confine him immediately. You must be really firm once he starts to mature and spray. It is, however, an almost impossible task to keep him trained.

The only real solution to this particular breaking problem is castration. A trip to the vet for this relatively simple operation is the best thing you can do for your cat. If you do plan on doing this, however, do it fast. Otherwise the habit may become so ingrained that you can't stop it at all. Once the spraying habit is well established, it is often almost impossible to stop the spraying, at least by castration alone. However, if it is not a firmly established habit, castration will cure it—especially if you add a little training. And it *will* stop the "old tom" odor, no matter at what age it is done. And even if it doesn't stop him from spraying, this operation may make it possible for you to train him to confine his spraying to the litter box or toilet.

If your cat is altered, you probably won't have to worry about territorial-marking problems in your home. But even an altered cat, of either sex, may break training upon reaching maturity and try to mark off the whole house as his or hers. This happened to one couple with an altered male; a couple of examples of who was boss straightened the whole thing out.

If a stranger—animal or human—comes into your house, your cat may react as if his territory were being violated. He may then break training and start leaving his mark around to reestablish and reaffirm it as his. It is a warning to one and all that he doesn't want anyone to encroach on what is his. Your cat might even go so far as to actually urinate on the visitor or one of his belongings to show his possession of him.

One cat peed on a woman when she came into the home of a friend. This had happened to her a few times before, so she thought cats disliked her. It turned out that rather than hating her they simply got great pleasure out of annoying her. She had a great fear of cats, and her fear was quite visible. Cats, therefore, simply took advantage and rubbed it in. Intimidating people they know fear or dislike them is a favorite pastime of many cats. The way we got this woman to stop the harassment was to force her to screw up her courage and chase the cat whenever he made the slightest move toward her. She had to learn to exert herself.

Remember, your cat is a creature of habit and tends to relieve himself in favorite spots, just like plenty of people who feel uncomfortable anywhere but on their own john. Once a cat starts to go somewhere outside the box the smell gets into that area and he will keep returning to that spot over and over. And if a cat gets into the *habit* of going elsewhere than his box or the toilet, drastic action may be required. Therefore, after it happens more than once you will have to confine your cat and retrain him.

One client's cat broke training because of an unfortunate incident: something fell on him while he was using his box. The placement of the box had to be changed and the cat had to be gently coaxed back into using the box. At the same time he had to be shown that going anywhere else was absolutely *verboten*. Make sure nothing bad happens with or to your cat while he is in his box or he may never use it again.

Another owner found damp spots on his bed. He swore his cat wouldn't do such a thing as urinate on the furniture. He was convinced it was caused by moisture in the air generated by his wife running overly hot baths. He knew the cat used the box because he found feces in it. We had him put a plastic covering on the bed. Miraculously, a yellow puddle appeared from nowhere. In this case the original trap turned out to be the solution. Apparently the urine ran on the plastic and got on the cat's feet. He preferred the way the litter soaked it in better and went back to using that.

Still another client who had a perfectly trained cat in her home got a new kitten. Her new arrival wouldn't use his box and insisted on going on the floor. It turned out that the older cat kept chasing the new one, refusing to allow him to use the box. The problem was solved simply by getting a second litter box and putting it in another room at the farthest end of the apartment from the original box. This way the older cat no longer felt as if the new intruder was infringing on what had been exclusively his for as long as he'd been in the house. Each now has his own private "territory," and they're both happy with the arrangement.

In another house two cats had been living together and sharing the same box in harmony until a visitor came to stay for a couple of days. Then suddenly one of the cats started peeing on the visitor's bed. It was assumed that the cat didn't like her and was exerting his dominance, but in this case a more obvious solution was the answer. It was simply that a second box was needed. The two cats had continued sharing just as long as they were still very young. But once they both reached maturity, each wanted his own box. The friend's visit just happened to come at a point in time that coincided with this development in the cats' lives. The visitor's bed had been set up at the other end of the house from the litter box, and the cat just took it over as his new box.

Usually you won't have problems of this sort with two cats of different sexes. Problems arise when you have two or more of the same sex. However, it's still wisest to give them privacy.

Another client had a problem getting her cat to go into a litter box. She was really upset: "My cat must either hate me or else be just plain stupid!" When we asked her why she thought this she replied that she had bought a beautiful bed, expensive bowls, and a modern new litter box for the cat. She had put all these things in one corner of a room, conveniently arranged so that her cat wouldn't have to go far to eat, drink or relieve himself. "But what does the stupid cat do—he goes to the farthest end of the house and uses the sofa as a litter box!" Simply moving the litter box to a different spot and an explanation of why soon settled the problem.

As usual, it is people who cause most of the problems with their pets. Not just because of what they do, but also because of what they don't do. Lack of correcting your cat is one of the worst mistakes in working with your cat. Cleaning up without correcting him gives your cat the go-ahead to do it again. If you aren't consistent with your cat, he won't know when you're serious. Lots of well meaning people would rather clean up the mess than listen to the harangue that comes down on the cat if caught. Everyone involved in training the cat has to feel responsible. Every time the cat messes he has to be reprimanded.

If your cat breaks, use the vinegar method when you clean it up. Make such a procedure out of it that the cat will never think of doing it again. In fact, the threat of going through the whole catastrophe another time should keep *you* motivated. Catching the cat in the act is the best way to stop him. This is hard to do since the first thing a cat learns fast is that if he does it in front of you, he gets punished. But if you do catch him in the act, a magazine thrown and a good "no" followed by the vinegar technique should really put a stop to it. Remember that to make sure your cat doesn't do anything bad or develop unwanted habits, you must make sure there is plenty of bad experience connected with the action.

For a single transgression, reprimand him with the vinegar method. If he goes outside of the box or away from the toilet more than once, it's already become a habit. His misbehavior has become well established. The vinegar method won't work overnight in this case. You have to chip away at the habit, bit by bit. Therefore, confine him for a few days in the bathroom wherever you keep his box. Feed and water him in the confined area, but at a distance from the box or toilet as when first training him. Let him out only when you can watch him. If he goes near the spots or starts to go toward them, throw a light magazine at or near him, and as it lands say "no," calmly. He won't know where it came from and will be duly startled. This should put the right amount of fear into him to reform him of his bad behavior. After he has used the box for one or two full days let him out, but watch him. Every time he makes a mistake, take him over to the spot and punish him with the vinegar method, and put him back in the bathroom. Obviously to rehabilitate a cat can take much time and effort. Just keep in mind he is in the bathroom *not* as a punishment, but so you can control him.

Confinement can also be used for other purposes. At one household the problem was doubly bad because two cats were doing the dirty work. We had to confine one to find out which was the culprit. The owners never seemed to be able to catch anyone in the act, so they had to single out the culprit somehow.

For a cat that has a favorite spot or spots where he constantly messes up, there is another trick that can be used in conjunction with the vinegar treatment and confinement. Arrange a piece of chicken wire or window screening over the spot, elevating it an inch or two off the floor by placing it on blocks or something similar. This obstacle should make it uncomfortable enough for the cat to realize he is not supposed to go there. If your cat is urinating on carpeting or furniture, you can also try laying plastic sheeting over the spots the way we did to trap and cure the cat that was leaving "damp spots" on the bed.

If your cat is toilet trained and breaks training, punish and confine him as you would for any mishap. However, if after confinement he continues to refuse to use the toilet, you may have to go back to a point in the original training procedure where he was comfortable. This means setting up the box with its toilet seat attached (see Chapter 15), and testing to see how far back you have to go for him to feel comfortable and to use the box. You then start his training again from there. You may even have to start from the very beginning. Some people push their cats too fast.

A "dirty," non-housebroken cat, one who urinates all over, is not a very desirable commodity. His urine leaves a definite smell and mark that is almost impossible to clean and deodorize. There is no positive way of cleaning a cat's urine so that it doesn't leave a stain or odor. Some say immediately using just plain cold or tepid water and a mild soap is best to draw it out. You can use tomato juice to neutralize the smell, but it stains— so confine it to areas where this doesn't matter. Try calling your dry cleaner; he might be able to offer advice. But if there were any product that really did the job, the inventor would make billions. It would be as great an invention as the safety pin, and we all know about that. Some people have had success with various commercial products available in pet stores; however, none have worked for us.

Aside from the "willpower" discipline factor, which only you the owner can produce, some cats really are difficult to train. There are many people including breeders who say there is no way to reform a dirty cat. We disagree. There is, of course, the occasional cat who for some unknown reason is "dirty" permanently. However, the vast majority of dirty cats are that way for a good reason. They can be trained with perseverance, consistency and know-how. This book should instill all three into you.

9

STOPPING POTENTIALLY DESTRUCTIVE HABITS AND RECHANNELING THEM: Chewing, Scratching, and Destructive Jumping

Your cat's claws are one of his main weapons, a major means of survival and his first line of defense. Thus every instinct in his body is attuned to keeping them in good working order. To do this your cat *must* scratch his claws against something. The purpose of this is to peel off the outer shells that grow over claws, and to keep them sharp and in condition. At the same time it keeps the muscles and tendons of the legs in tip-top shape.

Therefore, as soon as a kitten comes into your home you should set up some kind of a scratching post and train him to use it. If you don't he will scratch the furniture. Scratching is a subconscious instinctive action that cannot be stopped completely, and as such must be channeled into non-destructive areas. The way to do this is to give your cat an object or objects which he is allowed to scratch, and to stop him from scratching on anything else. If you make his scratching post tantalizingly appealing to him he will definitely go there. But you had better get that post immediately so that the scratching habit does not become established. The damage a scratching cat can do is really incredible. One friend went out and bought two new white leather couches only to come home a day later to find the sides perforated with holes. Another had an entire wardrobe of clothing along with shoes and boots demolished after leaving her cat for a weekend. Stories like this are rampant, but don't despair; it doesn't have to happen to you.

Whether or not you are planning to declaw your cat, you should set up a scratching post. You can't declaw a kitten before he is fairly mature (at least three months), since it can cause growth problems with the development of the paws if done too early. Thus by the time you get it done he can already have inflicted some heavy-duty damage to your belongings. If you have a large apartment or house, or if you have two or more cats, put up an additional post or posts at widely separated locations.

A scratching post doesn't have to be a "post"; it can be any object that he can really get his claws into. Even a chair will do, but if you give him a chair for this purpose, make sure that he only uses that chair and doesn't try any others. As children we saw plenty of homes each with a comfortable, old, and obviously well clawed armchair which was assigned as "the cat's chair." This was his for lying on, scratching, or doing just about whatever he wanted. Oftentimes, however, these chairs became the cats' simply because they picked them out as their scratching posts. Don't let this happen. If you want to give him a chair, fine, but you should assign the object he is to claw rather than having him tell you what he wants. If he does tell you, he might end up taking the entire house.

Whatever you pick out to give your cat as a post, it should be large enough to allow your cat to stretch out full length while scratching. It should also be a sturdy structure he can feel absolutely secure using. If it tends to move around, your cat may refuse to use it. This is why cats love to use furniture for scratching. It suits their purposes perfectly.

Cats scratch by stretching out and pulling their claws back toward them. This is the best way for them to sharpen their claws and make sure there are no hangnails or jagged edges. They like best to lie flat, letting their front legs hang down, and scratch by pulling their claws back. Of course, they will scratch anything and any way they can, but this is their favorite way and they will gravitate toward using an object that allows them to do it comfortably. This makes the plush arms of couches or armchairs especially popular. Danish modern or chrome furniture is not exactly their style.

Unfortunately, most commercial posts aren't strong or comfortable enough to allow a cat to scratch on them properly. Often there is nowhere for a cat to sit; or if there is, the post isn't large enough; or maybe it's unstable or even covered with the wrong material. Therefore, if you can't find a strong post which looks as if your cat can really enjoy scratching at it, it's best to construct one.

One good choice is to take a piece of tree—a log or large branch—four feet high and eight to twelve inches in diameter, with the bark still on it if possible. (Cats love to scratch bark better than anything; it's a carryover from their wild heritage.) It doesn't have to be a straight piece—it could even have some smaller branches on the sides for him to chew on—but it must be absolutely level on the top and the bottom. The posts provided for the big cats in the N.Y. Central Park Zoo's cages aren't any larger than this (though they should be), and in fact are often smaller, so this should be an adequate size for your cat. The only additional thing the big cats do have is an overhanging ledge which enables the cat to let his legs dangle, and thus scratch toward himself the way he prefers. Your cat doesn't absolutely need this ledge since there should be enough room for him atop the trunk, but it can be a useful addition for many cats especially if you use a thinner log—or have a larger cat.

Fasten the post securely to the floor in an upright position by screwing it into the floor or a base with angle irons of a size adequate for the log you have selected. (The salesperson at your local hardware store will help you choose the right ones.) Using extra-long screws, attach it to the floor or, if you don't want to mark up your floor, attach it to a solid, perfectly flat, square piece of lumber with a surface area about three or four times that of the base of the log. Don't use nails hammered through the bottom since they not only pull out easily, but also make for an uneven surface, causing instability.

After your cat wears the bark off this log, either replace the log entirely with a new one or "reupholster" it by covering it with carpet—preferably wool. You could leave the wood plain, but it is not the best of scratching surfaces. Besides, your cat may associate the plain wood with your furniture and start on that. When he then discovers that scratching finished wood is not as enjoyable as raw wood, he may turn his attentions to the materials next to the wood, such as the cushions on your couch.

If you don't want to use a log post or simply can't find a log, try building a post. If you elect to do this, build a solid rectangular box-type structure out of heavy wood with about the same dimensions recommended for the log. Cover this with carpeting and secure it to the floor or a base the way you would the log, making sure that it cannot fall or move around. If your cat's post, of whatever type, falls or is in any way insecure, you might have to forget about getting your cat to use it again.

Some people take catnip and put it between the carpet and log or wooden structure; others smear it on the plain bark where it can get between the grooves. This makes the scratching post even more inviting for the cat. However, you may occasionally find a cat who doesn't like catnip. Also, there are several varieties of catnip and a cat may prefer a specific type. So before adding catnip to the post, test his preferences with a catnip mouse or toy.

Once you are sure he loves it, mix the catnip with just enough water to give it a paste-like consistency and paint it on the wood; this way you can be sure it is well distributed. Once on, but before it dries—and it dries quickly, so be speedy—put on the carpeting by tacking it on solidly with long thin nails. (If you have bought a readymade post, try sprinkling the catnip into the pile. It isn't as effective but it could be an added incentive to get your cat to use it.)

If you wish, you can even grow, dry and cure your own catnip. It is a low-growing, spreading plant, with ornamental foliage. It thrives best in hot, dry sunny places but it can be grown under other conditions. Tea made from catnip leaves is said to aid digestion and an upset stomach by reducing gas in the intestinal tract. Cats, however, rarely eat catnip, simply inhale it. This way it affects them by acting as a mild mental and nerve stimulant.

Some people recommend cork for the scratching post rather than carpeting, but cork breaks off easily and is messy. Others think that if they use carpeting it will encourage him to scratch the carpeted floors. Don't worry—he won't confuse the carpet on the floor with that on the post. It is just not situated properly for him. His scratching technique requires a little different set-up. But if he does start on your carpeting, stop it with one of the methods which we will explain.

Whatever you decide to construct, give or buy for your cat as his scratching post, make sure that your cat can sit atop it comfortably and scratch from above. Make sure it's tall enough so he can stretch out full length while exercising. And make sure it is very secure. If these criteria are followed, your cat will probably prefer sitting atop and scratching this post even better than your couch—especially if you teach him not to go near anything else.

You can, of course, make or provide a post that is much larger than the one we recommend as a basic post—just be certain it is right for the cat so he will use it. Some people build huge structures containing hidden lairs, platforms and hanging branches where he can lie and play the "leopard" role. This habitat-type structure allows the cat to sleep, scratch, chew and

STOPPING POTENTIALLY DESTRUCTIVE HABITS

just plain enjoy himself all in one spot. In most cases, a small well-constructed post serves the purpose just as well if not better since it keeps him much more in touch with the human environment. If you want a sociable cat, it's best not to give him a place where he can hide from humans and encourage him to use it. (Give him a comfortable window seat where he can sit and look out at the world from behind a protective window instead.) However, if you are out a lot and want to develop an interest for your cat while you're away, there is nothing wrong with this kind of toy. The same is true if you, like so many others, simply want to indulge your cat. But in most cases it's best to try to keep him in touch with the human element in your home.

Some people don't mind that their cats scratch. In fact, they love it and use it to their advantage and amusement. We remember one friend who, when she found out about her cats' love of scratching and using their claws, had one of her living room walls carpeted to match the floor. When we told her about cats loving catnip, she had the carpeting ripped up, catnip spread under it, and the carpeting replaced. The cats now run up and down on it and scratch to their hearts' content all day long and thus keep their claws in fantastic shape.

Another client who has a house full of plants had a huge tree cut down and installed in his house so his cats could lie up in it and claw to their hearts' content. He wedged the tree right between the ceiling and floor and secured it tightly to both. It sits in his foyer and looks fantastic alongside all the other plants. He also has a couple of smaller logs distributed at strategic points around the house, but it's the big tree his cats love. Each one has a special branch that's all his, and none of the others encroach on it.

Although most people can't or don't want to go quite this far in catering to their cats—or themselves—there are variations on these more exotic arrangements that can prevent or solve the problem of scratching cats. Just keep in mind that scratching posts don't have to be ugly. If done right they can be attractive additions to your home. Be as conscientious about them as you would your own conveniences. The purpose of all these contraptions is to stop the cat from scratching anywhere but in the prescribed areas. Therefore making his post as tantalizing as possible makes good sense.

To get your cat to use his post, take him to it and make a scratching motion with his paws; encourage him to use it by giving him a treat. Show him it's good to be there. If your cat is already scratching at your furniture—perhaps even chewing it—you are going to have to break an already established habit. If your cat is using a post, and he starts scratching elsewhere, you have to stop him before it becomes a habit. He doesn't know he's doing something wrong until you show him; to him it's a natural action. You have to make it really clear to him that he has only one choice. He must use what you give him to scratch upon, and nothing else. If you never let him get away with scratching anywhere but on his post, there should be no problem. It's all a question of habit.

The first line of attack in stopping your cat from scratching, as with all bad habits, is to try to catch him in the act. If you are lucky enough to do so, throw something near him, such as a soft magazine, and say "no" as it lands. However, since your cat will usually do his scratching when your back is turned, you will probably have to set him up. First confine him for a day; then let him out and watch him carefully. He's sure to check out certain spots anew to make sure they are still around and that everything has remained stable. At the same time he will want to sharpen his claws so as to prepare himself to face anything new that may have come into the house while he was out of circulation. Hold a magazine under your arm and watch him closely. When he goes to his favorite spot, throw your magazine and again, as it lands, say "no." If he is a real scratcher, he will definitely go to that spot. He won't know you're watching out for him.

Setting booby traps around the spots he likes best and trying to get him in the act that way is another method you can use. You won't have any trouble locating his favorite spots—they'll be quite visibly clawed. To set a trap, take a dowel stick or chopstick and a book or plastic bowl and balance them together by setting them at angles to each other. They should be very precariously balanced so that when your cat goes to scratch, the cat will hit the stick and the book or bowl will fall down and scare him.

You should also clip your cat's claws as an added precaution against scratching. Your cat will scratch somewhere whether you clip them or not, but, his scratching is more controllable when his claws are being kept in good shape by you. Clipped claws won't accidentally dig into the furniture when he is walking across it. In addition, if the claws become jagged or extra long, the urge to scratch is even stronger than usual.

If his claws are too long, they will keep being pushed up into the sheath, into which they no longer fit properly, as he walks, and they will not lie flat along the bottom of the foot, as they should; thus the cat will not feel comfortable. If the edges are jagged, the claws will irritate or even cut into the sheath. If the cat's claws feel uncomfortable, he will start scratching anywhere he can when the urge hits him. Cats can feel when their claws need "trimming," so be sure to do it for them!

Some cats, however, are chronic scratchers, and for these more drastic action may be necessary. The best way to describe a chronic scratcher is a cat who really likes what he is doing. When your cat claws up the furniture, it's not that he's spitefully trying to get back at you for something you've done, or showing you he is resentful at being left alone—though sometimes you could swear it is. A cat's attention span is too short to make him capable of revenge. He's simply getting involved in a good thing.

One sure way to cure scratching is, of course, to have your cat declawed. We take no stand on this subject one way or the other—it's up to the individual owner to decide. It is the most positive cure there is. It is not advisable in all cases, but in some where all training methods have failed there is little other choice. However, cats can't defend themselves without their claws. No declawed cat should, therefore, be left outdoors; he can get hurt too easily. Even in his own backyard he may have to defend himself if another cat comes into his territory and attacks him, or if a hostile dog comes by. In addition, without claws cats can't climb, so they can no longer get up trees or other safe areas to get away from dogs or annoying children.

Other than these, there are no apparent adverse results, and since you should really confine your cat indoors anyway, even these shouldn't be of any major worry. Most people would rather their cats didn't climb with their claws. After all, if a cat likes to go up high into lairs on shelves, he has to climb via your clothing or other belongings, digging in with his claws as he goes and damaging whatever he uses as his ladder.

Declawing is a skilled operation requiring expert veterinary attention. But, once done, cats do not suffer any psychological damage whatsoever from the operation. In fact, they really don't even realize that they don't have any claws, and they will keep on scratching and even kneading after their claws are gone. Only now you have no need to supply a post since they can pretend to scratch anywhere and never do any damage. However there is a disadvantage to this "ignorance is bliss" blessing: if you let your cat outside, he might find out too late that he doesn't have any claws.

Despite the controversy surrounding declawing—and there is plenty, with some people completely in favor and others absolutely refusing even to think about it—it is a far better solution to declaw a cat than to get rid of him because he is an incorrigible scratcher. Innumerable cats get dumped at pounds or thrown into the street because they have scratched up the furniture. Some misguided people think it is a kinder fate to dump their cats than declawing them. For these people a few days being stranded out in the wilderness without food or shelter are in order. If there is absolutely no way you think you could ever live with a cat whose claws might someday rip up your furniture, clothing, or whatever, have him declawed. Don't let people tell you it's cruel. In fact, oftentimes it's kind. If it's a question of getting rid of the cat or declawing, you know what you have to do.

Another instinctive act involving claws and paws which cats like to indulge in is kneading. In this action, the cat lies down and takes his two front paws and presses them one at a time against whatever he is lying on: your lap, a pillow, your couch. He doesn't actually pick them up, but rather simply presses down with one paw at a time. Cats love to knead. And, like scratching, it is an action which doesn't seem to stop even when a cat is declawed. Cats knead when they are truly happy and content. Usually they won't hurt and their claws either don't come out at all or are barely visible. But when they really get involved their claws come out and can hurt. And if he does this while lying on your furniture or clothing, it can damage them by pulling threads. If this happens, he should be stopped. Train him *not* to bring his claws out by slipping an emery board or strip of rough sandpaper under the tips of his paws. As he kneads, the emery board or sandpaper will cause an uncomfortable feeling against his claws. This way he will not stop kneading, but will simply learn to keep his claws in. The only other solution is to reprimand him with a "no" and even a slap. However, if you do this he may never knead at all, and most people we know love the idea of their cat's kneading against their laps as they hold them. It's like purring. Therefore, the solution must be something that will annoy him only when his claws come out, and this must be done as subtly as possible—an emery board or thin strip of rough sandpaper is perfect.

Besides scratching and kneading, some cats have the bad habit of chewing. Teething is apparently a primeval urge ingrained in us all, and when teething a cat may well tend to chew. A stick—good raw wood—is something they like to chew on; thus a log scratching post can serve a two-fold purpose. Cats also enjoy a good piece of natural rawhide. If you do give your cat leather, it can drift over into a passion for your leather shoes, so be careful. In the same vein, try not to select toys made of materials similar to those found in your household furnishings or personal clothing. If you do, you could be encouraging your cat to claw, bite, and chew your good belongings. A cat won't know the difference; it all looks, feels and tastes the same, and besides it also has your smell on it, making it even better and more tantalizing.

We specifically warn people to train their cats not to chew electric wires. To do this take a bottle of Tabasco, let him taste it straight, and grow to hate it. Then coat the wires with it. Wires of even 110 volts can kill or at least harm your cat, especially a kitten. If he does bite at it, the only thing you can do is to pull the plug out in hopes of saving him.

Besides biting on electric cords, cats love to grab at dangling cords with their claws. Even with Tabasco a dangling cord is irresistible, and when your cat plays with it the lamp or appliance may come tumbling down on him. If you catch him in the act, reprimand him immediately. Otherwise, use a booby trap. Take a piece of cord and attach it to something light such as a disposable tinfoil baking pan and allow the cord to dangle. As soon as your cat starts pulling on the electrical cord, the pan will clatter down and startle him.

The same thing holds true for any other dangerous objects.

Don't wait for situations to occur—set them up. For instance, set down a fan with something dangling from it. His curiosity will bring him over to it. Never call him or even tempt him over to it. When he starts sniffing at the fan or playing with the dangling string, give him a good whack and tell him "no."

You might think that this is a bit harsh because you actually enticed him to do it, but just think of what the blades can do to him if he tried to play with the fan any other time.

If your cat starts chewing your belongings, try using the Tabasco method to stop him. Take the object your cat has chewed and spread Tabasco sauce on it really heavily (it's already ruined and there's no way to bring it back). Take the cat over to the Tabasco-covered object, open his mouth, and place the object in it. There should be enough Tabasco where you put his mouth to taste really awful. It should be a bad enough experience that your cat will never think of going near it again. Let him go immediately. Just remember to get him really well the first time. Unlike a dog, who will sit passively for reprimands, a cat is not going to hang around for any further correction. With a cat you've only got one chance, so take advantage of it. After doing this leave the Tabasco-tasting object around as a reminder.

For larger stationary objects or ones which you can't get your cat's mouth around, you'll have to use a slightly different approach. Objects which cannot be damaged by Tabasco should be smeared with it. Then take your cat and an open bottle of Tabasco over to the Tabasco-smeared item. Let your cat first get a sniff of the thing, then open your cat's mouth and smear a small amount of Tabasco on your cat's gums and let him go. Every time he goes back to his chewing spot the Tabasco will be reminder enough.

Things that can be damaged easily might work better with the black pepper treatment. In this case, sprinkle black pepper over the object in question. Take your cat over to it along with the pepper and blow the pepper into your cat's nose until you're sure he hates it. The next time he goes near anything that smells of it, he should steer well clear. (You can also use the pepper in place of Tabasco. Simply mix it with Vaseline and smear it on as you would the Tabasco. Just be sure to blow the pepper into his nose first.)

Cats have an inordinately strong fondness for chewing and clawing plants. They eat them because they like the taste or for use as roughage to help digestion. They also use them as a means of self-medication to force regurgitation of hairballs, or even as a source of vitamins for any deficiency they may have.

A dieffenbachia* could probably solve your problem permanently. But more standard remedies include the same basic solutions used for scratching and chewing, with catching him in the act and reprimanding him on the spot immediately being, as usual, the best solution.

One of the more effective remedies for plant chewers is to first take white vinegar, lime juice or lemon juice and rub some full-strength on your cat's gums. Use only a few drops, just enough to make him hate it. Then in a spray bottle make up a mixture consisting of whatever you used to rub on his gums, plus a very small amount of commercial cat repellent, diluted with water. Spray the plants with this mixture. Now if the cat goes near the plants the smell should remind him of his unpleasant experience, and the new unsavory cat repellent odor should be an added incentive for him to stay away. If he is not immediately turned off and he does attempt to eat them, the taste will positively deter him.

Do not use a cat repellent straight on your cat's gums, at least until you check to be sure it cannot be harmful. And never spray any product directly at your cat since it could hurt him.

---

* The "dumbcane" is reputed to numb the vocal cords and cause dumbness for a short while after being eaten. To cats, however, it is more likely to be poisonous.

If you spray a repellent (and even ammonia the way some people do) at your cat, you may get it in his eyes, throat and/or lungs and thus badly injure him.

Today plants are really popular, and it is important that your cat learn to live with them. He must not interfere with them in any way. One cat we know used to sit and stare at his owner's plants until they drooped and even died from sheer intimidation. This strange behavior started only after he had been punished for clawing and chewing at the plants. In fact, it had begun after he'd been discovered with his front legs wrapped around a large palm and his teeth stuck into the leaves. A magazine had stopped his overt behavior, but there was no way to stop the animosity which the cat now felt toward the plants. He would just sit around and send out vibes of hate which the plants would pick up and then wilt. The only solution was to get hardier plants upon which the cat's intimidating stares seemed to have no effect.

In addition to harassing the plants themselves, cats love to claw up the earth around the plants. The way to combat this little habit is to get a piece of chicken wire and cut it to fit into the container and around the plant. Then cover this with just a thin layer of earth. When the cat starts digging, his feet will become caught. Chicken wire is wide enough to catch his feet and annoy him, but not hurt—it is just to make him feel uncomfortable. Soon the cat will learn to stay away; once he does you can either take the wire away or leave it, whichever you wish. It looks just fine, you can't even see it, and after a while it will start to erode, thus helping enrich the soil.

Other potentially bad or destructive habits are related to a cat's passion for climbing. One cat we know used to leap up onto shelves and knock things down. In this case the man was a collector of ceramics and the woman a cat lover. After about three accidents he was ready to get rid of the cat, she was ready to get rid of the collection, and both were about ready for a divorce. They finally called us and we told them to pack away the collection for a couple of weeks and give us free reign. We told them that for the next few days every time the cat jumped up he was to be slapped, told "no," and put down on the floor; or a magazine was to be thrown at or near him accompanied by a sharp "no." After this, and when their cat had a good idea that he was not welcome on the shelves, the owners were instructed to reinforce the lesson by adding booby traps. This way the cat would learn that it was also taboo when they were not around.

We set up one-inch blocks or strips of wood across the shelves and laid chicken wire on top of them. Thus, a space of about one inch was left between the shelf and the wire, so that every time the cat jumped on the shelf he would catch his feet. After this happened a couple of times the cat was leery about jumping. We then cut holes in the chicken wire just large enough to fit the ceramics, and replaced them on the shelves. We then took the cat and placed him on the shelf to show him that the wire still remained despite the fact that the knick-knacks were back. The wire was left up for a couple of weeks to let the lesson really sink in. It was then taken off and the people told to save it in case of relapse in training. The owners were instructed to watch for any transgressions and to correct him immediately.

Never let your cat get away with anything which could be harmful to him. No matter how bad you feel, you must reprimand him. Often people's guilt feelings prevent them from doing something which in the final analysis is the best thing for their cat.

When Christmas comes around pay particular attention to the way you decorate your home. Dangling tinsel is very tempting and can be potentially harmful. (Metal tinsel contains lead that can poison your cat, as can holly berries.) And if he leaps up for the decorations, he can topple the tree. For your own safety, never use candles. A cat can make a mistake and knock down the tree, but he can't open the door and run out when a fire starts.

In rare cases cats have been known to deliberately knock over ornaments shortly after they have been disciplined or even out of jealousy over a visitor in the house. Here, you must try to catch him in the act. This means setting up a situation that triggers such an action, then hiding and waiting to see what happens. If he does anything overt, reprimand him. Otherwise simply correct him in the appropriate manner through booby traps or any of the other means available.

Another solution and perhaps one of the best for stopping cats from going where you don't want them is to buy a box of balloons. You can get about fifty in a package for about a dollar or so. Sit down on the floor and start blowing the balloons full of air. When your cat comes over to see what you are doing, burst one in his face. It won't hurt him, but it certainly will startle him, which is what you want to do. Repeat this with another balloon and another until the cat is scared by the loud bangs and simply goes away from them. Your cat won't go near the balloons now because he feels they might explode if he does. So take the balloons and tape them right to wherever or whatever your cat has a habit of leaping up on. (Be sure to remove any knick-knacks during training, because if the balloons burst and frighten or startle him, he may become erratic and possibly do even more damage.) Since he has been shying away from the balloons he will probably stay off. After a week or so take the balloons down, and your cat should be cured. The only drawback to this technique is that when friends drop in to visit and see the balloons they will probably ask why they weren't invited to the party.

While you are doing this to him, don't say anything. Some

people call their cat to them, and then do it. If you do this your cat probably will never come to you when you want him. Just keep your mouth shut.

Incidentally, once your cat is shy of balloons you can also use them to keep him out of the garbage. Smear some tempting food on them and tuck a couple under the lid. The smooth surface of the balloons will cause his claws—front or back—to come out and dig in to get his footing and a secure traction. The balloons will therefore burst, scaring him away from the garbage.

Despite all these ploys, the best method of all for stopping potentially destructive or dangerous habits is to catch him right in the act and stop it on the spot. But if *you* don't catch him, at least make sure he does get caught—even when you are not around. Your cat must know that he can be reached no matter what, whether you are in or not. His bad behavior must be made unpleasant, uncomfortable and thus undesirable for him to do. On the other hand, always remember that good acts should be rewarded. Cats really have to be shown what is good and what is not.

One lady had her clothes and accessories scratched and chewed by her cat. She couldn't afford to support the habit very much longer. Our advice was to booby-trap her shoes and accessories with balloons that pop or cellophane or aluminum foil that crackles. The idea of the booby trap is to surprise—not hurt.

Use your common sense and think of how you can stop your cat's bad habits. Often you'll find that the same thing is so effective it can be used over and over in many different situations and problems, with only a simple adjustment. Thus the cellophane and aluminum could also be effective for stopping a cat from jumping up. The crackling might surprise him enough to stop him. Once your cat catches on to the whole thing, though, it's time to move on to another ploy. And if possible, try to replace a bad habit with a good one. Thus if you want him to stop scratching, give him a place where he can scratch; if he isn't allowed to sit in one place show him where he can sit, and give him a treat there to show him it's okay; and if he likes to chew your plants, give him a nice fresh raw wood stick as a substitute and some toys. Stop destructive habits before they start—and that includes ones destructive toward people and other animals as well as property.

10

AGGRESSION: Why Cats Fight and Kill, and How to Stop Them

Cats fight and kill for possession of territory, sex, protection, food and sometimes, as in the human brain, something goes wrong with the mechanism. No one wants a cat who is vicious and bites and scratches people, but certain cat owners are drawn toward the idea of a pet who can take on the local birds and other small wildlife, in addition to other cats and even the local dogs. Often it's the owners who need watching, not their cats, who are only behaving in a way that they feel their owners approve. These people don't want to correct the cat because they claim he's only doing what's natural—they don't want to "break his spirit" or "destroy his independent attitude." But what if we always acted "naturally"? Today we all have to make adjustments to fit into the social structure, and cats are no exception.

More often than not, such owners are using their cats to express their own repressed aggressions or fantasies. All we have to say to those who feel it is all right to let their cats fight other cats and even dogs, or hunt and kill birds and other small wild animals, is that allowing or encouraging bloodshed is cruel and unnecessary. Just imagine a twenty-five-pound Maine Coon cat attacking a visitor's five-pound Yorkshire Terrier!

Owners of bird killers have a special responsibility to stop their cats. It is selfish and stupid to allow this behavior to continue. To stop it take a toy canary, either the plastic kind or one of the ones covered in feathers. There is also a toy bird on a string available that flutters when waved in the air. This could be one of your better bets as a decoy. Attach one end of a length of string to the toy and the other end to a stick or—better yet— hang it on a long fishing pole. Then tease or tempt the cat by pulling the toy along the floor in front of him. Cats rely on vision when hunting so he's sure to go for it. And when he does make any overt move toward it, throw your trusty magazine and say "no."

Don't worry that tricking him with a toy bird will stop his playing; it won't. He'll just associate the decoy with the bird, and not with the act of playing. But make sure that the decoy you use is a good facsimile of a bird.

If you own a parakeet or other pet bird, you should definitely take this precaution. And if you have a cat you want to let outside, you should teach him from the outset not to chase and kill birds. The quick movements of birds attract a cat's attention and he goes after them for fun as much as anything. Even if he doesn't start off killing, but merely chases birds for fun, stop him. If you don't, it's sure to become a habit that will eventually turn to killing, whether deliberate or accidental. Discourage it before it starts by tempting him a few times with the decoy, and reprimanding him for chasing it. Do this even before you allow him out for the first time. This way you can feel pretty confident he won't bother with the local wildlife.

Once he no longer chases after the decoy when tempted with it, you can be fairly positive he has learned his lesson. Now let him out, but watch him anyway. If he makes a wrong move, throw your magazine or keys. (When outside, it's a good idea to tie a bright colored ribbon or string to your keys so they'll be easy to locate after they land.) In addition, try teasing him with the decoy bird outside a few times in the environment in which he will find real birds. Once the habit of chasing and killing birds is well established there is really little anyone can do other than to reprimand him with a sharp slap and a "no" if you catch him. It is, however, very hard to control the situation outside, so thoroughly instilling the lesson while he is inside is the best way to teach your cat.

As an added precaution against bird killing you can hang a tiny bell around your cat's neck. If you do use one, hang it only on loose elastic which your cat can slip easily if it gets hooked or entangled on something. If you don't, your cat could possibly throttle himself. Some people use brightly colored elastic as a further safeguard since it will tend to attract a bird's attention even if a cat is standing dead still in one of his hunting stalks.

Drastic action is called for if your cat is already a bird killer. One cat, Mike, had a favorite game. He would lie on his back as if sunning himself up on the terrace surrounding his owner's penthouse apartment. But every once in a while, as a pigeon flew over him, he would quickly strike out with his paw and kill the bird. To combat this we took the standard toy on a string decoy and attached it to an extra-long fishing pole. We then secreted ourselves on top of the roof one story above the terrace and waited. When he went out on the roof to lie in wait for his quarry we dangled the toy bird over his head. The moment he went for it, we let loose with a water hose. His bird-catching habit ended after about four good drenchings with the hose.

Hunting in which a cat recognizes, kills and eats prey is basically a learned behavior, but the senseless chasing and killing of wildlife for the sheer fun of it has no value above giving him a few moments' pleasure. Mice and other vermin are, however, another story and you should consider yourself lucky if he develops this type of hunting without a mother's intensive training. Very few people would want their cats to stop this activity. If, however, you have a pet mouse, gerbil, or hamster and want to discourage your cat from annoying it, follow the procedure used with birds, substituting a mouse decoy.

Stopping a cat who attacks and fights with dogs can be a damaging experience for all parties concerned. It must, therefore, be handled with utmost delicacy. Bodily interfering in a cat-and-dog fight is sure to end with your being the one who gets hurt, so you have to control it in other ways. One friend's next-door neighbor owned a cat who had the bad habit of jumping on big dogs' backs and digging in with his claws. The cat would stay on the dog's back digging his claws deeper and deeper until the dog got to the point where he had completely exhausted himself by aimlessly running around in circles. Then, when the cat felt the moment was right, he would leap off and beat a hasty retreat.

The cat's owner loved to watch, and laughed hysterically every time his pet attacked a dog. He would even reward him with a treat afterwards. We took it upon ourselves to stop this problem behavior without the owner's knowledge. To do this we stationed ourselves outside our friend's house and waited for the right moment. As soon as the cat made his move we quickly turned on a hose which we had previously set up just outside the door. The hose was long enough to follow the dog and cat, and the spray stopped the cat cold.

A cat nearly always wins in a one-on-one battle with a dog. Once he jumps on the dog's back and flails out at his head and eyes with his claws, the dog doesn't have much of a chance. A cat's defense mechanism lies not only in his teeth, which are strong and sharp like a dog's, but also in his long, sharply curved, retractable claws. If you compare the weapons of these two animals and take into consideration a cat's speed and agility, you will easily understand why a vicious cat can be far worse than a vicious dog.

However, except for some notorious dog-haters, most cats

147

aren't really looking for a fight. (The exception is a mother cat, who won't let anyone near her newborn kittens. In this case no matter what good friends they are normally, keep the dog away until the cat has calmed down and is more willing to share her new family with others.) There is no ancestral rivalry between cat and dog. In their natural habitat they have separate hunting interests and domains. Feuds mostly lie between cat lovers and dog lovers. And though really knowledgeable cats usually win hands down, they don't always. Thus, your cat, especially if young, could get hurt. Remember, defense is one thing, aggression another; stop aggression toward dogs immediately.

Caution is the key word when first introducing a cat and dog. Those claws are fast and it takes only a few seconds for some real damage to happen. The cat rises up on his hind legs and swings out with lightning-fast punches like a boxer—but he wears claws rather than gloves. We've seen a few claws that have remained stuck in a dog's eye. If you see any sign of aggression, throw your magazine, keys, or whatever is handy and when it lands the word is "no." Let him know right from the very beginning. The animal who makes the first move—whether cat or dog—is the one who should get it. If you do this every time you see your animal looking for trouble, the problem should be solved in no time.

Most pets in the same household ultimately become friends, but there are some who are completely incompatible. You could spend forever trying to work this one out, but often the best solution in a case like this is to try to get a home for one of the pets. Don't do this right away; try to remedy the situation. Make sure you aren't causing the problem by paying more attention to one than the other. Jealousy may well manifest itself in aggression.

Cats living together usually get along. With tigers brought up away from their parents but kept together in captivity well into maturity there was no animosity or fighting for supremacy. But if two non-related cats are forced to live together, one boss might evolve. Then if a strange new cat is introduced he may well have to be shown his position in the hierarchy of the household. In the standard ritualistic encounter the top cat arches his back, spits, thrashes his tail, and bares his claws. The newcomer then either fights or submits by giving the submissive gesture of flattening himself on the ground—but he will not roll over to yield the way a dog does. The dominant cat may then seize the other by the scruff of the neck and straddle him for a few seconds in a symbolic gesture of dominance. If, however, there is actually a fight it can be very vicious, since both cats go at it with everything they've got, and many battle scars will probably be received on both sides.

Most cats will go to any length in order to avoid the ultimate conflict, which then occurs only as the last resort. Thus, in his house a cat may often allow others in and around it. In fact, there may be only one spot in the entire house that he considers to be his alone and for which he will fight to defend against intruders. A friend's two altered female cats constantly bicker over the possession of any new objects that come into the house. Each will rush to it, trying to get there first, and the winner then sleeps or sits in or on it all day until it is really established as hers. This goes on even for a silly thing like a cardboard box that is going to be thrown out the next day anyway. But these cats have never actually fought; each one recognizes that possession is nine-tenths of the law and leaves it at that. The possessor simply gives the intruder an aggressive stare and that's it.

To keep your cat nonviolent when another cat visits, don't rush their introduction. Let them get acquainted slowly; they want to be sure of each other. Leave them alone, but don't wander off too far—and be sure to watch them for any signs of aggression. Reprimand even a remotely aggressive act, but be sure to punish the more aggressive of the two. Usually they'll stay away from each other, and as long as you don't push them there won't be any problem. They'll either become friends or ignore each other. However, it is always wisest to remove the resident cat's food, water, litter box and toys. The newcomer is bound to show an interest in them, and your cat will want to protect his own things. If the cat is staying, either permanently or on an extended basis, give each a separate bowl and box, though they can share the water. After a while you may find they are sharing everything, but it is best to be careful at first and prevent fights over encroachments on each other's possessions. Putting these things away and watching doesn't necessarily mean there won't be a fight, but it does minimize the possibility.

There are various ways of stopping a fight if you are too late to prevent it. The first cardinal rule is that you can't get between the animals or they will shred you. One solution is to take a big telephone book or similar object and skim it across the floor at them as if you were bowling. Don't drop it from above, as this could badly injure one of the animals, breaking a back or something equally nasty; throw from the side where there is very little chance of an injury. Once they are separated, grab the more aggressive of the two. He really shouldn't cause any damage once the fight is broken up. The scare is enough to startle him out of his aggressive mood. But if you think the aggressor might start on you, pick up the one you know best and feel most confident with.

If you definitely feel that one or both might attack you because they are known as aggressive cats, use another method. Take a broom or a mop and push the more aggressive animal away. The soft head won't hurt the fighters and the length of the handle will keep you at a safe distance. Then chase the aggressor out of the room and close the door.

Another method, somewhat less effective, uses a chair with rungs joining the legs together forming an open box-like structure. Place this gingerly over the pair so they are in an enclosed area. The trapped feeling will give them something besides the fight to think about and they will both clamor to get away from the new threat. They can then escape in opposite directions without hurting themselves.

If the animals are outside fighting, use a hose or bucket of water. A good dousing is enough to shock anyone back to rationality, and usually works wonders. Or a very loud noise to startle them both may work. Use your common sense when acting in this situation, but act promptly.

Whichever method you select to use, once the cats are separated, move out fast. Since most fights are over territory and/or sex, simply removing your cat or removing the reason for the battle, even a few feet away, should cool things off. There really is no way to reason with your cat over fights. Cats don't think about the possible consequences of actions and injuries; they just charge right in.

Don't deny your cat the benefits of your own common sense. Why not castrate your cat to take away his urge to fight? Then, after he is altered, keep him in. Don't get into the old habit of "letting the cat out before going to bed"; rather, make sure he's in and keep him there. Even if your cat is altered, other cats or dogs may pick on him. It is best not to allow your cat to roam, altered or not, since fights will occur and he can and often will get hurt. Your cat will suffer, you will suffer, and the vet will get plenty of business. In fact, if you do have to break up a serious fight, it is a good idea to take both parties to a vet, since you can't tell what internal damage might have occurred.

If your cat or the other animal is hurt and you have to get him to the vet, you may well have to restrain or entrap him. There are times, such as when he is terrified or in real distress, when a cat will claw and bite out of reflex. One cat ripped his owner's arm to shreds. There was no apparent reason and she assumed he must have been upset by something. She was right, he had been. He'd been out the night before and was badly hurt. When she touched him, it hurt and he instinctively struck out.

To restrain a distraught cat, throw a blanket or towel over him and let him tangle himself in it. Then carefully pick him up, put him straight into a carrier and get him to the vet. Be very sure to pick him up carefully, so that you don't injure him any more. A heavy laundry bag with a drawstring at one end, or a large zippered tote bag where only his head can stick out, are also good for restraining your cat and carrying him to the vet. (Incidentally these are also especially good places for feeding your cat medicines.) Don very heavy gardener's gloves if it will help you psychologically, though a suit of armor might be your only real answer.

Any cat you suspect has been injured should be handled with great care. Approach any injured wild strays with extreme caution. If you find you absolutely cannot go near the cat, there are humane cage-type traps that capture the cat in a trap laid with food. The local humane society can supply these or can help you find one. All cats can inflict very painful scratches and bites. Think about it, before you plunge in—it's you who will get hurt. A cat must be held so that he cannot reach you. If those ears are flat down and he is screaming in rage, watch out.

If you feel pretty confident that the cat will not attack you, there is another method you can use to pick up your cat to transfer him to the carrier. A cat has an inherited reflex action that causes him to curl up like a tiny kitten being carried in his mother's mouth when you grasp him by a large handful of skin at the scruff of the neck. Therefore, simply grasp the cat in this manner and hold him at arm's length so that no flailing claws can reach you. If the cat or kitten is just a little nervous or excited you can pick him up and control him simply by placing one hand under the chest, holding the forelegs between your fingers, and the other hand under the buttocks for support.

Don't play around with aggression. At first it may seem amusing but later it can become really annoying and dangerous. People often encourage aggression in their pets, either intentionally or simply through ignorance. Sometimes they even do it on the advice of so-called "experts." We read somewhere recently that the way to treat aggressive behavior caused by jealousy or rivalry over territory or even owners is to lavish attention on the aggressor to make him feel better. But this is about the worst thing you can do. Lavishing attention on your cat for aggressive behavior makes him think it's a good thing. You will thus be rewarding your cat for being bad. In the future he will, therefore, continue to behave badly. You have to show him that aggression is not good. Once aggression develops in a cat it may not limit itself to other animals but may also develop into aggression toward people.

People who are afraid of or dislike cats often display actions which are a little erratic—not quite normal—and the cat is attracted to the abnormality. He will tend to bully someone he can see is nervous by hanging around. And the more he hangs around, the more nervous the person gets, and consequently the more aggressive the cat becomes. Some cats absolutely revel in intimidating people in this way. Owners often don't recognize this as aggression, because their cat expresses it in excessive attention. They therefore assume their cats are being nice. If you see a friend squirm when your cat rubs against him, realize what's happening. Cats can definitely sense people who dislike them and will bully them if possible just to be contrary. Cats should be taught to treat guests with courtesy.

At first this kind of aggression may easily go unnoticed. A cat may simply develop the annoying habit of rubbing up against people, especially new visitors in the house. This leaves an odor on the visitor from special glands along his tail and head which excrete a substance when rubbed against something. This enables the cat to leave a mark on people or objects and thus claim them as his. The next step could be urinating on something belonging to the visitor, or even on him. After this—and possibly without it—outright hostility can follow. Stop it and have visitors stop it before it gets started.

If your cat gets overly "affectionate" in an aggressive manner, slap him or use the magazine method. All aggression toward people, even subtle signs of it, should be stopped immediately. One of our major tenets in working with cats is that there is no such thing as a friendly scratch or bite, though convincing cat owners of this is sometimes a headache.

Cats learn to scratch and bite at an early age. Small kittens nip at your hand and bat at you with their paws while you are playing with them. They have been used to playing this way with their brothers and sisters in the litter and to them you are just a substitute. But you don't have a fur covering to cushion the blows and thus protect you.

Kittens must be shown immediately that scratching and biting are not wanted, because a kitten's nipping and scratching can become a habit. It's far better to teach the cat manners while he is young than to wait until he's set in his ways. You've got to be vigilant in the beginning because the older a cat gets the more he learns that he can get his own way by biting or scratching, and the harder the habit is to stop.

A kitten or cat's claws come out in play simply because he hasn't learned to control them. Teach him how by telling him in no uncertain terms you don't want them out. Once you let him use them and he learns that they will elicit responses from you, he'll learn to use them to his advantage. Stop it early. Smack his paw hard and say "no." Don't worry about his becoming hand shy—he must be stopped. Don't pull your hand away in fright. If you do, you will be doing two things. First of all you'll teach him that you're afraid of claws, and secondly you'll get badly scratched as you pull your hand against his claws—the pulling action does the damage.

To stop any biting, flip him on the nose or side of the jaw

sharply with your hand. Don't pull your hand or whatever is in his mouth back. He'll think you are playing and thus learn to use his mouth in play. Additionally, if you pull your hand out of his mouth, as with his claws, the teeth will really scrape and hurt.

Don't let your cat get away with any aggression; stop it immediately, even if you think it could possibly be your fault. One woman was grooming her cat when he suddenly turned around and gave her a swipe across the face with his claws. She told us that she blamed herself for the accident, because she had pulled too hard on a bad gnarl. When he does it again, no matter what the circumstances, she'll probably find another way to blame herself. This is one of the most common mistakes when coping with an aggressive cat. What she should have done was slap the cat, no matter what the circumstances. Reprimand the cat firmly to establish that this type of behavior is plainly unacceptable.

If allowed, a cat might attack you as he would another cat if you go near his food. Or if you are a man and you own an unaltered male, he may not allow you near his mate in season. In one family with an unfixed cat, the cat and the owner, a sweet, retiring man, were in competition for control. The cat was winning because he had sharper teeth and longer claws. The man was really frightened of his cat and until he got over this fear nothing could be done.

In another household we ran into a behavior problem involving a cat who had bitten his owner quite badly. When asked if her cat had been declawed, she said no. Fortunately this case we could help, since a cat with his claws doesn't usually bite as his first line of attack, but rather hits with his claws and bites only as the final "kill" gesture. (Even declawed cats come at you with their paws first; they don't seem to know their claws are missing.) We, therefore, felt confident that her cat wasn't vicious to the point of really being untrainable. Something else was wrong here. And as it turned out, the problem was the result of the cat's having a bad back which hurt when anyone touched it. Biting his owner was his only way of trying to tell her something was wrong and not to touch. Remember, it is not always aggression that causes vicious behavior. In case of any sudden, seemingly unprovoked act of viciousness, take your cat to a veterinarian to see if anything is wrong.

The cat who ran up one client's pants leg, clawing both him and his pants to shreds, wasn't such a simple problem to solve. We told the owner that the only way to handle a cat like this was to hold his hand flat open and, when the cat came at him, to hit him away as fast and hard as he could. (The reason for the open hand is to give you as large a hitting surface as possible, like the new oversized tennis rackets on the market.) We warned the owner never to grab the cat; always hit him away so he could escape. But the owner couldn't bring himself to do it—he was too scared. Declawing was therefore necessary before we could even start working with the cat, since he was really a vicious animal. Even after his claws were removed, the cat still thought he had them and continued to flail at all visitors. Therefore, every time someone came into the house and the cat looked at them offensively a magazine was thrown at him before he could make his move. At other times we had the owner set the cat up and have us or someone else come through the door. The cat was allowed to make an overt attack and then a heavy magazine was thrown at him as he started. The cat still had his teeth and could hurt, so we had to get to him fast. This meant being sure to have something handy to throw when visitors came through the door.

Declawing is, of course, the most obvious solution for a cat who claws people, but it doesn't help the biting situation. Once a cat learns the bad habit of biting, it's hard to control. First he should be physically checked out by the vet to make sure he's okay. If he is absolutely impossible and you can't stop him by training you may have to have his fangs taken out. This should, of course, be absolutely the last resort and isn't really a nice thing to do. But if it's a choice between that and having him destroyed or dumping him—have the fangs removed.

Many of the big cats you see on television, in movies, or in shows have no teeth, or at least no large canines, along with no claws. As long as they are in captivity they don't need them. Many other big cats do have all their teeth and claws, however. In fact, Gunther Gebel-Williams, the tiger trainer, proved that to the world when he appeared on a national television show with only a swimsuit to show his scars—and he had plenty, even though he brings up all his cats by hand from tiny cubs. Everyone who keeps large cats with claws and teeth has to pay the price.

One woman's cat attacked every man who came into her house. Her solution was to lock him in the bathroom with a big DANGER sign on the door every time she was expecting male company. We finally cured the problem by convincing her to have the cat castrated. This is often the only solution to the problem. Once altered, almost all cats lose their competitiveness and they become much better and friendlier pets.

Another client's vicious cat came out of a public pound. He was so mean he would allow no one to touch him. It was impossible to know what had happened to him. He could have been beaten or starved. With lots of time, affection and good care he became a good pet. Even today he is still not the friendliest of cats, but at least he lives in harmony with everyone in the house.

Aggression is not always your cat's fault. Often owners provoke this behavior. One family had a problem with their cat's scratching the children. The kids had it coming because they teased the cat. Our advice to the parents in this case was to reprimand the kids, not the cat, for the misbehavior.

Of course, if your cat scratches or bites at children with no provocation—a very unlikely situation—you have to take the ap-

157

propriate action. We instructed them to keep a magazine or rolled newspaper tucked under their arms as often as possible, to be tossed at the cat whenever he attempted to scratch or bite. If the paper were held in the hand rather than under the arm, the cat would see it and anticipate what was coming, thus destroying our main weapon—the element of surprise. We told the parents to tell the children to "go and play," but not tease, and then toss the magazine at the cat if he went for them. We reminded them not to scream at the children or the cat, but just to toss the magazine methodically and say "no" when it hit.

In normal circumstances the cat must be reprimanded for biting, chewing or any kind of aggressive act. A firm reprimand at the first sign of aggression, playful or otherwise, is the answer—not excuses. Whenever he does wrong, correct him immediately, right there on the spot. A good hard smack is just about the best solution. If you've allowed it to get this far it's your fault and you no longer have any choice. Let him have it or he'll let you have it. As a cat owner, it's your responsibility to see that your animal behaves.

PART THREE

ADVANCED TRAINING

COMING WHEN CALLED

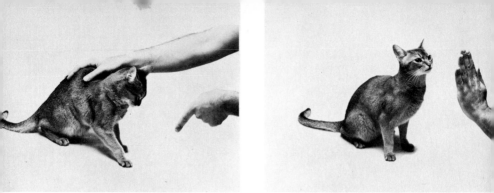

SIT/STAY

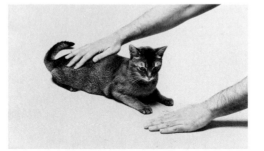

LIE DOWN

WALKING ON A LEAD

SHAKING HANDS

EATING OUT OF A CAN

WAVING

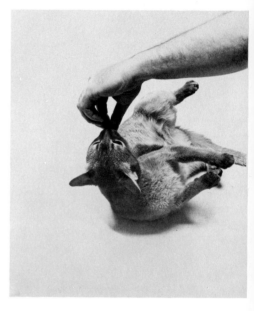

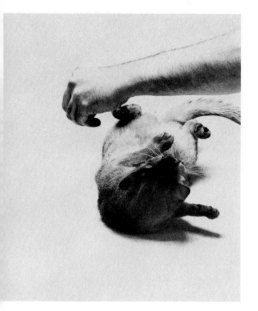

ROLLING OVER

SITTING UP
AND BEGGING

JUMPING

HOLDING YOUR CAT PROPERLY

TOILET TRAINED—IT CAN BE DONE!

A SCRATCHING POST

11

COME WHEN CALLED

"Come" is an extremely touchy command, requiring in our opinion the most work of any of the basic commands. Therefore, the best thing you can do is start working it with your cat from the very beginning. Try to teach him the command as soon as possible. But don't despair if he's older; he can still learn—it's just that kittens can't run very fast so you can catch up with them easily, making your job simpler.

After a certain age, *any* cat will be more set in his ways and affections. This is not to say that an older cat can't be taught new tricks, it just takes longer and requires more reinforcement. Therefore, it's impossible to overstress the advantage you have by trying to get in as much training at as early an age as possible.

If you carry your kitten around with you from a very early age, the cat may well look upon you as a parent figure. This type of behavior in animals is known as imprinting, and it seems to be an inborn instinctive process on which an animal's survival depends. Animals must learn early where their protection lies and to what species they belong. But a cat's critical marking period, during which time he will readily accept new owners as parents, is over very early. It has been proved that a kitten who has never been in contact with humans before three months of age never really learns to relate to them and is almost impossible to keep as a pet. He will consider himself completely a cat and if he takes orders at all it will be only from other cats. If, however, he is hand-raised and becomes very attached to humans he probably won't be able to develop close relationships with other cats.

Admittedly, imprinting in cats is not as enduring as in many species; many types of cats in the wild establish lone territories and cats are soon on their own. But with conditioning started at an early age and maintained throughout his life, a cat can achieve a lasting relationship with you.

There's no point in trying to teach this command to a cat who doesn't know or feel secure with you. There must be some rapport between the two of you. If you and your cat aren't on speaking terms, you can forget teaching him any commands. People often say, "My cat ignores me completely. I call him and call him, but he won't come." Or, "My cat only comes around when he wants." But what do they expect if they never pay any attention to him except when they want him to do something or when the whim hits them? Why shouldn't the cat act exactly the same way? You get response from your cat in proportion to the amount of love and effort you give him.

Teach your cat to come when called. You will find that the effort put into this command is well worth it. Once he learns it perfectly you will have established that you can control your cat. You can be sure he will come back to you and are therefore much more confident about your ability to train him, especially when it comes to the more complex tricks.

One cat owner who'd been persuaded to leave her cat alone for the first time while she went away for a ski weekend would have saved herself a lot of worry if she'd taught her cat the courtesy of coming when called. After having been away for only a day, this owner started worrying about her cat. She felt nervous and guilty over having left him alone. She was positive he was pining away with loneliness, or that something had happened to him. She rushed home expecting to find her sweet cat waiting nervously beside the door. When she got home, however, there was no cat in sight. She called him, but got no response. Visions of all the things that could be responsible for the cat's not being there to greet her flashed through her mind—He's been stolen! Somehow he's managed to get out, has run away, and is starving somewhere! He's dead!—so she rushed around the house looking for him. Then she methodically started searching every room in the house. She even called in a friend to help her out. Finally she found him lying comfortably on the top shelf in her closet, calmly grooming himself in his comfortable lair and completely ignoring her frantic calls.

Perhaps the first and simplest way to start teaching the "come" command is to start working with him around mealtime. Don't just put his food down, but call him every time you lay out his food. At the same time you call him, tap his bowl. When he comes to you, praise him for coming and then feed him. This will imprint in him to come to you for his food when you call him or tap on his bowl. At the same time it will start conditioning him to come to you when you call since he will associate the word "come" with food and rewards.

Once he's coming to you when you call him to his food, it's time to start calling him at other times of the day and in other places. Take him to as confined an area as possible, where there is no possibility of his running away from you. At first call him from just a few feet away—arm's length at most—so you can catch him easily if he attempts to run off. Remember to train in three-to-five minute intervals only, and make sure your cat completes each repetition of the exercise.

Since this is a command that, to have any meaning or effectiveness, must be obeyed by your cat when he is at a distance, you must get your cat's attention by calling his name before telling him to come. Therefore, before teaching the command make certain that your pet knows his name by repeating it often while you are playing with him. Then, when teaching him the command, call his name just once, say "come," and give him the hand command by making a large beckoning gesture toward you, usually with your right hand. At the same time hold a special treat such as an appetizing morsel of food in your other hand and tempt him with it. If and when he comes to you reward him with lots of praise and the special tidbit. Don't make it too much, just a tiny piece, enough to whet his appetite and ensure that he will come to you again in the future. You don't want a fat cat, just an obedient one.

If he does not respond to you or pay attention when you call his name and say "come," perhaps you could crumble or crinkle a piece of cellophane paper or make some other interesting noise. A sound, especially if it's strange, unusual, or new will usually attract your cat's immediate attention. So, to get his attention, make a strange sound where you want your cat to look or come. Not a loud noise, just something to excite his curiosity and get him to come or look over to investigate. Make the sound first, then call him using both voice and hand commands. When he gets to you, treat him and praise him.

If he absolutely refuses to come to you within the time allotted for the lesson—three to five minutes—go over, pick him up, and bring him over to the spot from which you called him. Then treat him. Never let him get away with not completing a command. If you do, he'll only learn that it doesn't really matter whether he comes or not. He must be taught that "come" means *come*, no matter what.

One woman whose cat refused to come when she called decided that it was simply because he didn't like his name. She therefore changed it. Then when he didn't respond to that one she changed it again. As far as we know she's still changing it on a regular basis, and her cat still isn't listening. Perhaps she'd be better off if she called him Stop, Stay, Come, Go or, better still, No.

What you name your cat has nothing to do with whether he

responds to you or not. It's your perseverance that's going to do it. Start slowly, repeating the exercise frequently for very short periods, and being sure he completes it every time. After he is coming to you consistently, increase the distance between you and the cat every few sessions until he is eventually coming to you from at least across a room.

Once he responds at this distance you need to take your cat to a new environment, such as a friend's house, and work with him there. This way you can reinforce his training and be sure your cat really knows the command. Make it a small, secure room where he has never been before, from which he cannot escape, and with absolutely no place where he can hide. The room you select should be as empty as possible so that you can easily catch him if he tries to run off. It's a real nuisance trying to drag a cat out from under a couch.

For this new training you will have to take along a piece of board with a string at least the length of the room attached to it, or a bunch of light aluminum cans with a few pebbles or pennies in each tied to an equally long piece of string. You will also need a completely enclosed cat carrier or cardboard box. You are going to be setting up a "trap" to encourage him to come to you on command. You don't want him to see what's going on while you set everything up, so he must stay in the carrier while this is going on. If your cat's carrier has peekholes or a clear plastic observation top, cover them, but make sure there are enough airholes to allow for adequate ventilation. Cats are so smart that if your cat sees you setting the trap he may well associate it with what's to come and never come when called.

Once you have everything you need, put your cat in his enclosed carrier and take him to the new training location. When you get to the room place the board or the bunch of cans up against a wall, but keep the free end of the string in your hand. Then put your cat's carrier with him still in it at the opposite end of the room and sit down next to it. You should now be sitting beside your cat's carrier and holding the free end of a string which is attached, at the other end, to a wooden board or pebble-filled cans leaning against the wall on the other side of the room.

When everything is all set up, let your cat out of his carrier. Reassure him that everything is okay. Then sit back patiently, relax, and just wait. Your cat will eventually start wandering around the room to check everything out. Some cats are more adventurous than others, but all cats must check out their environment before they can feel secure in it. When your cat goes near the board or cans, but not under them so he could get hurt, pull the string, causing the board to fall with a loud bang or the cans to clatter. *After* the noise, immediately call your cat to you by calling his name, saying the word "come," and using your beckoning gesture.

The noise will frighten your cat and he will naturally run to his carrier where he feels safe and secure because it is familiar. The box is right next to you, so he will naturally run toward you. When he comes to the box, take him in your arms, praise and reassure him to calm him down, then give him a treat as a reward for coming to you.

Next, switch everything around and repeat the command. To do this put your cat back in his carrier and move him to the other end of the room. Then set the board or tins at the opposite side of the room. Repeat the entire exercise. He will be more cautious this time because of what happened the last time he explored the room. But he will still check everything out anew since he didn't really have the opportunity to investigate completely. And besides, now it is all turned around and he will thus be a little disoriented by the changes. When he does start to explore and goes close to the board or cans, do as you did before— pull the string out and after the racket occurs call his name, say "come," and beckon him toward you.

Repeat this exercise for a few more times, keeping in mind that it's not going to take your cat long to get smart and catch on to what's happening with the cans or board. Get in a few good lessons and make them count so he remembers in the future.

You must always call his name, say "come," and use your hand command only *after* the cans or board fall. If you do it beforehand, the cat might associate the word "come" with the action that follows. Thus, he will not perform and may well run away and hide every time he hears the word. By the same token, be absolutely sure that the cans or board do not actually touch the cat or in any way hurt him. These aids are only supposed to fall near him, but *never* touch. As you should know by now the idea is to surprise and make your cat uneasy, not ever to hurt him. It is just to encourage him to come to you so you can show him coming when called is good.

After doing this shock-treatment training exercise, do not work with him on the come-when-called command for two or three days. Then, the next time you work the command, simply call the cat to you once. If he doesn't come, gently toss your keys or a magazine near him, but make sure you don't hit him. It's very important to try to make sure that your cat does *not* see the source of the magazine or keys. Therefore, toss discreetly. Then immediately *after* they land say "come" and give your hand signal. Repeat this process until he comes to you, and when he does give him a treat.

Just remember that if you throw the keys or magazine at him and he still doesn't come, you must not run after him screaming *"Come!"* It will only panic him if you do this and he may well run and hide. If he does run away, wait until he stops and then go after him. No matter how annoying or disobedient your cat is during these exercises, the only "correction" you must give him is the thrown magazine or keys. And these aren't really anything but aids for training. *You cannot hit him when you finally get him back*. That is why when we throw the keys, we say "come" only after they land.

The purpose of the keys is to give you some kind of control over your cat. If he seems apprehensive and runs off to hide, you must go get him, console him, and take him back to the spot where he was sitting when you first called him. You must then go back to the spot where you called him from, even if it is in a different room, and call him again. If your cat still refuses to come, go and get him. Bring him to the original spot you called him from and end the exercise there. You must make him finish even if you carry him through the command. Whether he does it well or not, he must come to you every time you tell him to do so, even if you have to go and get him. As with everything you want him to do consistently, never quit without completing the command.

If, after a few days of this type of training, your cat still refuses to come, you will have to use the shock treatment training again. Go to a different unfamiliar room and use the board or cans. But do not use this technique more than once or twice per week at the very most.

If your cat is really stubborn and absolutely refuses to obey this command, you can try another technique. This consists simply of putting a harness on your cat and attaching a six-foot training lead to it. (See Chapter 13, "Walking on a Lead," for information on the type to use.) Let the cat out to the end of the lead, then call his name to attract his attention and give a gentle tug on the lead. Immediately let the line go slack and use the command "come" while motioning for him to come to you. If you get no response, pull the lead, let it go slack, and call him again. After this if he still refuses to come, reel him in to you. Every time he comes to you, whether of his own free will or with your help, he must be praised and treated.

Once he starts coming to you after you give the lead only a

slight jerk, try calling him while holding the line slack and not pulling him at all. After he starts coming without a jerk on the line at all, don't stop pulling him completely. Alternate the times you don't pull the line with the times that you do. This will serve to reinforce his obeying the command. Just remember to complete each repetition of the exercise—even if you have to reel him in—every time you give the command.

Give the command "come" either before or after applying pressure to the lead. Never call your cat and pull on the lead at the same time. If your cat stops or tries to run away, pull him toward you. Once he is coming consistently without any pressure on the lead, but simply when you call him, try him without it. If it doesn't work, go back to the lead or try one of the other methods to encourage him to come when you call.

In teaching this command you can add variations. For instance, you can blow a whistle every time you feed and call your cat. This way he would learn to come whenever a whistle is blown. In fact, you can feasibly train your cat to come to any sound, signal, word, or combination thereof. Many people prefer other hand signals to the traditional beckoning one. Some pat their thighs, others clap their hands. But whatever you decide, select only *one* gesture for any command, and stick to it. No matter what you decide to use, your cat will begin to associate the word used with the hand signal, and with the treat he receives when he gets to you.

Just remember, your cat must know that when he comes to you after you call him he has a strong chance of getting something good—such as a special tidbit—in return. Coming to you must be a very rewarding experience. Thus, each and every time he gets to you lots of praise must always be given and when he is first learning the command a special treat should always be awaiting him. Get him accustomed to both praise and reward for deeds well done.

After a while, when he is really obeying the command, give

him the food treat on a random basis. Be sure you don't subconsciously set up a pattern, like treating your cat every two or three times. Space them out completely randomly and keep your cat guessing. This way he'll always come to you since he doesn't know when he's going to get something and when not. It will keep him on his toes.

No matter what, your cat should always be praised for coming when called since he must know it is a good thing. But it's really the occasional random treat that will serve to keep his interest aroused and give him a reason for coming. Praise, though nice, isn't the most important thing to him. Rewards, physical comfort, treats and the like are more in his line. Your cat will show up pronto if he thinks he will be rewarded for doing so in some gratifying way. Therefore, getting your cat to come when called is as simple as rewarding him for doing so. Make it pleasant for him to be near you.

Never, ever call your cat to you for punishment, medication, grooming, or anything that might in any way cause him discomfort. If a wrong association becomes attached to the command, it will be almost impossible to reprogram your cat into accepting it as a good thing. If you make a mistake and mess it up, you might as well forget using "come" as a command.

Since we don't recommend letting your cat outside other than on a lead, we don't want to dwell too long on training your cat to come back when called outside. Besides, it's one of those almost impossible jobs. The only way you could possibly do it is to make sure he is coming to you one hundred percent of the time inside first. Then work him outside the way you did indoors. Start him off in a small enclosed area such as a fenced-in yard. But always bear in mind that fences and trees mean nothing to your cat. He can leap over or climb them without the slightest effort and easily escape. Therefore, for outside training it is best to use the lead and harness technique with an extra-long lead, and bring along his carrier since it is familiar to him and he will just naturally tend to come to it. Once he is coming with reasonable certainty while on a lead, go on to try without it. But when first training without the lead stay very close to him the way you did when inside. Continue in the same manner as when training indoors.

At all stages of training in the come command, whether done inside or out, go back a step once in a while for review. In addition, once your cat has the command down pat don't let him forget his training. Issue the command every once in a while to keep him up on his lessons; don't allow him to go stale. Even when he is perfect, he must go back a few steps and be reminded once in a while. While practicing in the house, try to use distractions such as other cats or pets. Call him when he is really involved in playing with another cat or in a game of his own making, and make sure he comes to you. Responding under these difficult circumstances is the test he must pass before you know the command is thoroughly ingrained. Just remember that he must be perfect in one stage before going on to the next.

Never let any other people interfere while you are training. Sometimes another person will try to encourage your cat to respond to you by saying, "Go on over to her, that's a good boy." Too many voices can confuse the cat, so only one person should give the command at a time.

Keep in mind that your cat must always feel it is good to come when you call him. Too many people have a tendency to call their cat when they want to punish him. When the cat does something wrong in the house, they say, "Come here you little bastard, come here, why did you do that?" They then punish him. He thus learns *not* to come when called. His response will be to run the other way. No matter how angry you are with your cat, don't ever punish him when he comes after you call him or you might as well forget this entire command. Only good must happen to your cat when he comes to you.

171

12

SIT, STAY, LIE DOWN

"Sit," "stay" and then "lie down" usually come early in training because they are stationary commands. As such they offer the least possibility of confusion.

SIT AND STAY

The sitting and staying command have to be taught together. If not, you will be running all over the house telling your cat to sit. "Stay" is the thing that will keep him in position.

About four short lessons a day, each three to five minutes long are plenty for training. Do not get discouraged if the training doesn't seem to be working very fast at first. The first command you teach your cat or kitten often requires a lot of time and effort. This is especially true since they have no concept of what training is all about. Therefore, you will not only be training him to respond to the command, but also to accept working for you.

Eventually he will do what you ask if you insist. Just keep putting him through his paces over and over until you wear him down and get him to do what you want. When he first does sit, he may start to groom himself in a show of nerves or defiance. But you will find that he soon gains new confidence once he knows exactly what is expected of him, and learns that not only is listening to you the only way, but that it is also very rewarding.

To teach your cat to sit, use your three-foot dowel (page 105) teaching aid. Take the cat to a convenient corner in your home or put him up on a table covered with a nonslip surface such as toweling in a corner. The reason for using a corner when first teaching the "sit" command is to keep him in a somewhat restricted area and thus make his escape less likely. After all, here he's surrounded by walls on two sides and you on the third. This eliminates the confusion for a very young kitten and even for the older cat getting his first lesson in obedience.

The table in the corner is a good idea for many early training lessons since it allows the cat to be up high enough so you can sit in comfort while working with him. It also makes it easy to control him. But if you teach your cat on a table, you must eventually teach him on the floor also. Otherwise you will only be able to command him if he is at eye level and within easy grasp.

Don't take him to a corner where there is a lot of racket. A sharp noise could go off at the same time you give the "sit" command, and he might never learn what "sit" really means. You could tell him to sit until you're blue in the face and he will never respond.

In order to teach a cat to sit and stay, the first thing you have to do is to get his attention. Make enough of an impression to ensure that he knows you're around, the way you do with people when you shake their hands, or give them a hug or kiss. To do this, shake him slightly or tap him or the floor in front of him with your dowel. Be extremely careful to be gentle and not hurt him. Just get his attention. Any painful experience will only stop him from working at all.

A similar principle is used by the trainers of big cats. The crack of the whip in front of them in a circus isn't so much a threat of intimidation as so many people think, but rather attracts the immediate attention of the cat. This way if his mind starts to wander or it is time for him to go through his routine the sound of the cracking whip gets his attention immediately. You must have a cat's full attention before you can work with him.

Once you have your cat or kitten in the corner and have his complete attention to the extent that he is looking at you, put the dowel down and then do three things at once:

1. Point to the floor or table with one hand. Don't point to his tail because there are no eyes there, even though it is the part you want to sit down.

2. Place your other hand on his back and slowly move it down his back. When you get to the rear end, gently push down on his hindquarters to force him into a sitting position. Moving your hand down your cat's back before pushing him combines a little reassurance and praise with assistance in sitting.

3. Say "sit," *once.*

If he doesn't sit for you, again push him gently to a sitting position, point to the floor, and say "sit" at the same time. Keep doing this until you finally get him to sit down. If he is stubborn and won't do it, and you get tired of trying to get him to perform the exercise, hold him in position for a few seconds and then release him. Don't give in to your cat. Make him come around to your terms. Hold him down and say "sit." Hold him for a few seconds or so. Then pick him up and praise him. This way he will remember for the next time that you mean what you say. You must make him complete the lesson before you release him.

But stop the lesson before you and your cat get irritated—

174

three to five minutes tops. Remember that you're not reprimanding your cat, just teaching him to sit. Be patient, give all commands in your normal tone of voice and finish what you start. But again, never end a session unless the cat is sitting— even if you're holding him in position.

Keep repeating the exercise over and over. Gradually let up on the amount of pressure you exert on his back until your cat goes into a sit position with no pressure at all, but simply on the voice and hand command to sit. When your cat does sit for you, praise and pet him with one hand while holding him in place with the other for a few seconds. Then pick him up, praise him, and give him a treat.

Once he responds consistently with no assistance other than the actual commands to sit, he is ready to learn the "stay" command also. This command is, of course, connected with the "sit" command. After all, there's no point to telling him to stay unless you already have him in a specific position and spot. Therefore, after he sits, praise and hold him in place the way you normally would. When he is sitting comfortably, take your hands away from him and immediately push your right one straight toward him like a police officer stopping traffic. At the same time say "stay" *once*. This should freeze your cat in position. If he attempts to get up gently push him back down. After he stays, if only for a couple of seconds, pick him up, give him a treat and release him. Keep doing this gradually making him stay a little longer each time until you eventually get him to stay there for a count of ten.

After he's been doing this while you are sitting in front of him, try to get him to respond when you are not right on top of him. If you don't, you will always have to set him up before giving a command. You must get him to follow the commands when you are in a standing position. You probably will never get him to listen from across a room, but having him listen while you are standing is not too much to ask. If you are training him to sit down on the table, first try to do it from a standing position with him still on the table. Next move him and yourself to the floor and proceed to go through the commands there.

When he is obeying this stationary command perfectly on the floor with you sitting in front of him, try to get him to do it while you are in a kneeling position. This way you won't be making too big a jump for him to comprehend or accept at one time. Cats like to take it slowly and methodically. After he is doing well while you are in a kneeling position, try working him from a standing position. In this case you can't use your hand to exert pressure on his back to encourage him to sit. Therefore, take your dowel and tap very lightly on his rump as encouragement if he seems to be having problems. Remember never to hurt him during training or you'll never get him to respond. Your dowel is for encouragement *only*. It simply helps nudge him into position. If he refuses to sit, go back a step and build up again. And if he tries to get away without completing the command, again use your dowel. Simply place it in front of him and push him back into position with it. If this doesn't work, bend down, pick him up, and put him back into position.

Once your cat is sitting on command without any assistance and staying for a count of ten or so while you are giving the commands from a standing position, step back about a foot or so after you tell him to "sit" and "stay." You can't just turn your back on a cat, at least not at the beginning. If he gets up when you back up, let him move out only a couple of feet and then bring him back. Do not use the reprimand "no," or punish or hurt him, since he might confuse it with the command you are teaching him. It's important that you remain friends. If he gets up or if you catch him on the run, grab him as he is leaving and reissue the command. Say nothing else. Simply take him back to his sit position. Repeat the command again holding your palm before his face as if to push him. Again walk back a few feet. Repeat this procedure until he gets tired and stays.

Once he does stay he must now remain in that sit-and-stay corner until you release him. *You* must release him. Therefore, once he has remained sitting there, walk away a short distance, hold your hand out in the stay position as you did before and say "stay." Walk toward your cat. Don't say another word but hold your hand out in front of you in the stay position. Go all the way over to him and touch him, keeping him there, and say "good cat." Then immediately give him the voice and hand command "stay." Remember not to say anything to him before you touch him since he might consider this to be a release from the command.

Always remember to give your cat a relaxing remark and signal so he'll know exactly when he is released from his command. Many people like to use a word as a release signal. If you do, the word you choose to release him from the command should work something like the army command "at ease." It should be something other than "good cat" and the like. That's praise and he should continue with a command when praised. A common word like "okay" is not the best choice since it crops up so often in ordinary conversation.

With cats, perhaps the best release "word" is a hand signal such as clapping your hands, or even something more physical than that, such as picking up the cat and giving him a cuddle. Whatever your choice of signal, always use it when you've finished working with him so he knows the lesson is over.

At the end of the lesson, when he is finally sitting and staying, give him plenty of praise and a special treat. To praise him rub his ear or tickle him under the throat. But always make sure he is doing something before treating him. Don't just give him something for time put in. Rewards should be for tangible feats well done, responses to commands. Don't feel obligated to give unless he gives something in return. At the beginning, before he knows the command, you can reward him even if you carry him physically through the command. But when he has some idea of what is going on, don't give for the sake of giving. Show your cat that he gets something in return for something given on his part. Also, wait to give your cat his treat rewards or meal at the end of a training session. The smell of food in the middle of a session can be distracting to all cats.

Gradually increase the amount of time the cat has to sit or the distance you walk away. But don't turn your back on him until you are absolutely positive of him. First try to extend the time he will sit and stay while you are standing in front of him. Then another time see how far you can back up away from him. After he is used to sitting for a while, see if he'll still stay once your back is turned and you're not right on top of him. Then start varying the time and/or the distance pattern to test him. He must learn that "stay" means *stay*. When he is proficient in this exercise, try adding distractions like some small noises and see if he'll stay. If he won't, work him until he will.

Practice this exercise until your cat responds immediately to both voice and hand commands. After you have success, start to use just the hand command and then the voice. If he seems to be having problems, always go back and work on the weakest points. Then go on with the training again. And be sure you always reward him for doing his lessons well.

Once he does this and is really perfect in the corner, you are ready to vary the sit-and-stay exercise. Take him to the center of a room where there are no distractions around him and work there. Vary this spot by moving to a different one every few times you work the command. This way you can be sure he is learning the command and not just to sit in a corner. Follow the exact same procedure in each new spot as you did when first teaching your cat the sit/stay command in the corner. When he sits and stays almost immediately after being moved to a new spot, you can be sure he knows the command.

A cat is not supposed to do anything else, and should not be trained to do anything else, until the initial lesson is completed. If for any reason you are interrupted in the midst of a training session, *go back to it as soon as possible.* Otherwise, the next time you command him your cat may well feel that an interruption means he doesn't have to obey, and he will dawdle, waiting for the telephone or doorbell that means class is over. Remember that you are the one he learns from and if he doesn't learn it right, it is your fault and not his. If you can get the script and the movements down pat, your cat will listen and do as you ask.

You should not call your cat by name constantly when teaching him this or any new command. "Sabbath, sit," or "Stay, Sabbath," will tend to confuse him. Just say "sit" or the command for whatever you are teaching him. *After* you teach him the command and he is responding to it, it is all right to use his name before a command. In fact, it is absolutely essential in order to get his attention—how else can he know it's directed toward him? At the beginning you are right on top of him and can use more direct physical means to attract his attention, but as he becomes more proficient in performing the command you will be giving it at a distance and will need to attract his attention by calling his name. Call his name once and, when he turns and gives you his attention, issue the command. Do not keep on calling his name over and over except when he is still learning it. *Once* to attract his attention is enough.

If during training your cat manages to get away from the sit/stay position, you must go get him and bring him back to the spot. Take away his security spots, make him know there is no security but what you want. A cat must be forced back time and time again. He must be taught that he must finish a command you give. You must make sure he completes every command. It is extremely important that you bring him back each time to the exact same spot where you told him to sit-and-stay in the first place. He must learn that when you say something you mean exactly that and, thus, he must learn to sit and stay where you want.

Once he has learned the command, try teaching him to sit and stay with other cats and perhaps even dogs around. The very distractions that do make him leave the sit/stay position are the ones you should work on. Try to increase the amount of time he will sit and stay without moving when there are distractions around. At the same time always try to use your hand commands to get him to sit and stay. If your cat breaks the sit-and-stay for any reason—even if you caused it by adding distractions—you must start all over and make him go through with it properly before praising, treating and releasing him.

Remember to keep the sessions short and spaced well apart, be consistent and extremely patient, and always make sure your cat completes a command. He must learn that if he holds that sitting position when you say "sit" and "stay" and/or use the appropriate hand signals, it means that he will get rewarded. And this is what makes a cat listen.

LIE DOWN

"Lie down" is basically an extension of "sit," and it is even executed from a sitting position. Therefore, it is much easier to teach your cat to lie down if he knows the "sit-and-stay" commands. This way he is used to obeying commands already, is familiar with the position, and is thus more at ease and easier to work.

However, when you do first teach your cat to lie down, actually place him in a sit position, but do *not* command him to "sit-and-stay." Give *no* command except for one he is learning, which in this case is "lie down" or "down." If you give him the command to "sit-and-stay" first, it will only be confusing for him, and he may well learn to associate the "lie down" with the "sit" command. You will probably never be able to teach your cat to lie down straight from a standing position, but you should still make sure he understands the "lie down" command as distinct unto itself.

Although the "lie down" or "down" command is a relatively easy one, for some strange reason it tends to be something many cats are extremely obstinate about. Often you will find that when you tell your cat to "sit-and-stay," after a moment or so he will get tired and lie down, but when you *tell* him to lie down, he will refuse. Your cat must learn that you mean what you say, and that "sit" means sit *only*.

To make sure he does do this remember it is best, at least at first, to keep all commands separate until he has mastered each. In addition, to be sure he does keep them separated in his mind, be careful to keep the training periods separated by a reasonable length of time. This way you stand a better chance of not having him confuse this command with "sit" or any other command. Never mix basic commands until each is perfect by itself. If you go straight from "sit-and-stay" to "lie down" in one training session, he may simply learn that "lie down" is the final step and thereafter lie down when told to sit.

To teach the command "lie down," it is best to use the corner training area first. Place your cat on a table covered with a nonslip surface, then sit down on a chair facing him. Or, if you prefer, place him on the floor and simply sit comfortably on the floor facing him. Place your cat in a sit position, but remember to say nothing to him. Place one hand on his upper back and the other behind the lower part of his front legs. Give the command "down," and at the same time run your hand gently yet firmly down the cat's back carefully pushing him down. At the same time gently pull his front legs out from under him with your other hand. This way you will be gently forcing him to the lying position. Be very careful when doing this so that your cat doesn't think he is going to get hurt. In a cat's mind, pushing is an aggressive act on your part. Therefore, do it very slowly and gently so that he doesn't panic.

As soon as he is lying down, say "good cat" and give him a treat, but do not allow him to leave the lying position. Keep him there by holding your hand on him as you did with the sit command. Once he is lying down, and you have praised and rewarded him, push him gently back up into a sitting position, but without giving him the command to sit. Then repeat this whole thing over and over, until the cat eventually gets the idea of what "down" means. When he lies down with only a slight pressure on his back you can feel pretty confident that he has some idea of what the command means.

Now, instead of pulling his legs out from under him every time you give him the "down" command, give him the hand command for it. Move your hand, palm downward, straight down to the floor in front of him, thus showing the direction in which you want him to go. At the same time give the voice command. But still exert pressure and push gently down on his back with your other hand.

Continue this exercise, gradually exerting less and less pressure on his back. When he responds with little or no pressure, you know that he associates your word and signal with the act of lying down. Next still placing one hand on your cat's back, immediately give the command "lie down" or "down" *once*. If he refuses, exert the pressure. Give him the opportunity to do it by himself first; then if he won't, you complete it for him. However, once you feel he is going to lie down of his own volition let up on the pressure. And always make sure he completes the down command before letting him go. Of course, when he is

SIT, STAY, LIE DOWN

learning always remember to treat him for deeds well done. And
also make sure you keep the lessons short, simple and sweet.

After he seems to be responding simply to the voice and hand
commands without any assistance from you, he's probably mastered the command. Now take your hand off his back when
you give him the command. If he does not lie down, put your
hand on his back and exert pressure. Make sure you give the
command "down" only once. If he refuses, it means that he is
not quite ready for this step, so go back to where he *is* working.

If he lies down without any assistance, give him the "stay"
command immediately in the same manner you would with the
"sit-and-stay" command, by gently pushing your open palm in
front of his face and saying "stay." After he stays, praise him
and give him a treat. If he does not stay or even lie down but
runs off, follow the same procedure you did when teaching "sit-
and-stay." Make sure he completes each sequence you give him.
Continue this exercise until the cat lies down of his own accord
on both the voice and hand commands and also stays lying
down on command. Constantly review everything until he
learns it all perfectly. Most of the training is relatively simple.
It just takes a lot of patience.

When teaching your cat to lie down, it is most important to
remember three things: First of all, once he starts to lie down
on his own, release the pressure that you exert on him. Second,
as soon as your cat actually reaches the down position, always
release your hand command for the "down" position and change
it to a "stay" command. Third, don't keep repeating "down,
down, down," while you try to get him to lie down; as in all
commands, say it only once.

Once he is lying down on command and can stay for a count
of ten while you are right on top of him, it's time to get him to
listen while you don't have direct physical control over him. Do
this by following the same procedure used in the sit/stay com-

183

mand using your dowel as an aid. First make sure he is proficient at responding to commands on the floor while you are sitting. Then teach him to listen first while you are kneeling, and then while you are standing. To do this slip your dowel stick under his front paws and pull them out from under him gently, trying to get him to lie down. If he refuses, go back a step and work up again until he will. When he is responding, proceed to back away from him after he is staying on command. If he moves out, block his way by tapping the stick in front of him. But if he does get away, bring him back and put him through his paces. Get him to stay for increasingly longer times while you go ever farther away. Add distractions such as noises once he is proficient up to this point; then take him out of the corner and start varying the spots where you give him the command.

Remember to use as few words as possible, and isolate your basic commands. They don't need to learn all the complicated innuendos of our language. Consider how hard it is for small school children to learn the meaning of prepositions such as *in, out, through, to*. Spare your cat the bother, he's never going to have to use them.

When he is proficient in the "lie down" command and can link it with "stay" perfectly, you are ready to join the "sit," "stay," and "down" commands together. Before doing this, however, isolate the separate commands and review any weak points. You must be sure that your cat won't learn or doesn't anticipate the command to lie down right after the "sit" command is given.

After he is thoroughly versed in the "lie down" command you can start telling him to sit before telling him to lie down. However, it's a good idea once all three commands—"sit," "stay," and "lie down"—are thoroughly learned to sometimes tell him to "lie down" after "sit" and sometimes not. Don't let him learn to anticipate by always giving the three commands in the same order constantly. Sometimes give just the commands "sit-and-stay" and sometimes "sit, lie down, and stay." This should keep him guessing as to what you expect. And once he has it all down pat, always remember to give him treats on a random basis so he keeps on doing it.

If he balks at any step along the way in training, simply go back a step to review. And make sure he never gets away with not obeying. If he ever runs off while you are teaching him, go get him and make him go through with the command you were working on. Do it over and over until he is proficient. And when he is perfect, praise him each time and feed him randomly to keep him interested. Keep in mind that you can't rush a cat or treat him harshly when working or you will never get him trained. In working with cats, "Slow and easy does it every time."

This whole process probably sounds repetitious. Of course it is, but the results can surprise you. It's all a question of perseverance.

13

WALKING ON A LEAD

Cats walking on a lead are not as uncommon or unnatural a sight as one might suspect. In fact, lately we've seen more and more people walking cats on leads. Cats love to go out by themselves to roam, exercise and have fun. In earlier times they could do so, but today with the crowded conditions of modern society it is *not* a good idea even for an altered cat to wander on his own. This doesn't mean, however, that your cat has to be deprived of one of his favorite pastimes. It is just that now you are responsible.

Training your cat to walk on a lead is a must when you take him on long trips in a car, for he will need to exercise occasionally. In addition, lead training can often be the basis for helping you in other lessons. And from it the cat learns a very important concept—that you represent security.

Each cat has a different personality and each will react differently to the idea of going outside on a lead. Some cats take to walking on a lead immediately; others need more encouragement, incentive and time. In fact, not all cats have a suitable temperament for lead training. A very shy, retiring cat isn't the best of subjects for lead training. In general, however, if trained properly and given a definite feeling of security by your side, a cat will learn readily. In fact once your cat gets into walking "tied to you," you'll soon find that he really enjoys your jaunts together. Any early resistance is simply a result of his innate instinct to be in complete control and to check out everything on his own terms. The idea of being under someone else's control is alien to him. Once he gets used to the safety perimeters you will establish, however, he'll function just fine on the lead.

It isn't that your cat doesn't like to go out of the house to new locations and explore—he does. It's just that he likes to do it quietly, on his own terms and at his own pace. In addition, and perhaps more importantly, he want to feel sure that he has a secure, familiar place to return to.

Very few cats will follow you around. Cats walk a few steps, then stop to look around and make sure everything is safe. Therefore, you cannot expect your cat to master the militaristic command of "heel." He can, however, easily learn to walk alongside you. And you will definitely be able to take your cat on enjoyable walks and not have to worry about his getting away.

Be prepared to put some time and effort into teaching this command. Like all other commands, walking on a lead can and often is a slow and somewhat difficult lesson for your cat to learn and for you to teach. But the end results are more than enough reward for the effort.

If you do walk your cat and use a lead, the lead can often be the source of unexpected problems. Be sure to watch your cat and lead so that you know where both ends of the lead are at all times. This is especially true if you ignore our advice and use a collar on your cat. For example, if the end of the lead gets stuck in a closing elevator door as the elevator begins to move, the lead will strangle your cat.

For training your cat to walk on a lead you will need a harness and a six-foot training lead. Do *not* use a choke or any other type of collar; use a harness. The adjustable nylon or leather kind you find in local pet shops or advertised in cat magazines is good. The most desirable is the nylon figure-eight harness that is made in one piece, but if you cannot get this type, a leather or a felt-backed one will do. Since cats have an uncanny knack for slipping out of almost any type of restraint, make sure the harness you purchase is adjustable. Fit the harness very carefully, making sure that it is not too tight but at the same time not loose enough so your cat can worm his way out of it.

We see no justification for using collars, especially chokes, on a cat. These bite into the cat's neck at the slightest tug of the lead. A cat must not be punished by an abrasive collar while he's performing properly. And if you use a regular collar, a cat can easily slip out of it, and you can lose your cat. This is true whether it is too small, too large, or even the right size. In addition, you shouldn't use a collar because cats tend to freeze when any pressure is applied to it. Thus once a cat stops and you have to apply even the least amount of pressure on the lead to get him to move again he will become even more rigid and absolutely refuse to budge. Some people master the technique, but we haven't had much luck with collars on domestic cats. We have trained some big cats to walk on a lead with collars. But these cats have less fear than small cats in a new environment. If, however, you insist on using a collar, choose the lesser of two evils and make it a regular leather one. _Never_ use a choke.

In selecting a lead, choose a plain all-cotton six-foot training lead. These are usually made of an army green canvas belting. This is the one lead you can feel secure with. It is strong yet lightweight, just perfect for controlling your cat. Don't invest in a chain lead. Such leads are usually too heavy for training kittens and cats. In addition, they slip easily through your hands.

The purpose of the six-foot training lead is not only to keep your cat from running away, but also to teach him to stay by your side. Therefore, in selecting a training lead, length is a most important factor. Some owners, who want to give their cats free rein but are scared the cat will run off, invest in one-hundred-

188

fifty yard clotheslines. We've even seen some people with the new small hand-held fishing reels, using the line as a lead. If a cat is then allowed to run in the park, the final result resembles Charlie Brown's kite, especially if the cat panics and runs off. Even the standard ten-foot lead is a bit much. A six-foot lead is long enough for your cat to move about easily, but still short enough for you to control him. (However, if you insist on giving your cat free rein, it would be better to use an extra-long lead than to allow him to remain loose in any strange outdoor area. Your cat should have some kind of restraint since he may become frightened and escape, then become so nervous he cannot be caught.)

Once your pet is perfect on a lead you can, if you wish, switch your cat's lead to a thin strong nylon one. You can even make one out of clear nylon fishing line. Use this if you really want to make an impression: it looks as if you have a cat who walks and stays at your side without a lead. On TV and in the movies many of the big cats you see, especially those who have all their teeth and claws, are controlled in just this way with an invisible nylon cord. The owners simply attach it to the cat, using it to control him as they lead him through his paces.

In order for any lead to work, it must be attached to the cat. In one commercial—not one of ours—a leopard was supposed to chase after a girl. The cat was held on a nylon cord as they ran him through his paces. But when the cameraman looked through the camera, he felt that the nylon was too visible. Apparently the sun was hitting it from just the right angle and it caught the light and showed up. Rather than adjusting the camera angles and set-ups or rescheduling the shoot for another day, the director talked the leopard's owners into letting him off the lead. This was, to say the least, a mistake. And during the shooting the cat got carried away with the chase and grabbed the girl. Luckily he didn't have any teeth or claws, but he still had enough strength to break a few ribs and do plenty of damage.

To train your cat to walk on a lead you will need to use your three-foot dowel or a thin cane in addition to the harness and cotton training lead. You will be using the dowel to push or tap your cat into position during training. Pulling on his lead is not always effective, and bending down to adjust your cat's position is not always comfortable for you, so use your cane or stick to help out. A cane is like a neutral authority symbol which can quite graphically circumscribe the designated boundaries of your cat's freedom. Your cat will learn quickly exactly how far he is allowed to go and where he is supposed to remain while he is walking by your side. This aid is, as already mentioned, not intended to hurt, but simply to help you keep your cat in position.

Start training your cat to walk on a lead early. In fact, since you must start training for this command in the house it is possible to start him when he is a very young kitten. He can even begin before he gets all his shots so that by the time he does get them you can take him out immediately and he will already be used to walking on a lead. This way you have the added advantage of being able to take him outside as young as possible, and walking on a lead outside will become second nature to him.

In training your cat to walk on a lead the first thing you must do is get him accustomed to the apparatus to be used. After a while your cat should ideally come to consider the harness the link by which his owner's lead and his owner is attached to him —it should provide him with a sense of security.

Put the harness on your cat, making sure it fits correctly. Your cat has to learn to live with it, so put it on the right way and make sure he is comfortable in it. If he shows any reluctance to having it put on him, proceed slowly. Hurrying him at any point in the training may frighten him and discourage him from lead training for life. Let him become used to his harness by wearing it around the house for about a week. Don't attempt to attach the lead to it for at least that length of time. Just let him get used to it alone first. Soon he should be acting as if he were born with a harness on. Once he seems to be completely accustomed to wearing it, you can remove it and put it on only when working him. Some people leave it on all the time, but this is really unnecessary.

The next step is to attach the lead to his harness and get him used to that. If he is reluctant, give him a treat and reassure him. Leave the lead on only for a short while the first time he has it on and let him drag it around for a while. When he has had it on for a few minutes, give him a treat and take the lead off. Do this a few times until he doesn't object to it any more.

Next, put the lead on him and hold it, but let your cat wander wherever he wants. Don't try to force him to do anything. You are just trying to get him used to the lead. However, if he balks at having the lead on him and fights it or simply lies down and refuses to move, coax him into taking a couple of steps, then treat him for it and remove the lead. Don't reward him unless he does something. If you reward him for fighting the lead or lying down, he'll simply learn that this is the thing to do when he is on the lead because he gets treated for doing just that. On the other hand, *never* drag your cat around on a lead. This will only serve to teach him that lead training is unpleasant.

In breaking the cat to the lead, a toy or food is used to distract him but you should only actually give him a reward when he does something. Make him walk a couple of steps. You can do this by simply making him walk to get food which is being dangled in front of him like a carrot in front of a donkey. If he continues to fight the lead, drop it and let him drag it around for a while. Then treat him after he has walked with the lead whether held by you or not. Of course, this is all done in the house so your cat can't escape.

After he is walking where *he* wants to go with the lead on without any bother, it's time to teach him to walk where *you* want him to go. The correct position for walking your cat on a

191

lead is to have your cat standing on either your left or right side, and close enough to you so that he is easily controlled. (With dogs the accepted side is the left side, but with cats select whichever side you wish.) Whichever side you select, always use the same one when walking him.

To hold the lead correctly, make sure that your thumb is in a forward and downward position. You should not be exerting any pressure on the lead at all, and it should have a little slack to it. Simply let your arm fall naturally at your side wherever it feels comfortable.

When first teaching your cat to stay by your side on the lead, you must allow him to walk very slowly, perhaps one step at a time. At first just getting him to go a few steps is an accomplishment. Coax him along with food treats and/or a toy. Don't try to force him to stay too close but give him a somewhat free rein. This exercise is just to get him used to walking along beside you at your pace rather than at his. Gradually build up the exercise until finally he is walking at your pace rather than his and you can walk him all over the house.

Once he is walking along with you comfortably around the house, it's time to start defining just how far he is allowed to wander from your side when being walked on a lead. A cat should have a reasonable amount of freedom. Perfect precision cannot be expected from a cat. However, if he starts to wander too far from your side, it's time to stiffen up and draw the line. Allow him to go out a foot or two to the front, side, and back of you. Farther than that is too far. After all, you must have some control, so once he goes outside these boundaries you must bring him back.

To control your cat on a lead, always apply gentle pressure to stop him from going where you don't want him to and also to direct him to where you want him to go. Apply steady pressure on the lead until the cat goes in the direction you want, then release the pressure immediately. All cats will fight the lead if you try to jerk them along quickly, since it could hurt them. In fact, they may well develop an incurable hatred for it. Just use a steady directive pull on the lead. When he is back where he should be, release the pressure. The idea is to make the cat uncomfortable, not to hurt. And if he is hurt, he may never obey the command. Make the pressure slow, steady, almost gentle—you don't want him to be really aware of what is going on. You just want him to get used to walking beside you. Once the habit of walking close to you on a lead is established, he'll tend to stay there.

In addition to pressure on the lead, you can also use your dowel or cane to help keep your cat in place. Every time he goes outside the limited "secure area" in which he is allowed to wander, use the stick to nudge him back in. Just gently tap him toward you with it; this will push him back in place. Remember never to hurt your cat with the stick, it is only for gentle encouragement.

It is almost impossible to get a cat to "heel," but he should stay within the boundaries you set up for him. If he moves out in any wrong direction apply slow steady pressure on the lead, and/or tap him back to you with your stick. Always stand your ground and make him come back to you, don't you go to him. Never change your position for him. Once he comes back, praise him and slip him a treat.

When first walking with your cat, stick to walking in a straight line. Once you feel he is completely proficient in walking in a straight line then you can start going around corners and changing directions. As he becomes used to it, gradually increase the length of time he is on the lead. Get him to the point where he'll stay close by when you walk him all over the house. To be really trained, your cat should be walking along with you while you hold him on a slack lead.

Both you and your cat must be completely comfortable when walking. If he seems to be having difficulties at any point, go back a step to where he is comfortably proficient and work from there. Don't push him beyond the point he is ready for or all your training might fall through. And remember to give him praise and to slip him a treat now and then for work well done to ensure he will keep on working.

After he is really working for you around the house and walking close to you with ease, it's time to start him outside. When first taking him out, do so slowly and with extreme caution. Carry him around in your arms first, then put him down for only a few seconds. Pick him up, reassure him that everything is fine, then put him down again. Don't expect him to do anything but be bewildered for the first few times. It's enough just to get him out and used to the idea of the great outdoors.

Each time you take your cat out he should stay on the ground for longer and longer periods of time. But do not work him at first, simply let him wander around or sit down and look everything over. Never force him beyond his limits and always reward and reassure him. At the same time you are doing this, work him extra hard indoors so that he keeps in good practice. Extend the time he spends outside with each lesson. Soon things should click in his mind and you will find he is starting to walk along beside you on his lead. He will automatically transfer his in-house lead training to the outside.

Only after he is somewhat secure outside should you start using the stick and the steady, slow pull on the lead to define his boundaries. These actions are designed not only to give you control but also to give him a feeling of security with you outside. He must learn that he's secure within the boundaries you set for him, but that he'll be made uncomfortable once he goes outside of this secure area by your side.

When first taking your cat out it is very important that you do as you did when you started training him inside: keep walking in a straight direction. Turning around and making sharp left or right turns can be confusing to the cat. Make it simple at first by keeping both of you in one straight path until he gets some idea as to what is expected of him. Once he's doing well in a straight line you can start adding the complicated turns. And always remember to praise your cat and give him a special treat when he walks with you and does well. In fact, when you're walking him and he is doing well it's a good idea to slip him a little something every once in a while to reinforce his training and keep him working well for you.

It's necessary to teach your cat to walk on a lead in the house thoroughly before going out because many of the aspects of walking outside take a cat a long time to get used to. It's best not to ask him to concentrate on both new environment and learning a new command at the same time. Cats become extremely attached to their home environment, and can find it difficult to adjust to new environments. Therefore, it might be too much for your cat to face too many new things at one time.

The object of lead training is to get your cat walking perfectly at your side. This means that your cat is right at your side within his allotted security area at all times. In other words, he must learn to follow your movements—not a natural thing for cats. Most owners never achieve this. And many others don't care to. They like their cats to wander a little and explore. But it's best not to let your cat constantly get to the full length of he lead because then you no longer have control. He is too far for you to protect him from danger; six feet is far enough to allow him to dart into the street in front of cars if you are standing on a curb. Therefore, at some point he must be taught not to go off street curbs without you. Don't do this until the cat is really working one hundred percent of the time outside.

For this lesson you will have to use your housekeys. Lead your cat right up to the curb. If he moves off, the keys are to be dropped in front of him. (Make sure you're not standing over a drain!) If he doesn't go off, he is to be given a tiny treat. Cats understand this small amount of pressure from their master and the keys are usually needed only a few times as reinforcement. Make sure the lesson is well learned. Your cat should step off the curb only immediately after you. Some people never even allow their cats to walk in the gutter, on or off the lead, and thus the cat never learns to go in it. Simply pick the cat up at curbs, carry him across the street and then put him down. And if he does attempt to go off a curb by himself, use the key method.

Training your cat so you can control him off the lead is almost impossible. Therefore, if you are planning to try to teach him to walk alongside you without one, he must be perfectly lead trained. Additionally, he has to be trained to "come" every time you call him both inside and out. If you are a nervous person and tend to panic easily, don't attempt to walk your cat off the lead except within at least a semi-confined area. Don't be ashamed or embarrassed to admit to yourself that you couldn't handle the possibility of trying to control your cat in an emergency. Be honest with yourself, it's the best policy in this case.

A cat might be perfectly controllable on the lead but feel free to take advantage of freedom when he sees it. Therefore, work with him in a confined area when you first take him off the lead. Make sure he is perfect here before trying him in a semi-confined area, and finally go on to work him without any restrictions. Work him step by step in each area as you did when you first started teaching him how to walk on a lead. Simply place your cat by your side where you would normally want him to be when on a lead, and start walking while calling and coaxing him. When he comes along with you at your side give him a good praising, and a tiny treat now and then. Try to train him in different locations. Your cat should then tend to stick by your side for security since the area is strange to him. However, if he refuses to walk along with you, put the lead on him and work him that way. After you feel he is ready, try him without it once more. After he does it, gradually increase walking off the lead the same way you did walking on the lead. But off-the-lead training for cats is almost impossible. Cats are too curious about their surroundings and get startled too easily by unusual noises to be controllable without a restraint.

In training your cat to walk on or off a lead alongside you, patience is imperative just as it is with all training. Always be consistent with your cat. He will listen and become used to new places and things if you insist and if he feels secure walking with you. Let him know that if anything distracting happens you expect him to turn to you, to trust you, and to wait for your command.

Often people don't want to pull on their cat's lead because they think it hurts their cats. If done gently but firmly, it actually doesn't hurt one bit. It's just a way of telling your cat that you're in charge, and he's going to have to follow whatever you say. There's no need to speak to the cat, just pull on the lead and gently nudge him with the stick. He'll get the message if you give it to him. And it's your duty to do so.

Remember that your cat shouldn't be forced to be in a heel position like a dog. He must feel he has some kind of freedom and decision-making of his own. Besides, you don't want him to get under your feet. But you should give him an area in which he must stay and, no matter what size area you restrict him to, you must make sure nothing but good happens to him in this area. Only good things are allowed there. So don't let any dogs approach too close on his walks, or let balls get thrown at him, or any of the myriad other things that can happen when he goes out on a walk.

On the other hand, if your cat makes any overt move after a dog while out on a walk, pull the lead firmly and say "no." Keep pulling until your cat stops. Make sure he understands that he is not to act in this way. And if he simply gives out an aggressive hiss, tap him firmly with your dowel to distract his attention and let him know you don't want him to do it.

Noises, especially loud, sudden, new ones, are a source of aggravation. They scare the cat, making him want to run away. To combat this set up a few noise tests *inside*. But do so only *after* he is walking really well on a lead and feels secure. His reaction will probably be to freeze, a common phenomenon in cats, for a few seconds, move his ears around trying to pinpoint the source, and then hightail it in the opposite direction. Take the few seconds that he freezes to pick him up and show him it's okay, that he's secure with you. Comfort him, praise him, show him the noise is absolutely no danger to him—at least as long as you're around. Then put him down, make him walk a couple of steps and give him a treat. Whenever you take him out you must always be on the alert to expect an adverse reaction from him to noises.

If your cat is really upset by anything in the street, take him in your arms and reassure him. Don't rush him back to the training, but then again don't commiserate with him to the point where he won't work. One client picked up her cat every time he was in the least bit apprehensive, reassured him and also plied him with special treats so he wouldn't be scared. All she succeeded in teaching her cat was that if he acted nervous and scared she would pick him up and give him a treat. Now she walks around carrying her cat all day long. She should have picked him up and reassured him, then put him down and tested him by making him walk a few feet and only then treated him. In fact, whenever you take your cat out you should, before returning home with your cat, always make sure that you end the lesson by making the cat walk a few steps. When he does, praise him, give him a treat, and then take him home.

New sights will excite your cat's curiosity and cause him to walk slowly and check everything out. The saying "Curiosity killed the cat, but satisfaction brought him back" is a true one. In fact, if cats could drive cars, they would make some of the worst "rubbernecks" around. Therefore, when you take your cat to new places, don't expect speed. Once he is used to an area and has checked it all out he will tend to speed up and simply watch out for any changes. After he knows an area it doesn't stimulate his curiosity any more; thus as a place becomes more and more familiar, the faster he will travel through it. How many times have you said, "It always seems faster on the way back?" This is simply because on the way back you are familiar with the terrain, and are thus more relaxed, not so alert, looking for signs and the like. Therefore, it seems and is better, faster and easier. The same is true for a cat in his travels.

Cats love to run away outside on their own. They feel completely secure doing so because they are moving at their own pace and under their own direction. They are free to hide and explore as they wish. When you are walking your cat, however, you are in control—not him. He is therefore at first insecure and unsure of how to react. In fact, no matter how much time you put into him he will never put his absolute trust in you. He will always be on the alert. But the more times you take him out the more secure he will become. The trust and ease of walking he achieves is directly related to the amount of time you put in on his training.

14

ADVANCED TRICKS: Shake Hands, Wave a Paw, Eat out of a Can, Roll Over, Sit Up and Beg, Jump, Retrieve

Teaching tricks to a cat is not dependent on the intelligence or even the docile nature of the cat, but rather on a smart or at least a very persistent owner who knows how to handle cats properly. Some of the tricks in this book may seem incredibly advanced, but if you work you can train your cat to do them. Nor are they the last word in cat training. They are simply a primer to show you what can be done. It's up to you, the individual owner, to think of new stunts and try them out. Just be careful that nothing you ask your cat to do can hurt him. Because of the remarkable physical agility your cat's ancestors have endowed him with, there may seem to be no limitations on the tricks a cat could feasibly perform. But always keep in mind that your cat really has only *one* life.

Some exercises are well within your cat's capability, but are simply too complex for anyone but a very experienced trainer to teach. One woman had seen a Siamese do a somersault and jump through a flaming hoop on television. And she wanted her very own acrobatic Siamese. We told her that her cat could probably learn the stunt, but that we would have to teach the cat personally and that it could be a very long process. These professional trick cats are trained from tiny kittens (or cubs). Another asked us to teach her cat to cha-cha like the cat in a commercial. We told her it was impossible, that it was done through trick photography and optical effects produced in developing the film.

We would never attempt to teach owners to teach their cats any complicated tricks that could cause physical injury to either cat or owner. We feel that the average person, no matter how well trained his cat may be, is not qualified to teach certain things, because great precaution and many years of experience are required. We don't want to see any cat get hurt, so stick to the simple but effective tricks that both you and your cat can handle. Don't expect too much of your cat. Allow him his cathood.

Don't try to make an animal go completely against his nature, because it is so much easier to work with what is already there. Cats have certain strong points and certain weaknesses that should be taken into account when training. Tricks involving the sense of smell aren't best for your cat. Use your common sense along with your imagination and think up little tricks for your cat to learn in accordance with his innate abilities. This is why it is so important that you read this book through before you begin. Like most people, you are probably anxious to rush straight into the fun part of training. But in order to do a really good job, you should have some background knowledge about your cat. Now is the time to put all that theory in the early parts of the book into practice.

If something is too difficult for your cat to do, he usually won't do it. But since he can't anticipate or reason very well, he must learn by trial and error, and thus an eager owner can easily push his cat too far. When teaching your cat to do anything, check ahead of time to be sure he is perfectly safe. There should be no surprises, otherwise you'll scare him and he'll never trust you. Surprises have a place, but for reprimands only.

The one trick we absolutely refuse to teach and see no point in your cat's learning is the "speak" command. You don't want to turn your cat into a noisemaker. If you teach him to meow by saying "speak" when he meows and treating him, you might end up with a cat who meows incessantly because he thinks he'll be rewarded if he does so.

It's always a good idea to make sure that your cat has a thorough basic obedience background before you attempt any tricks with him. You will find that you can teach some tricks without any of the preliminary basic lessons, but in general, trick training will do no good and could become frustrating to you if your cat doesn't understand the basic commands. If your cat has no background in listening to you, why should he suddenly start doing tricks? Start him off simply, then work up. He must get used to working with you, and you with him. Besides, the basic commands are often integrated in some way with the performance of other tricks.

If you have already taught your cat to sit, stay, come, and walk on a lead, and you find any of these commands isn't working, go back and work only with the exercise he is weak in. Do it over and over until the cat responds perfectly. Only then can you go on with other commands. Always go back to any weak points you find in his basic training, or you might never be able to do the more complex ones.

Your three-foot long dowel is your most important aid for teaching your cat tricks. And a table placed in a corner is your best bet for a location to teach many of them. Cover it with a towel so that your cat's footing will be secure; he will thus be more comfortable about performing certain feats. If you use the floor, you should be just as careful about the floor covering.

Placing your cat on a table when first teaching him a trick is often far superior to working him on the floor. It puts him at a level where you can easily get his attention and where you can conveniently work with him. When he's on the table you won't have to be constantly stooping and bending to reach your cat and place him in position. At the same time, it makes it easier for you to prevent any premature departure from the training session on your cat's part. Getting a cat to do things at a distance, at least in the early stages of training, is almost impossible. You must keep him within your reach or at least within a short distance so you can easily control him.

When teaching a cat any new command or trick, hand commands are often the best way to communicate and get him to respond to you. If a cat learns to respond to the basic hand commands from the very beginning, these could feasibly eventually be linked together to form a more complex command which he will be able to perform by watching your hands. You probably won't get the response a conductor gets when leading an orchestra, but you could get something of that feeling if you wear a tux and use a baton as your aid when working him!

Some people, when working with animals, and more especially when teaching tricks, give hand commands that do not direct the cat, but only look good. Ideally, your hand commands should eventually become the trigger for any trick. For instance, in teaching a cat to roll over, you constantly use the words "roll over" at the time that he actually goes over. This way he eventually learns to associate the word with the action of rolling over, but at the same time he will also learn your accompanying gesture. At first this gesture must be very expansive, but eventually you can do it in a more contained way, so that finally a very small, even almost unnoticeable gesture might possibly be enough to trigger a command.

Trick training requires you to do all the things you did when teaching your cat his basic obedience, so review the tips we've given you so far. Remember that as with all training, when teaching your cat tricks, work only until your cat reacts to the command a couple of times correctly. If he refuses to obey, work him for about three minutes and then walk him through the trick. Be sure not to spend too much time on each session. If you do he will only become bored and may well refuse to do anything. After he has been walked through it or has done it of his own free will, reward him with a special tidbit. Always make training a rewarding experience for your cat. Most cats see no purpose in doing tricks which have no clear benefits for them. Therefore, unless your cat thinks he is going to get something for performing, he probably won't do it. Even after he is performing a trick really well, continue to reward him on a random basis; he may decide not to bother doing it any more if he thinks there's no longer something in it for him. But be sure to reward him only if he completes an exercise, even if you have to walk him through it.

When first teaching him a trick, and in fact until he really has it down pat, select a quiet room to put him through his paces. Make sure there aren't lots of people around or other noisy or unpleasant distractions. Once he is doing the trick well you should start bringing in the distractions to make sure you can control him at all times, but at first there should be absolutely none.

It is important that you teach only one exercise at a time. Don't try to teach your cat too much at one time; he will only become confused. It is best not to proceed to a new trick until the previous one has been thoroughly mastered. Don't leave anything half done. But, if your cat is having terrible problems with a trick no matter how hard you work, and he absolutely refuses to obey, leave it. Go on to another, then come back to it after the new trick has been thoroughly taught. Never let a second one go, however, since it will then become a habit, and he will learn that being stubborn and refusing to listen can get him out of his lessons.

Once your cat does learn a command, make sure it is learned thoroughly before going on to new ones. Each trick should be isolated until your cat really knows it. Therefore, if you want to review tricks, do so at different periods during the day. And whenever things aren't going right with a trick go back to the stage where your cat was doing the right thing.

Be sure, before you start a training session or even simply issue a command, that you have the time and are prepared to make your cat complete the trick. Remember that cats are not always consistent, so don't get upset if he misses once in a while. Just be prepared to walk him through the command if he misses. This is true even if you are putting on a show for friends. Don't be embarrassed if he messes up—no matter how little your cat does people will be impressed.

SHAKE HANDS

One of the simplest but most sought-after tricks is having your cat "shake hands"; that is, extend his paw when you make the gesture of wanting to take it. This trick is taught basically with body language. Put your cat on the table and make him sit-and-stay. Extend your hand as you would when you go to shake hands; with your other hand gently push him to one side, throwing him slightly off balance, while at the same time saying "shake hands." He will automatically lift his paw. When he does, take it immediately, saying "good kitty," and give him a treat. After a while eliminate the gentle push and simply extend your hand and say "shake." If he refuses to do it, nudge him with your extended hand right behind the elbow of the leg you want him to raise up. This will automatically force him to raise his leg; as soon as he does, say "shake" again and take his paw. Then give him a treat. Soon it will connect in his mind and he'll lift his paw when you simply give the command. Once he is doing it perfectly, don't treat him every time he responds but only randomly as with all commands.

By placing your hand close to the paw you want, you may

eventually be able to get him to give the paw of your choice on command, even to the extent of teaching him to respond to "left" or "right." But whether you or your friends approach him with "give me five," "put 'er there," or whatever, he will still understand and shake whenever he sees a hand coming in the appropriate gesture.

WAVE A PAW

What your cat cannot reach with his mouth he is sure to try to grab with his paw. Use this principle to teach him to extend his paw on command to give the impression of waving. It is a gesture almost identical to shaking hands, only in this the cat must raise his paw much higher.

Put him on a table and have him sit-and-stay. Hold a treat just far enough in front of his face so that he cannot reach it with his mouth, but must extend a paw to try and grab it. If he attempts to get up and come forward toward you, push him back down into a sitting position. Keep pushing him down until he goes for the treat with his paw. When he goes for it, give it a name such as "wave" and reward him by giving him the treat.

Repeat this over and over, and reinforce the waving response by rewarding the cat immediately, thus conditioning him thoroughly. Now move him to other locations, and teach him the command there. After a while he should wave as soon as you hold your hand up in front of his face and say "wave," with treats being used only occasionally to keep him on his toes.

For speed training cats in commercials we don't bother to imprint the command. We simply use the initial training step and dangle something such as a toy or tidbit in front of them, and get them to bat at it. Thus when the picture is taken all you see is the cat looking as if he is waving, but only because you don't see the object he is batting at on the screen.

EAT OUT OF A CAN WITH HIS PAW

Start teaching this command by giving your cat a taste of his favorite food on the outside of the can where he can easily smell and taste it. Once he licks the food off the outside of the can he'll start associating food with the can. After this get a supply of his favorite food in large-sized cans. Open one can and let your cat eat his meal out of a *full* can of food instead of out of his regular feeding bowl. If he likes his food, he should eat out of the can readily. But, if he refuses, feed him in the normal way. Then the next day try the can again. Keep trying until he starts eating out of the can. Once he does, feed him that way for a few days.

If he seems content with this feeding method, try feeding him out of a can that is only one-third to one-half full. With this he can no longer eat out of it with his mouth. Everytime he puts his head down into the can and attempts to eat, it will get stuck. Since it is mealtime, he will be hungry and will try to get at his food. He knows there's food in the can and so he will stick his paw in to get at it. If, however, he can't figure it out, don't starve him but rather go back a step and feed from a full can. Then the next day try a half-empty can again. Keep trying until he does it. This trick may cost you quite a few wasted cans of food, but it's a fun trick and once learned he'll do it every time—especially if he likes the food and is hungry.

ROLL OVER

When teaching your cat to roll over, you must remember that he doesn't really like to do this. It tends to throw him off balance, and a cat likes to be in complete control of his body at all times. Rolling over is not, however, harmful in any way, and it is an impressive trick.

This is one trick where it is best to train your cat on the floor where there is lots of room. You could train your cat on the table, but if you do be very careful to make sure your cat does not fall and hurt himself. If he does, he'll probably never do the trick again.

First, sit down in front of your cat and make him lie down. If he knows the command thoroughly, issue it; if not, gently push him down. Once he is down hold him there in a lying position. Take one of his special treats and tempt him with it, while still holding him down. When he starts to get interested in it, pass it in a circular motion over his shoulders and around his back very slowly, keeping it just out of reach of his paws and mouth.

His nose will follow the treat like a donkey after a carrot. His head cannot go around in a complete circle, and so he has to move his body around with his head in order to follow the movement of the treat. In this way he will naturally have to roll over, and while he is rolling use the command "roll over." After he rolls over completely, praise him and give him the treat. Repeat this exercise over and over, switching sides occasionally until he understands.

After you feel confident that he does understand, stop holding him down and simply use your voice and hand commands. When he is proficient with your leaning over him, try to get him to do it while you are standing. Simply stand up and make the same circular motion with the treat still in your hand and tell him to "roll over." Unfortunately, once you are standing your cat may well decide not to listen to just the hand and voice commands for this trick. Therefore, you will need to use your dowel. With this you can nudge him gently in the direction wanted and thus control him even when you are not right on top of him. Just hold his treat in one hand and give the circular motion command. At the same time take the dowel in your other hand and push him over with it as best you can, being very careful not to hurt him while doing so.

Once he rolls over with only a slight nudge from the stick, try him without using it. If he can do it consistently without any help from you, he's really got the command down pat. Now you can go a step farther and try to get him to listen from a distance. To do this simply step back a little and try him. If he listens, go back slightly farther and then gradually increase your distance. But if at any point he refuses to roll over, go back to the stage that he completed properly and work ahead from there.

Eventually you may no longer need to use a treat to tempt your cat if you don't want to, and the circular motion made with your hand will become the hand command for this trick. Ideally, you should be able to make a circular motion with one hand, saying "roll over" at the same time, and your cat should lie down and roll over. You may even be able to get him to do this with the hand command alone—with or without a treat— even from across a room. Simply call his name and when you get his attention, give the hand signal and he should lie down and roll over. If and when he does, reward him. But, even if you don't want to get quite that sophisticated, do keep working until he does this trick to your satisfaction or at least up to his limitations.

SIT UP AND BEG

First place your cat up on his training table, which should be covered with a nonslip material. Take your dowel and hold it out toward him, tempting him with it like a toy. When he starts to play with it his paws will naturally hook onto the stick. When they do, pull it up in the air and he'll go up with it. As he does say "sit up" or "beg." If he doesn't go up with the stick, keep trying until he does. When he's finally up, slowly withdraw the stick and he should remain sitting up for at least a moment or two. Treat him immediately while he's still up. If you don't treat him quickly when first teaching this trick, he won't still be sitting up. And the whole point is to treat him when he's still sitting up so he'll connect the action with the reward.

After a couple of lessons treat him only a second or so *after* you take the stick away. Gradually increase the length of time between when taking the stick away and giving him his treat. This way you will teach him to stay up longer each time. You may always need the aid of the stick to do this command, but hopefully it will only take a little encouragement to get your cat to do the trick. If you watch the big cats in circuses, you will notice that the trainer has to give gentle touches with the stick to nudge the cat upward. After your cat is obeying the command with only the upward movement of the stick, try to get him to respond by simply making an upward gesture with your open hand in front of him. This upward movement of the stick or your hand (either touching him gently or not as the need calls) is the usual command for him to do the trick. And this along with the words "sit up" or "beg" should get him to sit up.

Another method is simply to hold food above your cat's head and tempt him with it. He will naturally stretch out and up to get on his hind legs and grab for it. If he has claws he might in his excitement to get at the food inadvertently grab your fingers with them. Try once or twice to see how he reacts. If he tends to use his claws, attach the tidbit to a stick with a thin cord and dangle that above his head in the carrot-in-front-of-a-donkey method. When he stands up to reach out, gently push him into a begging position and tell him to "sit up" or "beg." When he does sit properly, reward him immediately by giving him the food. Keep doing this until he sits up as soon as you place your hand over his head and say "sit up." He'll be so used to getting a treat when he does it that he'll keep on doing it.

Always make sure your cat goes through with the whole command before treating him, even if you have to hold him in position after giving the command. Once he knows how to sit up on command with ease, add the "stay" command. This should be taught in the same way you did when you taught it in conjunction with the "sit" or "lie down" commands in basic obedience.

He'll learn this trick fast and soon be around the table trying out his "begging" ability, especially it would seem if you have guests to dinner. Don't let it turn into a begging habit, however. Train him so that he knows to do it on command only. This is quite simple to do. Just never reward or allow anyone to reward him for indiscriminate begging without being given the command. No matter how appealing it might appear, it can become a very annoying habit if rewarded. (This same fact holds for any trick. Don't reward him unless you ask him or it could become a begging action for the cat to elicit rewards.)

JUMP

Jumping is a good-looking and exciting trick. Four months of age is about the best time to start training your cat to jump. Before this time his bones are not developed enough to support the jump, and he could possibly injure himself. In addition, you'll need all that time to train your cat in basic obedience. He should have a reasonable knowledge of such commands as "sit," "stay," and "come" before you teach him to jump. A certain amount of control is necessary before you can accomplish this trick, but if you have started obedience training at about eight weeks of age, when you first brought your kitten home, your cat should be very well behaved by the age of four to six

211

months. Just remember that the more tricks you can teach a cat while he's young, the more they will be second nature to him. On the other hand, don't overlook the potential of an adult cat, just make sure he also has his basic obedience down before attempting this.

When you start teaching your cat to jump, get a hurdle that's not too high—say ten to twelve inches. It should be no trouble to nail a few old boards together, but whatever you decide to use as the hurdle, make sure it can be fastened securely in place. Since this trick, like all others, should be done indoors, we recommend placing it securely in the doorway between two rooms. Make sure it really is secure, because if your cat accidentally knocks it over, he might never want to try jumping again. Remember that once hurt, a cat will become frightened and never forget, so be very careful the first few times until he gains his confidence. This same principle holds true for any new trick, including any jumps over tricky or oddly shaped objects.

Set your cat on one side of the barrier in the doorway and sit or stand on the other. Tempt him over with a special treat. As he is coming over say "jump." If for some reason he won't come over for the food treat, you could also tempt him over with a toy and/or a strange but interesting sound like crinkling paper. When he gets over, praise him and give him the treat.

Use no other word but "jump" as he is coming over. With this as with all other commands, make sure that the cat completes the exercises every time you give the command. If he can't or won't jump, nudge, pull or lift him over. Even if he runs away you must bring him back and make him go through with the command. If he gets away with not doing it once, he'll try not doing it again and again.

Whenever he gets over the obstacle, no matter how reluctantly, praise him profusely and give him his treat. Then step over to the other side of the board and repeat the whole thing in the other direction. Remember that praise and reward are very important in training for this trick as with all others.

Use this barrier until jumping becomes second nature to your cat. Once your cat is jumping easily on command over this small hurdle, move over to the other side of this obstacle so that you are now standing alongside him. For this part of the training you must use your dowel as an aid. Stand beside him and point over the barrier with one arm extended, say "jump," and gently nudge him over with the stick. When he does this with very little or no assistance from the stick, try changing the object he is to jump. Move him to other locations and have him jump different obstacles of various heights and shapes. After he is jumping consistently, simply give the commands and start using random treats.

If you don't vary the position and type of obstacle your cat is to jump you may find that your cat will refuse to jump anything but the original hurdle. Each and every time you change to a new obstacle you probably will have to start him off again, to ensure that the cat knows what you are asking him to jump. This way he will at least have several objects he can definitely jump over on command.

Once trained, your cat should ideally be able to jump whenever you extend your arm, point your finger toward an object and give the command "jump." If he doesn't, go back to the stage he can do and start from there. This means that you might have to nudge him over with the dowel or even go to the opposite side of the obstacle and tempt him over. Once he really is good at obeying when you are standing beside him right in front of the hurdle, gradually move both yourself and your cat back from the hurdle so that your cat has to run a short distance to reach it before jumping. You probably won't get a flying leap out of him but you can try. Just keep him within easy reach so you can get him started if need be. Never push your cat beyond where he feels comfortable, and make it a rewarding experience for him.

We don't recommend using a harness as an aid in training the cat to jump. Some people might assume that it could possibly give them added control, but pulling your cat over or across means nothing. That action is merely a repetition of teaching him to come to you. You won't be teaching him "jump." The barrier itself isn't definite enough in these circumstances. To him it is just another thing he has to go over, around, or under to get to you. "Jump" must mean just that. Your cat must jump what you point to.

JUMP THROUGH AN OBJECT

Once your cat is bounding over whatever you point to, you can proceed to teach him trick jumping through something such as a hoop. Most owners don't realize that the concept of "jumping through" is not a natural act for an animal. Originally your pet learned the concept of up and over, not an unusual method of getting past obstacles. An animal is used to going to one side of, under, or over obstacles, and sees no point to going through them unless the aperture is like a doorway, enclosed on all sides, in which case there is no other way to go but through. To be able to jump through a hoop he must learn to go over the bottom, under the top, and between the two sides, which is slightly more complex than a simple flying leap over something.

To teach the "through" concept, set up the original hurdle you used when you first started to teach your cat to jump. Then take a Hula-Hoop, place it atop this obstacle and hold it in place securely. Place your cat on one side of the hurdle, and place yourself on the opposite side. Continue in the same way you did when first teaching your cat to jump *over*. The hurdle will form a barrier preventing his going under the hoop. Once he gets the idea and is jumping well, remove the hurdle under the hoop and simply hold it in place. Try to tempt him to jump through the hoop and hope for the best. He will probably dart under it. If he does, put him back and insist he do it properly even if you have to gently pull him through. Again, don't forget this is not a natural act for a cat, so use a great deal of patience and plenty of praise and treats.

JUMP INTO YOUR ARMS

Teaching your cat to jump into your arms on command is a fantastically effective trick. But your cat must first feel completely confident in your arms. He should therefore be carried around for at least a few days before you start teaching him this trick. Of course, it is by far the best thing if the cat is already schooled in the basic obedience commands.

When you feel your cat is ready, put him on a table or some other flat-topped secure structure which is at least at waist level. Be especially careful that the top is covered with toweling or other nonslip material. When he is sitting up there, give him a treat. Then offer him another one, but this time hold it away from him slightly and make him reach for it. When he does give it to him. The next time hold the treat further away, making him stretch out even farther to reach it. Once he is accustomed to having to reach for his treat, move back a step from him and tempt him with the treat; at the same time hold out your arms in a welcoming gesture prepared to catch him, saying "jump." He probably will simply try to reach out farther in his attempt to get it. If he can reach it and does grab at it with his paw you must give it to him. Then next time back up further to a point where he can't reach it with his paws, but must jump in order to get the food. Don't let him fall, especially in the early stages, or he may never do the trick. If he looks as if he is reaching too far and may topple off, catch him before he falls. Then treat him. He reached your arms, even if in an odd way, and

215

thus must be rewarded. This will encourage him to try to get into your arms again. Thus you will be reinforcing this response in the future.

Patience is very important in this trick. Your cat will eventually jump to get at the treat. But it takes time and you must keep tempting him and tempting him until he does it. Make him stretch farther and farther. Keep repeating this exercise until your cat finally leaps directly into your arms when you ask him to do so. When he does, lavish praise and treats are in order. This is basically just like teaching him to go over, only we widen the distance he has to jump across instead of up and over.

RETRIEVE

The ancient Egyptians are reputed to have trained caracals as retrievers to bring back birds. They used a boomerang-type stick to knock down the birds, and the cats would go get them where they fell in the papyrus reeds and mud flats. Hopefully you don't want to go that far, but simple retrieving is a fun trick. It is excellent exercise for your cat with a bare minimum of effort on your part. Test your cat to see how much natural retrieving ability he possesses. Use an article he likes, such as a small ball, a toy mouse, or a crumpled cellophane wrapper. Cats play at retrieving because chasing is natural to them. Tempt your cat to your side and allow him to investigate the article you are holding. Don't call him to you, because you are going to tease him, and he must never be greeted with unpleasantness when called. When his interest is aroused in the object, throw it out a short distance and watch his reaction. If he runs out after it, you probably have a natural retriever. In this case tempt him to come back to you while still carrying the toy in his mouth. If he brings it back, give him a treat—he's retrieving.

216

Try him a few times. If, however, he stares at you and the object doesn't move, don't despair—he can still learn.

Cats have a poor sense of smell but great eyesight, so cats rely almost entirely on their eyes when hunting. Therefore, you can't train your cat to retrieve by scent but only by sight and/or sound.

To teach "fetch," take a favorite toy of your cat's. Tie a length of string to it and attach that in turn to a stick to make a fishing-pole-type contraption. Tempt your cat with the toy. Dangle it in front of him, let him chase it along the ground and say "fetch." While he's playing with the toy, take it away from him and give him a special treat in exchange for it. Repeat this process a few times. Then when you play with the toy and the cat, pull the toy toward you, thus forcing the cat to follow the toy toward you; as he does, say "fetch." If he picks it up in his mouth, keep reeling him in like a fish on a hook, but do so very slowly with an almost imperceptible movement so your cat hardly knows what's going on. When he gets almost all the way over to you stop the pressure and offer him a treat. He should drop the toy and take the treat, thus making an exchange. Repeat this over and over again until you feel that there is hardly any or no pressure on the string when the cat comes toward you. When this happens a few times in a row, take the string off the toy, throw it out by itself and say "fetch." Give him a treat and plenty of praise when he brings it back to you. Your cat is now retrieving for you. If he doesn't bring it back, however, go back a step and reattach the toy to the pole; also, use the random method of reward. (On very important occasions when you want to be positive he'll do it, use treats every time you give the command.)

After he's become really good at retrieving the original toy, change the object you throw and tell him "fetch." If your cat doesn't chase the new object, attach the original toy to it. Tease him with both the toys and get him interested in them, then throw the new/old toy out to see if he'll get it that way. Repeat this until he retrieves it. If he refuses to go out after them both, attach them to the string, thus going back a step. When he is retrieving them on a string, take them off and try again. After he is retrieving them both for a while, detach the new object and throw it out alone to see if he'll get it. He will probably retrieve it alone now because he's so used to it.

Once he can retrieve two different objects he'll probably go after any object you throw out for him to retrieve. Just get his attention, let him see you throw the new object out, and say "fetch." This should be his signal to get it and to bring it back, and thus get a treat in return. If he does not retrieve it, get the original toy and tie it to this new object and work from there. Do this with every new object until he finally understands the command and fetches anything you throw out, not just a few certain objects.

Just remember that a cat, no matter how well trained, may well have his own preferences and prejudices as to what he wants to fetch. Some objects are not built to fit in the mouth of an average-sized cat. After trying and failing to pick them up, they get frustrated and give up. For those cat owners who complain of their pets' reluctance to fetch, we tell them to throw something cats can and will handle. If you want your cat to retrieve, find out what he likes the best. Cats, like people, are partial to different things.

Always remember to tempt your cat with the object you want him to retrieve; only after he is really interested in it should you throw it out a short distance. Repeat, increasing or decreasing the distance according to how the cat is responding. Some people throw a toy across the room and expect the cat to fetch it even when his attention is elsewhere and he doesn't even know something is being thrown. The cat, therefore, doesn't get it. The cat's owner then gives up in disgust without even trying and blames his failure on the cat's lack of intelligence. Do one step at a time, and if your cat isn't responding to training go back a step to where he was. Never work longer than you can keep your cat's attention, three to five minutes at most.

Repeat these exercises until he's really got "fetch" down pat. And if he breaks down anywhere along the line—for instance, if he goes after the object but refuses to take it in his mouth and bring it back—go back a step and review until he is perfect. When he's really good, treat him randomly so he'll do it more readily. There should be no rhyme or reason to the way you reward. Keep him guessing; he'll keep on retrieving if you do. And no matter what, once you throw out an object and say "fetch" make sure he completes the command, even if you have to walk him through it.

15

TOILET TRAINING

Teaching your cat to use the toilet, and possibly even flush it, might be the solution you're looking for. It eliminates the need for a litter box and all the often unpleasant things associated with it. The only problem that could arise is that if your cat doesn't flush it—as he probably won't—an unsuspecting visitor in your house might have good cause to wonder about your diet and/or physical makeup.

Cats can be taught how to use the toilet simply because they have superb balance and are built right. Their normal squatting position insures that he/she will urinate or defecate right into the toilet, once sitting straddle-legged atop it. Even an unaltered male is physically capable of using it, though whether he can be stopped from spraying around the house is another story.

The main trick in toilet training is just to be consistent, persistent, and above all patient. It doesn't really require any major effort on your part. It's mostly time that is needed for the cat or kitten to make the adjustment. You must teach him slowly and methodically. Be sure he knows each step thoroughly before going on to the next. If necessary, go back a step, but never push too hard or too fast. If you go beyond your cat's limits, you can ruin the whole thing. A friend skipped ahead in school because she was bright. However, this caused her to miss out on two years of basic math which she never managed to catch up on, so that today despite her artistic success she still can't do math. If you skip the basics with your cat, he may never be able to tackle advanced feats.

The first step in toilet training is to make sure your cat or kitten is completely litter trained. If he isn't, wait until he is to start. It is best to start with a young cat or kitten since he has yet to be deeply imprinted with the habit of using a box. However, even an older cat can be trained; it just takes longer. The older and more strongly imprinted a cat is with the box, the harder it is.

For training you will need a spare toilet seat minus the cover. In addition, get a plain, shallow litter box which fulfills all the normal requirements for litter boxes. Make sure it is as shallow as possible, while still allowing enough room for both the cat's litter and the cat to be there (say four inches deep). If you can't find a shallow box, use one a little deeper. Whatever box you use, make sure it is the right size. When the spare toilet seat is placed atop it, there should be an overlap of one-half to one inch all around except for the hinge side, which should fit flush. At the same time the box must be strong enough to hold the weight of the toilet seat and cat on it.

If you have an extra toilet, reserve it for your cat during training. And if not, share yours with him. Place the shallow litter box on the floor beside the toilet, which from now on should always have the seat down and the seat cover up. There is no need to keep your regular toilet seat cover closed; cats are very surefooted. We've never heard of one falling into a toilet yet—even the clumsiest. And since there is no way a cat can use a toilet without the seat being down, you might just as well get used to its being down at all times. Without the seat, the span is too great and the balancing area too small.

Once you are positive your cat is completely litter trained to this particular box, place the toilet seat on top of the box and attach it securely. In fastening it to the box, attach only the hinge portion of the seat to one of the narrower sides of the box with screws, glue or tape. This way once the seat is attached to the box it will open and close the way a seat does on a toilet so that you can lift it up to easily clean the box. Whatever you use to fasten it, be sure that it is very solidly attached. Your cat will be using this "training contraption" for as long as it takes to get him toilet trained, so make sure it is right. Many people make the mistake of not securing the seat to the box properly and thus ruin the whole toilet training process. If the seat is loose and slips around or if your cat knocks it off and it falls, you might just as well forget the whole thing. The cat may not even use the box again, let alone go near a toilet seat.

Once your cat is using this new litter box with the toilet seat attached, start constructing a support or base under the box to raise it up off the floor. Some people use a pile of telephone directories; others, some of the larger-sized magazines. These both make for a solid, regular-shaped, secure stack. You could try using newspapers also, but once unfolded, newspapers never get folded back quite the way they were. Therefore, the stack is not always quite regular. Whatever you use, make sure it makes a very secure base.

The idea here is to slowly raise the box higher and higher until it reaches the height of the toilet. You do this by elevating it at a rate of about one-fourth to one inch every few days, depending upon the size, age and willingness to learn of the cat or kitten being trained. Keep in mind that a young kitten can only jump to certain heights until he has had time to grow and develop physically.

Keep raising the box continually so that the cat has to jump higher and higher in order to reach the top. Don't worry that your cat can't or won't use the box as you raise it; cats jump easily. It's the security of the structure that's really important.

A cat has a superb sense of balance, but the box must be stable enough to hold steady every time your cat jumps up to use it.

A cat can reach the height of a toilet without an ounce of effort, but you should still take your time getting him prepared. Make sure your cat is using the box at each new level to which it is raised. If he refuses to go that height, lower the box until it is back to the point of security where he will use it. Don't forget to correct him with the *White Distilled Vinegar Method* (page 91) when and if he makes a mistake. Even if you consider yourself responsible for pushing him too fast, he must be reprimanded for all mistakes. After he is again using his box regularly, start raising it again—but more slowly this time.

When the seat is raised to the exact height of the toilet with the seat down, leave it at that level for a while. Now is the time to make sure your cat is balancing on the seat when relieving himself. A very small kitten will go inside the seat into the box. As he gets larger he will start to feel slightly cramped, and then will tend to balance himself on the seat rather than stepping into the box. Some cats, however, never make this transition no matter how large they are, and you must force the issue. Don't bother to do anything overt until the seat on the box is level with the toilet seat. But, unless he is still too small, at this point it's time he learned how to balance himself on the seat.

One very important point in training your cat is that you don't rush the training. Many cats will learn right off the bat; others take more time. Work slowly at your cat's pace. A cat will usually make his move when he is ready, but sometimes if he is consistently stubborn you may have to force the issue. If you do, force it in such a way that he makes the move by himself—"with a little help from his friends."

First take a thin piece of wood one-eighth to one-quarter inch thick, two inches wide and one inch longer than the length of the litter box. Place it over the box but under the seat so that it

223

YOU CAN TRAIN YOUR CAT

lies flat. Now put the seat down. The hole into which your cat
has been jumping is now cut in half. He therefore has to start
balancing himself in order to use the box. If he refuses to use it
with this setup, reprimand him for going outside the box. Remove the wood and go back a step to just using the box for a
few days.

Then try placing a piece of string across the box the same way
you did with the wood. This way the hole is again cut down,
but this time with a far less objectionable obstruction. With
this your cat will still be able to go into the box, since there is
nothing solid to block his way. The string simply makes it uncomfortable for him, may possibly force him to start balancing.
If this doesn't work and he continues to go inside the box, tie
another string across the box in the other direction. With the
second string his feet will become a little more entangled. He
will therefore try to balance himself somehow in order to relieve
himself in his litter box. Using the box should be ingrained in
him by now since he has used it so much, and also because he
has always been punished for going anywhere else—even if he
messed up because you made the litter box uncomfortable—so
he realizes that no matter what, he has to go in his box. If he
won't balance and refuses to use the box with the string, take it
off and go back a step to where he is willing to use it.

If all else fails, a more direct approach might encourage him
to move out of the box onto the seat. Gradually remove the
amount of litter in the box until the bottom is barely covered.
Then replace the litter with newspaper or a paper towel. Your
cat won't like this and may tend to squat on the seat. If that
doesn't work, try a little water in the bottom of the box or a tray
filled with water in the center. This should do the trick. If nothing works, go back to the litter and try again. This is the part
where your patience may really wear a little thin. But keep going, because it will work.

Use one of these techniques at a time, not all at the same

time. Each of these little tricks is designed to get him to start balancing. Be persistent; keep on trying until he starts. Once he learns that the toilet seat is the place to sit—and he will sooner or later if you insist—remember to keep the box at the exact level of the top of the toilet until he never makes any mistakes. Then maintain the status quo a little longer, trying to get him to make the transition to the toilet of his own accord.

Once your cat is balancing on the seat and the box is the same height as the toilet, your cat may well tend to become confused and start using the other seat on the john without any further encouragement. So hold it here for a while to see if he'll simply transfer over by himself. If he does, be grateful for it. And if he doesn't, go on to the next step the way we usually have to. But before that, be sure he is really balancing on the seat.

If your cat doesn't make the move over to the toilet, go on to the next phase. First, raise the box slowly until the bottom of the litter box is level with the toilet top. When it gets to the right height, gradually move the box over on top of the toilet. This can be a tricky maneuver, so be careful that the box is secure at all times. Balance the box on both its base and the top of the toilet, which should be exactly level with each other at this point. Each day move it further over. Soon the litter box should be resting atop only the toilet.

Leave the base where it is. This way you can simply move the box over if you or a guest want to use the toilet, and then replace it. Once the cat has been using the box atop the toilet, balancing perfectly, and making no mistakes for about a week, remove the litter box completely and leave just the toilet. The first day you take the box off, *confine* your cat to the bathroom for the entire day. If he goes on the floor, you know he's not ready. Reprimand him using the vinegar method. Put the box back on the seat. And keep him confined until he uses the box. After he uses it just once, let him go.

225

If, of course, he uses the toilet it's all done. Sometimes it happens on the first try. More often, however, it takes longer and you have to repeat the final step several times. But once a cat is hooked on going in the toilet just once or twice it's all over, the transference has been made.

If there are any relapses in the training, go back a few steps and build up again. If you follow all the instructions carefully, everything should work out fine. But, there are many variables involved, so follow all our instructions carefully or you could easily mess up the training.

The time it takes for toilet training varies with each cat. Some do it in no time while others take seemingly forever. If your cat appears to be having difficulties, don't push him, but go at his pace—slow and sure. Cats will not do anything unless they feel absolutely secure about it. It takes time to build up this kind of trust. And keep in mind that a kitten will not be ready to make the final step until he is the right size and age—at least five to six months old.

Once he's mastered using the toilet, teaching your cat to flush it once he gets off it is very difficult. In fact, it is almost an impossibility, but it can be done. The main problem is that many toilets require a lot of pressure to flush, and so your cat may not pull hard enough for it to happen. However, some cats do catch on. Try to tempt and trick your cat into flushing. Hang a catnip toy or other tempting object on a chain attached to the flush handle. This way the cat may play with the toy, inadvertently pull on it, and thus flush the toilet. If you see or hear him doing it, praise him and give him a treat to encourage him to do it again in the future. Don't worry about the noise and swirling water startling him. You flush so often the sound is a familiar one that means nothing to him. But flushing is really unnecessary—especially as he may decide to flush it in the middle of the night or ten times in a row just for the fun of it.

With a toilet trained cat you will, of course, be eliminating the need to clean up the box. This means that neither owner or cat will ever get turned off by a foul smell and a dirty box. However, even when your cat is toilet trained, there is still some work that has to be put in. The door has to be left open at all times (as with a litter trained cat). The toilet lid must be kept up and the seat kept down. In addition, neighbors or visitors should be made aware of the fact that they are sharing the toilet with a cat. Not because they might not want to do so, but because they must be told to keep the cover up, the seat down and the door open when they leave. A note impressing them with these things and at the same time excusing an unflushed toilet might be a good idea. If these things aren't done, your cat can't use the toilet and may well go elsewhere—like on your bed or couch. Make it a good-sized note and attach it where every person who uses your bathroom can and will read it. Flashy letters on the inside of the toilet cover are a good idea. It can even be part of the decoration.

16

PROFESSIONAL SECRETS: Training Cats for Movies and Commercials

We use "rapid" training for film and commercial use. This training is not merely in the interest of speed, but to overcome the myriad distractions that conspire on location to reduce a cat's attention span. By using this technique, we don't give the animals time to make mistakes. Before they know it they have done what the script calls for, as many times as the director wants, and the commercial or film has been shot.

A cat often misbehaves on the set for exactly the same reasons he does in any new locale. There are odd sounds, strange smells, new people, alien surroundings, and often other cats to contend with. The heat of the lights is another problem for animals that are supposed to appear cool and collected. In addition, the amount of people, activity, and noise makes a cat simply want to run and hide. Therefore, special techniques are called for.

Most commercials and movies demand constant improvising, because the more you get the cat to perform, the more the director wants. For one commercial all the cat was supposed to do was sit and look good. In the end she was eating out of a can with her paw, and balancing atop a narrow fence.

Getting a cat to perform tricks before the camera requires the same basic training techniques used for all the commands taught

228

in this book. However, the main problem with commercials and movies is that a cat usually has to perform a feat twenty or thirty times in a row—or rather, the trainer or handler has to be able to make him do so. From what you now know of a cat's capacity for boredom, you can see that this is not easy. Therefore, when cats are in the act, you must get the shot when you can because a cat's attention span is limited. And unlike humans, the concept of "stardom" is not an incentive.

In getting what is wanted we make use of a cat's natural innate abilities. For example, a cat's eyesight relies basically on its ability to see motion. Therefore, when we want to get a perked-up, wide-eyed, happy look on a cat's face in a photograph we get him to concentrate on a dangling moving object. We keep this just out of camera range wherever we want him to look. This attracts the cat's immediate attention and when he first catches sight of it, he perks up to see what it is and freezes in that position as if he were sizing it up before chasing it. This freeze may only last for a second or so, just enough time to get the shot. But if we have to get a lot of pictures, we change the object used to attract his attention frequently because cats become bored easily. Once a cat has satisfied his curiosity about what it is he loses interest. Sometimes even such things as birds in cages are used. We often use our parakeet, Saturday, as the stimulus for cats in commercials. She is so accustomed to cats now that you can put just about any kind near her, big or small, and it won't faze her at all—at least as long as she's safe inside her locked cage and they're outside.

We even used a cat's automatic programming to react to movement in one commercial to get a cat to close his eyes on cue and roll his head back as if he were falling asleep. Actually he was wide awake. It was just that his head and eyes were following the movement of an out-of-camera-range pocket watch being swung gently back and forth in front of him like a pendulum. The movement of the swinging watch gradually got smaller

229

and smaller, and the watch was at the same time slowly moved to one side. On camera you, of course, simply saw the cat's reaction.

Stock shots are thus frequently accomplished through little tricks. These include such things as the just-mentioned toy dangling off-camera to make a cat perk up and look attentive and excited. A clap of the hands will more than likely get a momentary confused, apprehensive, sad look. When recording live, however, one cannot make any noise at all, and this is where hand commands and other techniques are important. But this fact is often actually a boon since cats react badly to noise.

In working with cats professionally we also use their tendency to develop habits easily. We have found through working with so many cats that if you can coax one through a routine a couple of times and make it very rewarding for him, the chances are great that he will repeat that same routine over and over in anticipation of receiving more rewards.

If possible, we like to introduce a cat gradually to his trick and rehearse it slowly before shooting. We also often find it is easier to use a cat who is familiar with working. Once he goes through the work procedure a couple of times it is much easier the next time. The sets used for filming, especially interior ones, are remarkably similar. They all have just about the same type of equipment and crews in varying amounts and size. Therefore, even though the actual location is strange to a cat, many of the elements are familiar and thus reassuring to him.

But paradoxically, sometimes bringing a cat into a strange place can be advantageous in training. In fact, we often use a cat's apprehension and loss of self-confidence when first coming into strange places. This fact combines with his potential for developing habits in quite a few situations. In these circumstances we substitute an even more gratifying reward for the food treats—an escape to the refuge of a known secure spot. In strange places, if doing a trick ensures returning to a place where he feels secure, your cat will do it. Therefore, in training for many jobs we often use a "security box," usually his carrier (as we did when teaching him to "come") or an area which the cat is very familiar with. The reaching of this security is reward enough in itself and we often also add a treat as further incentive.

We used this method of training in one commercial with a black cat who had to jump across a ravine, prowl through undergrowth, follow along the beach, and end up lounging on a cushion-covered couch. The cat's own personal carrier in which he was always transported was used as the security box. We placed it on one end of the set and him on the other. He would then automatically head straight for his box every time he was released. At first he rushed straight across, but as he became more adjusted to his environment and felt more at ease, he slowed down to his normal pace. The set and props were then changed around him so that on film it looked as if he were continually walking through a new environment. Every time he was released he headed straight for his box—through the different scenes.

This cat was also trained for the jump scene by the security box method. First we set up a short leap where the cat had to jump from one pile of cushions to another. The box was placed just beyond whichever pile the cat had to jump to. We then gradually made the space to be jumped across wider and wider, until finally it was the right width required for the shot. Once it was right, the camera was focused directly on the center of the jump and thus only caught the cat in mid-air pictured against the backdrop of a full moon.

The carrier thus came to symbolize the trick to the cat. And as soon as he saw it he either ran or jumped to get to it. In this way the object became his voice and hand commands. Thus, a sign such as a box or other object can be used as the trigger to get your cat to perform. Often we use training aids like this with cats, because they frequently have to be taught through subterfuge and tricked into listening.

Many of the commercials you see on TV with cats are done with the help of special camera tricks, dubbing in of voices or animal sounds, and also, and perhaps even more importantly, with optical illusions (commonly called opticals) created in the developing of the film. The latter includes such things as running the film backward, or forward and backward to give a dance effect; using slow motion; stopping the camera to get a freeze action such as a mouth staying open or a paw raised; and repeating the same few frames of the film over and over so that it looks as if the cat is constantly meowing, "talking," or licking his chops. And when you do see that cat licking his chops over the fantastic food being advertised, it's probably because he has some even more delicious stuff like sardine oil rubbed on the outside of his jowls and is simply licking it off, not only because it tastes great, but also because he wants to be clean. Additionally, such props as false legs or tails for cats are used. These are manipulated by behind-the-scenes prop men to give the impression that a cat is lifting something, clapping his paws, or doing other feats that are obviously impossible for cats.

Of course we do commercials that include such stock production tricks, but we also do many others that require a lot of work be done by the cat with no optical effects whatsoever. These include one commercial where we had to train a cat to shop by herself. She had to leave her house, walk down the street, check out a few store windows, go into a supermarket and knock her food off the shelf. To get a cat to do this commercial we had to use quite a few different techniques and tricks, and it involved a lot of hard training.

First, to get the cat to walk out of the house and down the footpath leading through the garden, we set up her "security box" at the bottom of the path so that she would head straight for it when she came out of the door. But we didn't want her to rush straight for it. We wanted her to hesitate, look around, check everything out first, and then stroll down to it leisurely but with purpose. To get this reaction from the cat we hung a toy that fluttered above her head just outside the door, but out of camera range. This way, every time the cat came out she looked up at the toy to check it out before going on her way. It thus looked as if she were checking out the weather and area, then saying to herself "What a fantastic day!" before starting out on her stroll. This interruption in her walk also acted to break her concentration, and got her to slow down her pace as she headed for the box.

To get the cat to walk down the street and around a corner we simply tempted her with a piece of food on a string a few feet in front of her and out of camera range. We pulled it out of sight around the corner, and the cat naturally followed it. But to get the cat to check out all the store windows we had to do some rehearsing to condition the cat to stop and look in each window. To do this we put some food on the ledge of each window and walked her past holding her on a lead. We stopped wherever we had placed a treat, showed it to the cat, and let her get it. After this, every time the cat went by the windows she would stop to look for a treat on each window ledge and thus appear to be looking in the windows. We walked her through a couple of times with treats to make sure she had it down pat. Then we started the filming. Now, however, there were no treats on the ledges since it would be seen on camera if she stopped to eat. Because the food had been there once, however, the cat always stopped to look; and when she didn't find anything, she hurried on to the next window in hopes of something being there. Every few takes we ran her through the routine with treats but no film in the camera to keep her doing it.

Teaching her to walk through the right doorway into the store to get her food was accomplished by tempting her to follow a tidbit on a string, and rewarding her every time she went through the door. The door itself was pulled open from inside by an invisible nylon wire. Soon the food on the string bait was no longer needed and she invariably walked through the right doorway since she knew a treat would be awaiting her every time she did. (An electronic eye was supposed to open the door automatically, but unfortunately the cat was too low for it to operate, and thus the need for the invisible wire to open the door.)

Casting directors sometimes ask us to do almost impossible tasks. In one commercial all we had to do was find four "alley" cats and four backups, ranging in age from eight weeks to one and a half years. All these cats had to have identical markings since they had to cover a span representing the growing cycle of a kitten to a cat. They didn't want any purebreds with their standard markings, but only ordinary cats they felt everyone could identify with. These cats were to be used not only for a commercial, but also for still picture ads where the photographs were to be placed side by side. This invited comparison and also demanded that the markings be very close in order for the cats to look right. And on top of this requirement, each kitten or cat had to do a different trick—even the eight-week-old.

When working with a group of cats, great care must be taken to make sure the right cats are brought together. First they must all be healthy, and then they must all be acceptable to each other. This means there must be a social setup amongst them. Cats aren't really very sociable—especially around strange cats. Two toms or two adult females will often fight. Therefore, we greatly prefer working with altered cats only. In fact, the only time we work with unaltered cats is when we can't find the equivalent look in an altered one.

Bringing in other types of animals along with cats also calls for special attention. In one movie we had to train a single cat to sit calmly in the midst of forty dogs. These were all friendly, but it could still have been a harrowing experience for the average cat if not handled right. We therefore introduced the dogs to each other first so that their problems could be straightened out before we got the cat involved. The dogs were brought together slowly, only a few at a time. First we brought in the very young dogs, then the females, and finally the older males. (This is the same pattern used when bringing a group of any type of animals together.) Only after everyone was really relaxed and getting along together did we bring in the cat. The cat and the dogs had to learn to live together, at least for a while, and so a confrontation of sorts was essential. They had to work it out for themselves—with close supervision, of course.

The cat was declawed, so he really couldn't do any damage, but our attention was invariably on him. No matter whether he was attacking or being attacked, he was sure to be the one at the center of the situation and thus the one to watch. Once all the dogs got a good sniff at him to allay any fears they might have about being in contact with each other, everything was fine. The cat simply stayed in one spot where he had first been placed since he felt safest there, and he wouldn't go anywhere near "those dogs." Any dog whose reaction or behavior toward the cat was in any way suspect was ousted from the set. The only problems that arose involved a cocker spaniel who lifted his leg and urinated on the cat to claim him as his, and a big black Dane who decided to mount him. Fortunately the cat decided to ignore both affronts to his dignity and remained motionless on his spot.

Little house cats aren't the only types of cats we have worked with. For one commercial we had to supply and train a leopard who was to be walked on a lead by a glamorous blonde. We trained him to walk along with us to perfection, and he looked fantastic. When we got on the set and everyone saw how great he was, each clamored to have his/her picture taken with the cat. The only reluctant person turned out to be the model hired

235

for the job. In fact, when she arrived on location and saw the leopard she panicked and ran back into the car. According to her the type of cat to be walked was never mentioned—though we found that hard to believe. She had therefore assumed it was a little house cat. After a few strong drinks and a lot of persuasive talk and promises of further work from the director and agency people, she agreed to do the job. If it hadn't been for the money and promises she would probably have gone home. Instead, however, she came out with her newly gained confidence but *not* her normal coordination. She stepped on the cat's tail, the cat gave out a roar, and as if on cue, the model passed out.

When we finally did get around to filming this commercial, we ended up having to use extra-fast commercial speed training. The tail-stepping incident and the apparent discomfort of the model had made the cat nervous and he no longer wanted to be bothered. We knew the model was useless to us in helping control the cat and that we would have to do it from off camera somehow. In this case we decided to use water pistols, which we squirted at him from both sides when he attempted to walk off the designated pathway. This water-gun method worked out fine for quick temporary control. It did not, however, effect permanent training. It was just annoying enough to get him to respond rapidly for that day, but this was all that was needed to complete the job. There was no other way we could have worked with this particular model: she was more difficult than the leopard, and there are many people we are called in to work with who are equally difficult.

Many problems emanate from certain actors and actresses who are not overly pleased about the idea of working and/or sharing the limelight with animals. Some are genuinely nervous about animals, but if this is the case, they shouldn't take on the job in the first place. Others would just rather not be upstaged by an animal, so we frequently have to work around the egos of these people. One child actor was so miffed at being upstaged by an animal that he threw a fit. His mother took care of this one when she got him alone; she wasn't about to allow him to make a bad impression and thus spoil his chances for further work.

To many producers and directors, the cats are animated scenery, and only the human actors are religiously referred to as "the talent." Many production companies don't care about the cat, just the film. There are so many people involved they forget all about the animal and can't figure it out when he doesn't perform perfectly each and every time. The animal is just thought of as a machine and expected to be perfect at all times.

In one commercial, the director kept throwing in new props and noises. This only served to confuse the cat. Once a cat learns a certain way it should remain constant, except for making things better for him, until it is all over. Once a cat gets used to one set of circumstances it is hard to change, especially when trying to train him to do new tricks so fast.

When training cats for cat food commercials, we don't let our cats eat anything but the food at the job on the day of the actual commercial. We also feed the cats the same food to be used on the job for a few days in advance so they are accustomed to that particular brand of food. If you feed cats a completely new type of food on the set, you could have problems and they might refuse to eat. This is not necessarily because they don't like the food, but simply because they are not used to it and are cautious and picky when eating.

We always make sure that all our animal talent is treated humanely. There really is no entertainment value to be gotten from seeing animals misused, so we refuse to work when an animal has to be hurt in order to make him perform, or must work under dangerous conditions. Even when attending a movie with animals in it, we check to make sure it has a seal of approval issued by the A.H.A. (American Humane Association). If it does,

237

it means that the animals in the film have worked under supervised humane conditions. We ask at the box office to find out whether it does or doesn't have one. If there isn't one, we boycott the movie. This is the only way to ensure humane treatment of animals in films.

Unfortunately there are some owners who don't really know what love means. People tend to give so many of their own personal attributes, desires, and fantasies to their cats. Therefore, the idea of getting a pet into a commercial is often occasion for strange behavior on the part of many otherwise normal people. They will do just about anything to get their cat a part. One lady tranquilized her cat and starved him for days so her cat could get a job. We refused to use him and told her to think about how much she loved her cat if she could treat him like that. Don't confuse love with other things.

Some cats are useless for commercial and movie work. One cat came delivered to us in a cardboard box. When we took him out of the box, he ran and hid under the bed. We spent a good half-hour trying to coax him out. Another cat who came to audition for a part was very vicious. He wouldn't come out of his carrier. And if anyone attempted to put a hand in to get him out, a bite was the result.

If, however, your cat does perform well for you and you want him to do a commercial, he should do just as well and probably a whole lot better with an on-set trainer. If your cat lands a film or commercial job and is working, you'll probably be better off if you stay away. You won't be missing much. A location is usually a fairly dull place, with many different people milling about but very little apparently being accomplished. Once the cameras begin to roll the scene is usually repeated again and again, boring to tears anyone not directly involved in the work (and sometimes even them). Therefore, if you do attend, leave the day free and bring along a good book.

Stage mothers are not the most useful people on a set. So

keep out of the actual workings. Your cat will work better, get more work done, and maybe have a better chance of becoming a "star." Most television and movie tricks are within your cat's capacity. The only problem is that unless you understand the actual mechanics of filmmaking, you can't really do a thorough job. It's best to leave it to someone who does.

If you want your pet to be used in movies or commercials, and perhaps eventually become a "Patsy" winner, the animal counterpart to an Oscar winner, here are a few pointers:

• Be sure that he is outgoing and friendly, with an ability to accept new people and places.

• Have him thoroughly trained, at least for basic obedience and perhaps even for a trick or two.

• Be cautious of ads in papers or people saying they are looking for animal talent, who then suck you into paying for an "acting" class or photographs.

• Register him with reliable talent agencies. Include in his resumé a picture and all relevant information like size, color, and the like. Also list the tricks he can do. Fees are *not* required for listings, so if you are asked for money, go elsewhere.

• Remember that your main reward will be personal satisfaction rather than money. Unless they are well-known name animals such as Morris, cats do not receive residuals from commercials. And agents should and do take a fee for getting your cat the job.

Of course, some cats photograph better than others, and some cats react better than others on a set and under adverse working conditions. In fact, certain cats are just born "naturals," but a lot can be accomplished with training, so start working with your cat as young as possible.

PART FOUR

ADDITIONAL INFORMATION ABOUT CATS

17

WILD COUSINS

In one commercial we used a small black cat who, when viewed on television, looked more like a panther than anything else! Watch your cat stalking around after some unseen prey or just moving stealthily around the house. He looks just like a miniature version of one of his cousins, the wild cats. In fact, our little pet cats bear a remarkable resemblance to these cats. And this similarity is not restricted to physical appearance alone. Their behavioral and social characteristics are also strongly connected. In fact, the training techniques used for both are amazingly similar. The intensity differs because of the enormous difference in size, but amazingly there aren't any drastic changes in the methods—except, of course, for being a lot more careful.

Wild cats prefer warm climates and are most abundant in Asia and Africa, but are also found in America* and Europe. Interestingly, there are no cats known to be native to Australia or its surrounding islands.

* There was once even an American lion, which was apparently larger than the present-day lion or tiger. A skull resembling the African lion was found in Mississippi. It has a bigger muzzle and mouth but a smaller braincase and auditory area. (Probably meaning that it wasn't as smart as today's lion; it was more on the lines of an eating machine, such as the shark, but apparently not as successful.) Perhaps he was a Smilodon, the last of the saber-toothed cats.

It has long been supposed that all cats live solitary social lives in the wild. This is not entirely true. Cats are not always as alone as you might think: Jaguars mate for life and live closely together, sharing the hunting and all other chores. Tigers, though they don't live together, do mate for life, living on adjoining territories and meeting every few years for a few days to mate. Lions are actually highly socialized pack animals along the lines of dogs and wolves. However, unlike these nomadic-type animals, lions, like most other cats, set up very large permanent hunting ranges. Pumas, on the other hand, though complete loners, do not set up permanent territories but roam the way nomadic pack animals do. But the leopard is the embodiment of the stereotyped view most people have of cats. He fits the archetypical description of a cat: a complete loner with a large territorial hunting range which he/she controls absolutely, allowing no other cat on it, except to mate.

You can therefore see that cats in the wild have differing social orders and lifestyles. A cat can be a roaming, nomadic loner; a settled pack animal; or just about anything in between, depending on the circumstances of his life, his environment, how his ancestors evolved through centuries, and how he was raised. Adaptability is an extremely important, if often ignored, aspect in a cat's makeup. Use this malleability to mold your cat's nature the way you want it. The owner of a cat can have a tremendous influence on his cat's character and personality. In the wild, food availability would appear to be the major influence in molding a cat's lifestyle. The kind of social organization or lack of social organization which developed through the years was dictated by the imperatives of survival. A cat doesn't just go out and munch on some leaves or grass he finds around; rather, he has to go out and search for his food. He has to hunt it down, and for every quarry he catches, who knows how many get away? In addition, in times of drought or other natural catastrophes his food supply dwindles. Therefore in order to secure an adequate food supply at all times cats need large hunting areas.

All food hunting is done within a hunting range which the cat guards jealously. These ranges can be extremely large—a range of fifty square miles is about the average needed to adequately take care of the needs of a single tiger. All cats except the puma* hunt on territorial ranges.

In the same way, our pet house cats tend to develop ties with territories rather than people. In fact, they can become so strongly attached by habit and devotion to their environment that changes are difficult to make. This can cause problems if you have to move to a new house, or if you adopt a full-grown cat. Some would rather hide or go back to their old territories than go to a new home. A cat can even pine away in a new place or environment.

However, when the basic necessities of life such as food and shelter are provided, such as in your home, it is not necessary for cats to establish hunting ranges. In fact, litters of tigers brought up apart from their parent, but kept together in captivity well into maturity, did not establish separate territories. Rather they continued to play together and developed extremely close ties that remained intact even into maturity. (If one of the members of the pack had been a female and the others males, however, things might not have worked out so smoothly. At about two years of age the tiger matures and enters her first heat or mating cycle. Fighting for dominance and control would probably then develop amongst the males. This same thing holds true for our housecats, so if you're planning on getting a few cats, don't have more than one full-grown uncastrated

* The puma is a roamer whose range runs from Alaska down to the tip of South America. Unfortunately today, because of human expansion, the puma like so many other wildcats is an endangered species.

male if you've got an unspayed female in the house, even if they are related. Cats aren't particular, they have no ethics as far as a little incest is concerned. If you don't heed our warning you'll be in for two surprises—cat fights like you've never seen, and litters of kittens!)

If asked which wild cat the majority of today's domestic cats most resemble in personality, we'd probably say he reminds us most of the leopard. Leopards are real loners, and rarely ever meet another cat except to mate. They establish jealously guarded territories, keep their distance from all others, and communicate vocally from these territories. Like all cats, they mark the perimeters of these hunting ranges strongly with urine and/or feces. They spend a lot of time high up in lairs, surveying their territory, striking out to hunt from this vantage point; they even sleep up there for protection. (Lions will also sleep up in trees, but only low slanted ones which they can walk up. Leopards actually climb trees like a bear, digging in with their claws for traction.) Leopards even drag their food up into trees to protect it. They are amongst the smaller of the large cats, thus they have to protect it not only from the normal scavengers, but also from any of the larger cats. In fact, lions will often steal and eat a leopard's kill if they can get their paws on it. And sometimes, if extremely hungry, they will even attack, kill, and eat the leopard himself!

This comparison to such a loner may sound like a drastic description of your cat. Your cat may be nothing like this; he could be a friendly affectionate pet. Unfortunately, many a domestic cat is forced to adopt a loner's life. As a kitten he is taken away from his mother at a very early age, brought into some strange new home, and all too often generally ignored after the first couple of days when the initial "new toy" excitement passes. Because he is ignored (and sometimes because he is pulled around too much) by his new family, he assumes he is

246

supposed to live apart from others and, since animals adjust to just about any circumstances, he accepts the role given him and develops an aloof attitude.

In the wild the male and female cat basically think and feel the same way, except for the roles nature has given them. Lions are the exception, since lions live in a pride comprising several females, young males, and a dominant male. In this case the females do most of the hunting and the actual killing. The young males may act as decoys to flush out the prey. However, other than lions, most types of cats hunt and fight the same way, regardless of sex. In fact, jaguars hunt and fight as a team, interchanging roles as the need calls for it.

The private territorial hunting ranges of cats are generally respected. However, sometimes a cat has to leave for one reason or other, such as a flash forest fire. If at these times he chances to run into another cat in neutral territory, the dominant cat usually gets the right-of-way. Dominance in these cases is usually determined by a stand-off staring match in which both sit and stare at each other until one turns away or else sits down in a crouched submissive posture and lets the other pass. In a case of this kind, males as a rule won't generally fight. However, if they reach a stalemate where no one will give in, a fight becomes absolutely essential to establish dominance. Females are frequently less tolerant toward each other and will fight more readily in this type of situation.

This type of behavior also holds true for domestic cats caught in similar situations. This most frequently occurs with alley cats. The neighborhood stray population is usually a good example of the territorial aspects of cat life. These cats will not generally roam in packs the way dogs do; rather each will live alone. However, each neighborhood will have a dominant cat who will act like some feudal overlord who wanders around his domain at night seeking out females in heat and establishing his dominance over all the other cats living within it, often by fighting. High-ranking males in an area may thus occasionally visit the home territory of an inferior without any trouble, but usually territories are respected and guarded jealously.

18

WHEN YOU TAKE A TRIP: Traveling versus Boarding

If you are going somewhere you can take a cat, there's no need to leave him behind. Though basically homebodies, most cats can become good travelers and adjust to almost any given situation, especially if you get them accustomed to traveling while still a kitten. There are plenty of content cats who live on the roads in motor homes and trailers.

Many people feel that the easiest thing to do is to put the cat into a carrier when traveling and be done with it. For some people and cats this is by far the best solution. In fact for short distances, such as across town, a carrying case is often the answer, especially if you want to hop on a bus or in a cab. Additionally, if you are taking your pet on a prolonged trip, a carrier should be brought along whether you feel it is needed or not. You never know when an emergency need for one might arise. A cat should never be left free in a strange area. He might panic and bolt, and you'd never find him. Potentially new sights and sounds tend to make cats nervous. Cats grow attached to their environment and must become acclimatized gradually to new surroundings. Therefore, it is often kinder to certain cats to make these changes unknown to them when traveling. Many cats prefer to ride in a carrier, and feel more secure there than if allowed to be loose.

Cat carriers are luggage-like cases with airholes; they come in many styles and materials. The one you select should be well ventilated, have ample room for your pet to turn around in, and be easy to clean. It should be solidly constructed and have a good strong handle which is easy to grasp and hold. When in use the bottom should be lined with a towel or other easily cleanable padding. Some models have a see-through screen and/ or a plastic viewer, but try to make sure there is not too much of a view of the world. A small lookout plus many ventilation holes is your best bet. If it is too open it can only add to his confusion—you want your cat to see as little as possible of what's going on. A full view of a lot of activity will only make him very nervous. He needs as much of a closed-in feeling as he can possibly get without being cramped. It gives him a feeling of security. He can look out without anything's being able to touch him—like in his window seat at home.

These hand-held cat carriers are distinct from the crate-type kennels you should use for shipping a cat. For this type of transportation, buy or build a strong, properly ventilated crate. The new fiberglass ones sold at airports are excellent. Don't use a cage for the same uses as an enclosed carrier. The baggage-room circus is not something he should see.

Make absolutely sure that the cat is in a strong, proper-sized kennel. One Maine Coon (a prize winning show cat) weighing about twenty-five pounds was put into a kennel for a regular-sized adult cat. The cat died!

Many people ship animals in flimsy little slatted orange-crate type boxes that crush easily. However, a new law, The Animal Welfare Act of 1976, outlawing such practices has recently been passed. This includes regulations covering the shipment of animals. Hopefully it will eliminate much of the needless suffering and death caused to animals by the carelessness or uncaring attitude of shipping and transportation personnel. Up to now animals being transported had no protection. These regulations will be enforced by the U. S. Department of Agriculture. Your area office of this department will be able to give you exact requirements.

Before using the carrier or crate, get your cat used to it. The more familiar it is to him the better he'll adjust to it. A tranquilizer, if recommended by your vet, mightn't be a bad idea but it won't calm your cat as effectively as getting him used to his carrier or crate well in advance of using it. Introduce him to his carrier or crate in slow simple stages, preferably when he's sleepy, so that he'll relax automatically and even tend to doze off whenever he's inside. Gradually increase the length of time you leave him in there until he stays for as long as the traveling time is supposed to be. When you let him out again praise him and give him a treat; show him that everything is all right.

Many cats love to travel. However, for many people traveling with a cat can be fraught with problems, which may start when you simply try to get him into the car. Some cats love riding and will react enthusiastically but there are many others whose first car trip was to the veterinarian's office for inoculations, or who perhaps have been startled by cars as they pass by the house honking and creating a racket in the street. These cats look on anything on four wheels as a moving Iron Maiden.

You can get just about any cat to accept the car and even enjoy it but it takes time. You have to show him it's all right. Show him that a car is just like one big window seat for him. Let him know that inside that car he is absolutely secure.

To teach him about the car put him in his carrier (which he should be used to by now) and, with the car parked and quiet, put it into the back seat. Close all the doors and make sure the windows aren't open more than an inch or two so the cat can't escape. Open up the carrier and just leave him there. After about ten minutes close the case, with him in it, and take it back into the house. Another time let him stay longer. Wait until he comes out of the carrier by himself—he will. Cats are insatiably curious. It may take time but he'll do it and he must. Encourage him with a tidbit if you want but he must come out by himself.

Once he's coming out by himself almost as soon as he gets in the car, start the engine. Drive him first down the driveway, later around the block, eventually on more extensive journeys, never pressing him beyond his limits. If he seems the least bit fearful or upset, stop and continue another time.

Once you are driving with your cat there are some added precautions to take into consideration. Make sure you roll the window down just far enough so he can't possibly jump through. And pause to look around when push-buttoning a window closed. Many cats—and children—have gotten their heads caught in exactly this way. Look before you push that button. Teach him not to jump around in the car; it can be dangerous. If he were to get unruly while you were traveling at any real speed, it could cause an accident. However, seat belts are not for your cat and buckling him up could lead to injury. If seats are unusually smooth, it's a good idea to provide him with a rug, mat or towel so that his feet can enjoy traction without leaving claw marks on your seat.

Putting a harness and lead on your cat while he is in the car can also be helpful. This way you or someone else can hold the lead when the doors or windows are open. But don't use a collar and lead together in a car—a lead can catch on handles or gearshift and if he has a collar on, it can choke him.

If you absolutely can't control your cat while in the car, or if you are nervous about your cat's being loose, keep him confined to the carrier. Any cat who could possibly interfere with your driving, thus causing possible injury to you, himself or the car cannot be allowed the freedom of the car. Jumping around in the car is an absolute no-no.

If the trip is less than two to three hours your cat probably won't want or need a litter box, especially if you treat him like a child and make sure he uses his bathroom just before you leave the house. But if you are traveling long distances, you must take a litter box with you. (Unless, of course, your cat has learned to use the toilet, in which case you would simply take him to a restroom with you.) A metal box with a lid or one of the new disposables is best for traveling, but if one of these is unavailable you can take your regular one.

You should take plenty of rest periods with an opportunity for the cat to drink and relieve himself. Cats don't need a lot of exercise, but if you have taught your cat to walk with a lead and a harness, you can walk him to allow him to get a little air. Never allow your cat to remain loose in any strange place without some kind of restraint. There is the possibility he may become frightened and escape, then become so nervous he cannot be caught.

Never leave your cat locked in a car on a warm day since a metal car heats up very quickly, even in the late afternoon sun. Many animals suffocate each year in hot enclosed cars. Whenever you park, always make sure it's in the shade, and open the window an inch or two. But never leave it open too much or he may not be there when you return. He'll either bolt or someone will take him.

Certainly your cat should never be left in the car overnight. This should be self-explanatory. A car is not a home. Try to check in advance with the motel or hotel where you are planning to stay to see if it allows cats. Usually there is no objection to cats—as long as you provide the litter box.

Traveling by airplane is the way that will probably give you the most problems. A lot of airlines allow no animals to travel in the cabins at all. And others say that if you make special arrangements well in advance you can take only *one* cat in a carrier into the cabin with you. There is only one pet allowed per cabin in a plane, ever, so if you want to be the person who brings on that pet, reserve in advance. A lot of people want to

253

take their pets with them, and the airlines hold to the rule of one. A friend used to register for one and stash the other under his coat until he got on and then put it into the carrier with the other. After all, who would know then? But the last time he did it he got busted by the bomb squad for stashing a Persian. Apparently the anti-hijacking airport security spotted the bulge and dragged him in as suspicious. Imagine their surprise when out popped a white Persian!

Other than those lucky few who get reservations, the animals traveling by plane are stored and shipped in the cargo area of the airliner. Unfortunately most baggage compartments designed for carrying live animals are heated and pressurized but not air-conditioned. And if they are air-conditioned it is usually only while in flight. Therefore, if the baggage compartment gets overheated, especially in long layovers on the ground, it will not be cooled. And additionally, many baggage compartments are not adequately heated, so you should check carefully before consigning your pet to one. In these cases the temperature changes in the compartment are extreme. If it is extremely cold outside or if the airplane hits pockets of cold air, the temperature can drop low; then upon landing it can overheat rapidly because of the air-conditioning problem. Even the bigger and supposedly better planes have some pretty extreme temperature changes. Remember cats are critically hot when their body temperature reaches 103 degrees, and 105 degrees could be fatal.

As a result, we advise that if you must transport your animals in the baggage compartment, make sure you book onto a straight-through flight with absolutely no stopovers. Book non-stop also because your cat could get dropped off at the wrong place and sit there waiting forever. Every additional stop guarantees more loading and unloading. In addition, during the hot summer months, choose late night or early morning flights— and hope there are no ground delays.

Never feed your pet just before shipping; in fact, don't feed him for a good twelve hours beforehand. Water intake should also be restricted. Many animals die in flight simply because they regurgitate their food and then choke to death on it.

It is often best to ship your animal on one of the air-freight carriers which is temperature controlled for shipping all animals and cargoes. The thing to do here is to arrange your schedule so that you will be at the airport on arrival of the plane with the cat. This means you may have to get a friend to put the cat on the plane, and have him follow you to your final destination.

If you have to ship your cat without you, check out everything as you would for yourself. Put him on an express through flight, and be sure there will be someone there on time to meet him. Inform the person who is going to pick up the cat of the arrival time, flight number, and bill of lading number. If there are any changes in plans, tell him. If your cat doesn't arrive on time, get a trace out on him. He may have been put off at the wrong airport or loading dock.

In the final analysis it still boils down to one thing. Cat-owning passengers should apply common sense when shipping their pets and always remember that animals are *not* baggage but living, breathing creatures. It's up to you to ensure the safety of your pet. Precautions, plus some advance planning with airline personnel, should ensure you a happy, healthy pet when you get wherever you're headed. But it's up to you to make sure that he is going to make a pleasant adjustment.

When traveling by railroad, your cat will usually have to be put into the baggage car. However, with special arrangements you may be able to keep him in his carrier next to your seat. If that's the case, get the permission in writing because the conductor might know nothing about it. And if you are taking a boat, you can often take your cat in a kennel on the same boat so he can take the voyage with you.

Of course you know that flying and any other form of transportation is not free. Rates vary but usually they are computed by weight. The exception is boats, which charge per trip, usually a real bargain. (The best bargain in town for your cat is a trip on the Fire Island Ferry. Dogs have to pay, but cats go for free! Perhaps the owners are cat people.)

If you are traveling extensively you should know that each country and even most states have regulations regarding the transportation of animals. Health and entry requirements for pets vary from country to country. The ASPCA issues a booklet at a nominal charge called "Traveling With Your Pet" which gives a complete rundown of the regulations. However, sometimes it is best to get the information directly. This means contacting the Agriculture Department of the states you will be traveling through or getting in touch with the consulate of the country you plan to visit.

Keep in mind that there are some countries which will not allow your pet to enter at all, such as the Soviet Union. Then there are others such as England, Ireland, New Zealand, and Australia which require extended quarantine periods. Even one of the United States, Hawaii, has a quarantine on all animals entering, no matter what health certificates you have for your cat.

Before going anywhere with your pet, make sure he is in good health and that his inoculations are up to date. In addition, when traveling with your cat keep in mind that you must watch out for any health problems that could afflict him. Avoid taking your pet to some of the more backward countries since they have no regard for animals as pets and thus have no medical facilities for them. You might enjoy roughing it, but your cat doesn't. And when traveling anywhere watch out for ticks, fleas and any of the many other parasites cats can pick up. If you see anything abnormal or your cat is hurt, get him to a vet.

If you are staying for a short visit or an indefinite extended stay, keep in mind that your cat has to become acclimatized gradually to new surroundings. Thousands of cats have made the fretful transition from Connecticut farmland to teeming Manhattan. In the transition from city to country or vice versa, basically the same problems are encountered. A cat unaccustomed to the noise of a country farm or to city noises can become confused. You must show him it's okay.

When we go on vacation, it's usually to a place we can take our cat. However, some cats are such bad travelers that it is better to leave them home. Also, there are times that a person has to get away from all responsibilities. At such times, we try to have our pets taken care of by someone who knows them and whom we can trust completely. This way we can be sure that they will not be spoiled or hurt while we're away. If we cannot find someone, then we put them in a reputable boarding establishment. It is better to put them in a good cattery* or kennel than to leave them with an irresponsible person.

Because you're going to have a good time, think of your cat. Give your cat the consideration he deserves and remember that he is not a car to be put in dead storage for any length of time, but rather a living creature for whom you are responsible.

If you are simply making a short weekend trip, it's easy to leave your cat home alone. Just put out an ample supply of water and one of the semi-moist or dry convenience foods. (Canned foods aren't a good idea since they dry out and become stale within a short time of exposure.) In addition make sure the litter box is cleaned completely and filled with a fresh supply of cat litter. This will last for the entire weekend. Cats won't use a dirty litter tray, so if you want to come home to a clean house make sure you do this.

For more extended trips, you can arrange for someone to come in to care for your cat on a daily basis—either once, twice, or however many times you feel it's necessary. The sitter should

---

* Catteries are the places where cats were and are still traditionally boarded. Today, however, most commercial kennels also have facilities for cats.

give him fresh food and water, clean his litter tray, give him some attention and check to see that he is in good health. If you can't find a friend to do this you can hire a professional "cat sitter."

To find someone like this get references from your veterinarian and/or friends who have used the sitter or perhaps your local pet store has a similar service. Before leaving, have the sitter come over so you can show her around and be sure she knows your cat and your house.

If you don't want to have anyone in your house or if making sitting arrangements would be an inconvenience, you may want to consider boarding. There are quite a few good cat boarding facilities available at reasonable cost. There is no real right or wrong way to approach the boarding issue. But there are some pointers to keep in mind.

You have two basic choices in boarding: you can send your cat to a commercial boarding facility or you can arrange for boarding your cat in someone's home. Ask your veterinarian to recommend a few places. He often hears reports from people about boarding places. Another good source of information is friends whose cats have stayed at a place and had good treatment. The classified ads are not the ideal way to find this type of facility since it is such a personal service and ads in newspapers and magazines mean nothing.

Before deciding, be sure to check it out thoroughly personally. Your cat can't report on the conditions unless he comes back really sick and then it's too late, so you have to make sure that they are right beforehand. After all, he can't just pack up and leave if he doesn't like it the way you can. If you end up settling for the wrong boarding facility, your cat might come back with worms, ear mites, respiratory illnesses, or just about anything else. And don't wait until the last minute to make arrangements. Just as with the better hotels, the better boarding establishments fill up very quickly—especially around the major holidays. Get your reservation well in advance.

Some localities have licensing requirements for boarding places but on the whole they are pretty well left up to the owners to regulate. Therefore, it is extremely important that you check out the place carefully before leaving your cat. Make a surprise visit, preferably during the week because many people visit on weekends.

Make sure that the kennel or cattery is clean and has competent help, with a veterinarian on call 24 hours a day. Ask for the vet's name and speak to him personally if you can. If you go to a place that holds approximately 60 animals, and you can only see one person working, it's obvious that he can't possibly take care of them all. Check for adequate heating and proper ventilation with no drafts. There should be no odor about the place, but neither should it be antiseptic-smelling as if covering up underlying odors.

Make sure you know what your cat will be fed, because a swift change in diet can cause diarrhea or loss of appetite and therefore a loss in weight. Check that he will get clean water at all times. Make sure the litter is changed frequently. In fact, to be sure you can even take his own box with him. Also you can order your own specific food—this will usually cost extra, but if your cat is a fussy eater or gets upset stomachs over changes in diet, it is a good idea.

Don't forget that when you send your cat to a cattery or kennel, he won't be let free to roam. He will be put in a cage (or pen) and there he will stay. This arrangement is ideal for many cats who feel more secure in a closed area. The same goes for some people who feel happier knowing their cat is in a cage where he can't run away or get into any harm. This way they are sure they will get their cat back in one piece.

But this is also exactly why it is so important that the cages be of adequate size, and extremely clean. The cage should be big enough to hold your cat's bed, litter box, feeding dish and water bowl, and still provide him with enough room to move around and not feel cramped. Some people take all their own equipment, but that is really unnecessary. One favorite toy is all that is needed. One client took so many toys to make his cat feel at home that after they were stuffed in he couldn't even fit the cat in the cage.

Make sure the bed area is raised a few inches off the ground so there are no drafts. Don't let him stay in one of those cages with wire bottoms that can catch his feet. The cage should preferably be open only on one side so that he doesn't become disoriented by all the activity and strange surroundings. Don't put him in a noisy, busy area. But by the same token don't get him stuck in some dark corner where he'll be forgotten.

Don't use a place where they keep a few cats in one cage, unless from the same household. If they do this there could be a fight, they could catch germs from one another, and they definitely won't be too happy about sharing with strangers. This means that even when cleaning they should not put one cat into another's cage so that they can clean his.

Additionally, make sure they have a definite policy about isolating females in heat. One female in heat can upset an entire cattery or kennel. The unpredictability of heats in cats makes it difficult for many owners to know exactly when their cats are in heat, therefore there should be a separate area for emergency heats.

If you opt for boarding your cat at someone's house, make sure they don't take in too many cats, causing overcrowded conditions. Check that they understand cats, really like them, and take care of them properly. Keep in mind that your cat might run out of the door, and you could lose him; that there are other cats coming in contact with him who could be spreading germs; that many cats do not like the company of other cats and might fight or become frightened; and also that some people keep cages you never see down in the cellar. Nothing takes the place of a personal visit to check everything over.

The place where you finally decide to board your cat doesn't have to be one of those new luxury pet hotels, it just has to give the very best of care and attention. And when you find a good commercial boarding facility, cat sitter, or home boarding, stick with it, because this will give your cat a feeling of security through familiarity.

19

TO BREED OR NOT TO BREED

Cats are prolific breeders and, if left alone, females can start breeding at about seven months and can have about twenty litters in a lifetime. With an average of three to four kittens in a litter, you can figure out for yourself the number they can produce.

The figure you arrive at might sound as though it could be profitable to breed your cat if you own a pedigree. But breeding, and even simply owning an unaltered cat, can be fraught with problems. Breeding is really best left to the professionals. A pro knows how to handle matters far better than you. The only benefit most people get out of breeding their female is that when she has a litter she is entitled to be called a "queen."

Still, there are some people who argue in favor of breeding. Some want their cats to be happy parents. Others mistakenly feel that breeding will make their cats more mature and stop them from roaming, spraying, caterwauling, and doing all those other obnoxious things that unaltered cats do. Others breed their cats so that the children can experience the "miracle of life." But consider what's going to happen to those three or four "miracles of life" when they get to be eight weeks old? Who's going to take care of them? And don't forget that a mother cat will defend her young, so if the kids think that they get to pull and paw at the kittens, they'd better think again.

Remember there are more cats than homes, so *not* breeding is the kindest thing to do. In fact, almost everyone who allows his cat to breed ends up with a litter he can't find homes for. It doesn't make sense for owners to insist on breeding more kittens when unwanted and abandoned kittens and cats are being picked up daily by the ASPCA and humane societies. These places are packed to overcrowding, and they are sadly forced by the lack of facilities and money and the overloading of unwanted pets to destroy them. Seven hundred thousand kittens and cats are brought into animal shelters each year, but only seventy thousand fortunate ones get adopted. Don't add to the problem.

Some people just dump their cats—Either throw them out or let them wander or take them to a dark secluded spot and leave them. They have even been found in garbage cans. Owners simply look for a spot that's relatively deserted and anonymous, free of witnesses who might make them feel guilty. People who discard their cats often hope they'll find new homes, but a dark, deserted alley is no home for a cat. People feel that a cat off the street isn't worth anything. Or that it can fend for himself. Of course, there are kindly folk who take in stray cats, but their number is dwindling due to a labyrinth of financial and legal restrictions. As for those cats who are let go in the wild, chances are they won't survive. And those strays and their offspring living in populated areas are increasing far more quickly than owners can take them in.

Since the average life of a cat is about twelve to fifteen years, this is the length of time it will take to solve the problem of strays. Some have advocated birth control elements in cat food, but at the moment this method hasn't proved safe. Look at the stink that just erupted recently over the risks involved in human

oral contraceptives. At the moment the method used for population control is wholesale slaughter.

If you insist on breeding, or if your cat gets caught, there are
a few things you should know. For planned breeding we recommend that you breed only if your cat is a good, healthy purebred. Don't breed "mixed" cats, not because we don't love
them and think they're equal in every way to purebreds, but
rather because they are so plentiful and so cheap that in our
society, where money is the measure of worth, they are considered expendable by many people.

The only time breeding is really worthwhile for the average
person is when you have good *guaranteed* homes in advance. A
casual "I'd love one!" doesn't mean a thing; get a real commitment from someone who will really care for the kitten. But we
think even this shouldn't be enough to persuade you. Tell anyone who wants a kitten to do a kind deed and rescue one at the
humane society.

If you do decide to breed, keep these things in mind if you
want good healthy kittens. First, make sure that your cat is
healthy, and has had all her necessary inoculations. Then pick
a mate on the basis of physical fitness and a good disposition.
Choose for quality, not just of the cat himself, but also for
heredity. For instance, male cats with only one dropped testicle
should not be mated since that is a hereditary condition. And if
your female's father had or has only one, don't mate her either.
Her male offspring will have the same problem and her females
the gene for it. If not removed at a young age, undescended testicles can cause medical problems such as tumors in and around
it during a cat's middle to older years. Viciousness is another
hereditary characteristic which should be avoided. In fact, there
are many things you should know about genetics in order to be
a good breeder, and much study is required.

Inbreeding in cats can be either good or bad because it tends
to make a strain pure for characteristics good or bad. In the

wild, natural selection picks out strong to strong. Thus mixed cats are usually strong, healthy animals because they are the product of relatively natural selection. In fact, a strain of cats often begins to deteriorate when the cats are bred for a particular quality and other attributes are disregarded.

It is best for you to wait until the second or even third heat to mate your cat. Before that she herself has not really finished developing. However, waiting too much longer can be a mistake also since an older cat may not make such a good mother. If the male is too young, his sperm may not be virile enough. And if a stud is bred too frequently he won't have a good sperm supply, and a good sperm count is needed to cause pregnancy.

Cats are quite unpredictable when it comes to mating cycles and heat periods. A female cat (catta) has many heat periods during the year. But she usually has only a few peak periods, called "estrus," in which pregnancy can occur. Usually there are two, but sometimes three such periods in a year, each normally lasting fifteen to twenty-one days.

Theoretically the catta should be mated after the bleeding of the heat period has stopped, but while the vulva is still swollen. Cats have a vaginal discharge right from the beginning of the heat period but since they lick themselves clean it is hard to tell by looking. Thus the best way to tell when to mate your cat is by watching her behavior. The first sign of heat is usually a slight swelling around the vulva. Your cat will become affectionate yet restless, nervous and tense. This is the pre-acceptance period, which lasts a few days, during which time she will become increasingly, clawingly affectionate. The second stage is initiated by the willingness of the cat to copulate. In this period, your cat's voice will change to a more piercing and demanding tone, and she caterwauls constantly to attract a mate. She rolls on the floor and becomes even more of an affectionate nuisance. This caterwauling and rolling is usually considered the start of the acceptance period. Breeders usually wait two to three days after this outrageous behavior begins before putting her with a male. By then she should be ready; if not, she'll reject him.

Mating is not always as easy as it might seem. Many people assume they just put their cats together and they'll do it all themselves. Some cats are inexperienced, some females are vicious and won't accept a mate, some males are very rough in mating, and some cats do not like confined spaces. It's really hard for the novice; you have to get to know your own cat and his reactions, plus those of the potential mate. Therefore, use either an experienced stud and/or an experienced queen—it makes it a lot easier. Better still, take your female to a breeder who knows her business so she can oversee everything.

The actual mating game can be alarming for the unsuspecting, uninitiated owner. There is usually a good deal of growling, chewing and general mauling during mating. So don't get excited if you see a certain amount of squabbling. But if it looks like there is a real fight or that it is getting serious, break it up. It's best to let a woman do this, since the stud may take the man as a rival and attack him.

It is the agitation of the penis' being removed that causes the female to ovulate, and thus allows the mixing of the sperm with the ovum. The cat's penis is covered with small horn-like structures or barbs. There is no pain while inside, but when the male withdraws he does so quickly so that the barbs tear the tissue lining the vagina. It is this irritation which excites and causes ovulation in the female. This action also hurts, causing the female to cry out in her "mating call."

Copulation takes only a few seconds in a cat, but cats mate repeatedly to insure that the cat conceives. Once ovulation does occur it puts the brake on the mating drive and appeal—not suddenly, but over a period of days. This is done by a different odor transmitted by the female after she conceives.

The sense of smell in a cat is closely related to sex. The male picks up the smell of a heated female and goes courting. This is nature's way and in the wild it works. But in the crowded world of today, it can and often does cause a lot of problems when all the neighborhood toms come to visit your pet on the same night. The "natural" mating habits of cats are really quite turbulent. Once a female in heat gets outside, males gathered to court her fight for dominance. Oftentimes she will be surrounded by a circle of males each facing toward her. First one, then another will mate, usually in order of dominance.

If cats are allowed to mate at will, it is probable that a female will have a litter fathered by several males. The female produces several eggs for a litter, so that one egg can be fertilized by one tom, another by a second and so on depending on how many toms have mated with her and the number of eggs there are.

Since professional breeders keep their studs caged; if you use their services, you should bring the female there. If, however, it is a friend's male or if your female is nervous, it might be wiser to bring the male to the female. If a heated female is brought to an uncaged male's house, he will have a field day and start spraying up a storm, urinating to re-establish his own territory. So, in this case, let the stud cat do the visiting, put them in a small room together, and when the male has done his job remove him immediately.

Once pregnant, the gestation period will last fifty-eight to seventy days, usually an average of sixty-three to sixty-four. You won't notice anything for a few weeks, but then you will be able to tell—she'll get fat. During this time she should be watched for any unusual signs. If she seems to have any problems, take her to the vet. Besides, a physical checkup isn't a bad idea for every pregnant cat to be sure everything looks normal. The only way you can tell the number of kittens she is going to have is to have an x-ray or the newer and safer sound-wave pictures.

Take your vet's advice on the subject of diet during pregnancy, but in general she should be given extra nutritious foods with some vitamins and calcium added. Feed her extra meat for the last two to three weeks of pregnancy. But don't overfeed her —it will cause a difficult birth.

A pregnant cat will usually continue with her normal activity until two to three days prior to birth. You should allow her to continue this normal activity up until the last week or so and then you shouldn't allow her to jump around or get herself wet or damp. And starting about a week before she is due to give birth, make sure your pregnant cat isn't allowed on your bed or couch, since she may choose these soft spots to give birth later. If your cat is a longhair, about a week before the kittens are due cut the hair around her nipples, since a kitten can choke on loose hairs. Also, for all cats, wash her teats to be sure they're as clean as possible so the newborns will have a minimum of germs to contend with when they begin nursing. Even if you don't know the exact time she was mated you will be able to tell when it is time for her to give birth. During the last week or so of pregnancy she will appear restless, roaming back and forth throughout the house in search of a safe place to bear her young. Get in touch with your vet to tell him when you think she'll be due, and to get the telephone number where he or a substitute can be reached in case of emergency.

Most cats have a good maternal instinct and will search out a satisfactory nest prior to birth. It is, however, far better if you provide that "nest" for her. If she hides somewhere you may not know where she is giving birth and if something goes wrong you would be unavailable to help. Get a high cardboard box with one side cut out for her to get in and out, but too high for the kittens to fall out. It should have a top to make it nestlike, and also to keep it dark to protect the kittens' sensitive eyes. A towel over the top is adequate. As the kittens get older you can cut the hole in the side lower so they can come and go as they please. The box should be large enough for the mother to stretch out completely with plenty of room to spare for the kittens.

Pick a quiet, safe, warm, comfortable, draft-free location, well out of the way. In addition, make sure it is in a dark corner, since kittens have supersensitive eyes. Start putting her into the box in advance of delivery time. Get her used to it. Let her know that this is a good place for her to be. Your cat may reject this spot and go to one of her own choosing. Watch her when it is close to the time. And when she begins looking about for paper and rags to make a nest and starts acting completely different from before, get her wherever you want her to be fast, because she and her kittens will be there for the next eight weeks, at least. Try to steer her to your choice. Otherwise watch for her favorite spot and put her bed there. About a day before birth the stomach will drop and you might notice a vaginal discharge. This is the time to get her to the box as fast as possible.

Usually birth is a perfectly normal procedure without undue problems, but keep an eye on her when labor begins. If she seems to be having any problems, call your vet immediately. If the labor seems to be overly long or if she cannot seem to get a kitten out, get in touch with your vet.

In the actual birth process there is a semi-transparent membranous sac around each kitten, and each is attached to the mother by an umbilical cord which attaches it to the placenta. The mother removes the sac, cuts the cord and then cleans the kittens thoroughly, thus stimulating the body functions and circulation.

Sometimes, however, the mother doesn't do all that she should and you may have to help. If you can't get a vet, don't panic. Keep calm and don't interfere unless absolutely essential. Resist the urge to help unless you see a kitten in danger; your good intentions may be more disturbing than helpful.

If a newborn kitten doesn't begin breathing before the next one arrives, and only after the mother has definitely given up on him and goes to the next, help by gently swinging the kitten by its hind legs until he gasps for breath. If the mother doesn't cut the umbilical cord or doesn't cut it close enough, cut it to about one or one and a half inches with sterilized scissors and apply a drop of iodine or similar antiseptic to the end of the cord. If the mother can't or won't clean him, remove the membrane, and clean the nostrils to prevent suffocation. Most cats want no assistance but if one of the kittens gets stuck half in and half out, you may have to help. In a normal birth the head comes out first, if there is a breech birth—the tail and hind legs of the kitten are coming out first—you might have to help, since this could be fatal. Using a cloth, pull the kitten gently but firmly; don't tug, the mother will strain to help.

We don't like to give medical advice of any kind since we're not qualified vets. But, if there is an absolute emergency, and you have no hopes of getting a vet, you have to do something.

After birth there are some definite *don'ts* to keep in mind. Don't allow any strong light into the kittens' eyes and keep it that way for a full month after birth. A small amount of petting is good for young kittens because it makes the kittens more sociable pets, but don't bring in crowds of visitors; they will only interfere and upset the mother.

The mother takes care of feeding the kittens. All you have to do is leave her food near the box and make sure she eats well. The kittens can find their food source. And don't worry too much about cleaning the bed either; the mother usually takes care of that, but if it looks dirty help her out. You can also help by clipping the kittens' nails when they start to grow so they can't hurt each other and the mother when nursing. The greatest infant mortality rate is during the first week of life, so watch to make sure there is no suffocation and that each gets all the food he needs. If some of the kittens are getting pushed out at food time, if they don't seem to be getting enough food and are hungry, try giving them small amounts of warm water and glucose out of a plastic eyedropper.

After the first three weeks or so start to wean the young kitten to an adult-type diet. Begin the weaning with plain milk in a saucer or shallow plate then gradually increase the thickness by mixing the milk with a good quality nutritionally balanced cat or kitten food. Kittens are imitators and will soon emulate their mother's eating patterns. By the time they are seven to nine weeks old they should be in good shape, eating only solid food with water on the side and maybe a little milk as a supplement. Milk is a useful supplement for newly weaned kittens, but once fully weaned and eating all solid food well (which should be by the eighth or ninth week) they must be given water.

While nursing, the mother needs extra food at first so she can supply all the milk needed. But as the kittens grow larger and start weaning, her intake should be decreased since the kittens are not feeding from her as much. In order to get them to eat, as you will have to somehow, cut down on their milk supply from the mother so they will be hungry enough to try something else. The way to do this is to work on the mother. By the fourth week after birth she should be fed only what she would normally receive before littering. This will make her produce less milk, and since the kittens are now eating solids they don't need as much milk. If you feed her extra from now on, she will just get fat.

If the kittens lose their mother or the mother absolutely refuses to feed them, you might try to get a foster mother for them. Smear the kittens with the other female's fluids. Hold each kitten to the nipple; if she licks them that usually means acceptance. But keep watching; just let the kittens feed and then remove them, because if the foster mother doesn't accept them she may well kill them.

If you can't make these arrangements, get in touch with your vet about the best diet for them. Plain milk is not adequate. One effective recommended diet used by many breeders is a mixture of two cups milk, one teaspoon corn syrup, the yolk of an egg and a pinch of salt. Mix this very well and give it to the kittens during the first week every two or three hours around the clock—don't think you can sleep through the night! First feed them with a plastic eyedropper, one drop at a time. As they get older, change to a nipple bottle. After about one week, night feedings can be discontinued unless the kittens are really weak. At about two and a half to three weeks put milk around their mouths. They will lick it off and soon will learn to lap for themselves. At the same time you can start switching them to a nutritionally balanced cat food, weaning as you would normally do.

Once weaned, it's time for the kittens to go to their new homes. Hopefully, you've got good ones lined up for them. If you don't you may have a difficult time finding them. But before giving the kitten away check on the person to whose home he is going. Be sure each kitten gets a good home and make follow-up calls to see how he's getting on and to ensure he's being cared for properly. Never abandon a kitten.

As you can see, breeding has a lot more to it than you probably thought. Therefore, if you have a cat who has mated and you don't want her to have kittens, rush her to the vet before it gets to be too late. Don't let her carry unwanted kittens; it's cruel. The kindest thing you can do is to have her altered, thus avoiding the problem in the first place.

20

THE OLDER CAT

More and more infectious diseases are being controlled by modern antibiotics and vaccines; thus more and more cats, like people, have a greater chance of reaching a ripe old age. Many stay vigorous and active too as they age, but there are still a few considerations to keep in mind when your cat begins to get older.

It's your responsibility to make him comfortable and to adapt to his needs. Let him relax more; older cats need more rest and privacy than when younger. You're sure to find him lying out in warm, sunny places, trying to keep away from annoying noises and distractions or rough handling—especially by children.

As with cats of every age, it is best to keep your older cat indoors. A dog or unfriendly cat may only be a nuisance to a young cat, but can be fatal to your older cat with his slower reflexes and decreased physical agility. In addition, as he ages he becomes more susceptible to the elements, so that a cold or rainy day could cause pneumonia or some other such illness.

Therefore, if your cat has always been used to going outside now is the time to change his habits. Set up a litter box for him indoors. In fact, with all older cats it is often a good idea to set up several boxes. His bladder can't duplicate the feats it did when he was younger and he can't control himself the way he used to, so don't expect it.

Older cats are often not as fastidious about grooming and caring for themselves as they were when younger. It is up to you to take care of those of his grooming needs he may slip up on. Neglect of a cat's basic grooming can cause problems for him, and with an older cat these problems could be extremely dangerous to his health.

It's not a good idea to board an aged cat, even in the most comfortable of places. In fact, your cat may become so upset by his change in environment that he becomes physically ill. And, with the lowered resistance and resiliency of old age, he could easily succumb to diseases he may come in contact with. It is far better to leave him home, with a sitter coming in to care for his needs.

Most of all, don't forget to pay attention to him when he's older. Just because he lies around doing nothing, it doesn't mean he doesn't like to be petted and played with now and then. In fact, some older cats even become jealous and possessive in their later years. But when playing, don't roughhouse with him as you did when he was a kitten. You and your cat have enjoyed memorable years together, so in his old age you will want to do everything possible to make him feel loved and wanted and comfortable.

If your cat does stop playing, it might be an indication something is wrong. Watch your cat for any changes in his normal behavior or appearance. You must be much more aware when he is older. Even if he looks fine to you, things could be going on that you can't see. Prevention is the best medicine. Therefore, regular checkups are essential once a cat reaches a reasonable old age—no matter how well he appears. Your vet can often detect potentially serious and important changes in their early stages when there's a better chance of effective treatment. The commonsense approach to caring for an older cat is to be in touch with your vet so he can help you. Take advantage of the new advances made in medicine.

The regenerative powers of the aged are limited, so it is important to catch and care for any health problems early. For the most part, aging has the general effect of slowing down your cat's body processes. It is only when one part suffers damage that there is cause for alarm. This same is true of skin and especially teeth problems, which can fast become chronic if neglected.

Good nutrition is very important to your cat in old age. He may need a special diet. Or, because he may not want to eat as much as he once did or even may not eat enough for adequate nutrition, he may need dietary supplements. Your veterinarian is the final authority here. Smaller portions fed to him more frequently may be the answer. On the other hand, be extremely careful not to overfeed your cat. Obesity, especially in an older cat, can be dangerous.

Make sure your cat has plenty of liquids available at all times since an older cat often needs extra water. He drinks more as he ages because his kidneys are not as good as they used to be and therefore need flushing out frequently.

When—or why—should a cat be put to sleep? Your veterinarian is the best judge, but the main reasons for putting cats away are that a cat is in constant pain, cannot control any of his bodily functions, or is quite literally dying. Most cats die from aging of their vital organs such as heart, kidney or liver. But proper care and understanding can prolong a happy life for many years. Even a severe physical disability doesn't necessarily mean your cat cannot live on with you. A blind cat, a deaf cat, even one missing a leg can be cared for adequately and is perfectly capable of enjoying whatever life and senses are left to him. If however, the time ever comes when you must for medical and humane reasons resort to euthanasia for your cat, don't shunt him off to some strange place like the public pound to be harshly treated and left alone for the final moment. Your own vet can take care of it quickly and painlessly with a single shot—usually a sodium pentobarbital injection. Make sure he is treated with dignity and loving kindness to the end.

Animals do die, but that's something most books don't point out. And when they do, cremation is often the best answer. All cremation does is speed up the burning process which would occur as slow oxidation if the animal were buried. There are pet cemeteries, caskets, headstones—even funerals—available. But all these things can't solace a bereaved owner as effectively as a new pet.

If your last cat was a happy experience, it does seem a waste not to use the wisdom and experience you gathered from having lived with him. You should be an even better owner this time around. Besides, it's hard to beat the joy and satisfaction of having a cat for a pet.

Index

food (*cont.*)
  harmful, 53, 56–57
  labels on, 53
  purchase of, 53
  refusal of, 54–55
  taste of, 35
  in TV commercial work, 237–238
  see also diet; eating habits
food treats, as rewards, 103, 163
Foreign Shorthairs, 78–79
Fur and Feather, 47

gestation, preparation for, 267–270
getting lost, 94–95
grooming and brushing, 45–46, 59–61, 64, 100–01
grooming aids, 64

habits
  bad or destructive, 97–100, 126–42
  in TV commercial work, 230
hair balls, 61–62
hand signals
  in "sit" command, 177–78
  in teaching tricks, 203
harness
  for car travel, 252
  lead and, 187–88, 190–91
Havana Brown cat, 76–77
"heel" command, 187, 193
Himalayan cat, 80–81
Hula-Hoop, jumping through, 214–15
hurdle, in jumping trick, 212

imprinting, in kittens, 161–62

Japanese Bobtail cat, 60, 76–77
jumping habits, control of, 140–141
jumping out of windows, 96–97

jumping tricks, 211–16
  "jumping into owner's arms," 215–16
  "jumping through," 214–16

Kaffir cat, 29
Kaopectate, 69
keys diversion, in "come" command, 167–68
  see also magazine
kitten
  "action words" with, 105
  adjustment by, 48
  development of, 30
  feeding of, 55
  healthy and unhealthy signs in, 47
  holding and handling of, 25
  imprinting in, 161–62
  litter box for, 110–11
  vs. mature cat, 48
  newborn, 270–71
  nursing of by mother, 270–271
  selection of, 44–46
  sex determination in, 49
  training of, 18–19
  transporting of, 49
  unhealthy, 47
  veterinarian visits for, 66–67
  weaning of, 271
kitty litter, 108
kneading, vs. scratching, 135
Korat cat, 76–77

lead
  in "come" command training, 168–69
  types of, 188–89
  walking on, 186–99
  see also walking on a lead
leopards, 235–36, 245
  in TV commercials, 189, 235
licking, purpose of, 42

puma, 245
punishment, avoidance of, 92,
170–71
purebreds, 46–47

Queene Anne collar, for self-
suckling control, 101

rabies, vaccination against, 67
Rag-Doll cat, 82–83
reinforcement, positive, 103
reprimands
communication and, 93
enforcing of, 90
"No" as, 89–90, 123, 132,
150, 158
rewards and, 93
retching, 62
retrieving, 216–19
rewards
in advanced tricks, 206
as positive reinforcement, 103
Rex or Cornish cat, 78–79
"roll over" trick, 207–09
running away, 95–96

sardine oil, for hair ball, 61
Scottish Fold cat, 78
scratching
bad habits and, 126–42
declawing and, 134–35
scratching post, 126–31
"security box," in TV commercial work, 231
self-grooming, 100–01
self-suckling, 100–01
sex determination, in kittens and
cats, 49
"shake hands" trick, 205–06
shampoo, 58–59
shedding, 31, 60
shelf climbing or jumping habit,
140–41
short-haired cats, 45–46, 72–78

Siamese cat, 78–79
"sit and stay" command, 172–
180
repetition in, 179–80
"sit" command
dowel stick in, 173–74, 176
hand signals in, 177–78
praise in, 177–78
pushing in, 175
repetition in, 175
"sit up and beg" trick, 209–11
skin, anatomy of, 31
skin odor, 64
skunk, spraying of cat by, 60
smell
sense of, 35
sex and, 266–67
Smilodon, 243 n.
sodium pentobarbital injection,
276
Somali cat, 84–85
spaying, 50, 69
best age for, 51
Sphynx cat, 60, 78–79
spraying
by male or female cats, 118
in toilet training, 220
staring, aggression and, 41–42
stool samples, 67
suckling, breaking habit of, 99–
100
sweat glands, 31
swinging door, for cat egress, 110

Tabasco sauce, for chewing
habit, 137–38
tapetum, 33
tar, on paws, 59
taste sense, 35
teeth, 31
telephone book scare tactic, 150
temperature
normal, 63
taking of, 63

INDEX

284

INDEX

visitors
    aggression toward, 122, 153–154
    walking over, 98–99
vomiting, 68

walking on a lead
    change of locations in, 196–197
    control in, 192–93
    correct position in, 191–92
    noises and distractions in, 198–99
    patience in, 197
    "rehearsals" in, 194
water, for drinking, 57

water cure, for jumping behavior, 96–97
"wave a paw" trick, 206
whiskers, 32
    function of, 32, 35–36
whistle, in "come" command, 169
White Distilled Vinegar Method
    in litter box training, 91, 113, 123
    in toilet bowl training, 223
wild cats, 243–48
    food hunting by, 244–45
    territorial ranges of, 247
wildcat, 29 n.
windows, jumping out of, 96–97